*

WHEN
THEY ARE
THREE

*

*

WHEN THEY ARE THREE

Nursery Children in the Church and Home

By Sara G. Klein

ILLUSTRATED BY JACQUELINE C. STONE

The Westminster Press

PHILADELPHIA

Table of Contents

Preface

WHEN THEY ARE THREE is a handbook for teachers and parents and constitutes part of a curriculum course for the class for three-year-olds in the church school, and for the guidance of young children in the home. Included in the book is a discussion of the role of parents and teachers and of the child himself—his religious and emotional growth, his questions, his place in the family and in the church family. There is a section on the organization, program, and equipment of the nursery class in the church school; and teaching plans for fifty-two sessions.

The other materials in the course are four storybooks, illustrated in color, for the child, and a set of twelve large teaching pictures to be used in the church and the home. The pictures are enlargements made from illustrations in the children's books.

The four books should be read frequently to the children by their parents and teachers. They are based on religious ideas, appropriate for this age group, as follows:

In Our Church. The three-year-old has happy first associations with the nursery class and "the big church."

His Name Is Jesus. The three-year-old becomes acquainted with Jesus the baby and Jesus the man.

The Little Seeds That Grew. The three-year-old learns, through his own activity, that God plans for things to grow.

I'm Growing. The three-year-old experiences God's plan for people to love and help one another in the home and in the community.

The stories in the four books are reprinted on pages 215–223 of this handbook and are referred to frequently. It would be a good idea to become acquainted with them before reading the general material and teaching plans.

It is sincerely hoped that *every parent* of a nursery child, as well as the teacher, will have a copy of WHEN THEY ARE THREE. The material has purposely been addressed to both. For a more effective guidance of our nursery children, parents and teachers must work together; also Christian education is a seven-day-a-week affair. For that reason too, parents will find value in knowing the teaching plans and the program of the nursery class so that they can carry out the ideas during the week. In the chapters "'At Home in Church'" and "Three-year-olds at Work" there are practical suggestions for equipment and activities which can be adapted for use in the home. The study guide on pages 237–241 has been designed for parents' or parent-teacher study groups and classes.

It will be noted that the material in the first section on understanding children includes references to all the preschool ages. The other sections, however, are more closely confined to a discussion of the three-year-old, for they present the program and activities in the nursery class.

In churches with limited facilities a good program can be provided for the nursery class if careful planning is done and some adaptation is made. A complete list of equipment is given on pages 92–95, but there is really a minimum amount needed. Such equipment is marked. Although terms like "block center" and "doll corner" are used for the sake of convenience throughout the teaching plans, they represent places, however small, where materials are accessible to the children.

As each of us—mother, father, guardian, or teacher—plans for the welfare and future of a growing nursery child, let us read and ponder the words of Paul:

"So then neither is he that planteth any thing, neither he that watereth; but God that giveth the increase. . . . For we are laborers together with God. . . .

"According to the grace of God which is given unto me, as a wise masterbuilder, I have laid the foundation."—*I Corinthians* 3: 7, 9, 10.

Grateful acknowledgment is made, in the preparation of this book, to Elizabeth Cringan Gardner for writing the section "Teaching Plans for the Year in the Nursery Class"; to Dorothy B. Fritz and James D. Smart for their helpful suggestions and interest; and to all my former nursery children everywhere for having been "just themselves."

—SARA G. KLEIN.

WHEN NURSERY CHILDREN ARE THREE

*

*
*

CHAPTER I

They Learn from Us

ONE MORNING a young child was deeply absorbed in painting at the easel. After a while he called to the teacher, "Come, see what I made." Then he proceeded to name some of the objects he had just painted—a truck, a parking place, a garage. Down at the bottom of the paper were two more sets of lines and circles of color. "This," said he, pointing to one of them, "is a baby's cradle, and this," pointing to the other, "is the atomic bomb!"

How confusing it must be for our children: the baby's cradle, a symbol of home and security and kindliness; the atomic bomb, a mark of homelessness and disunity and destruction! It is we adults who have the responsibility of deciding where the emphasis of life will be—on good or evil, on love or hate, on faith or doubt, and as we make this decision, we pass on its influence to the little children of the world.

And so as we consider any curriculum course for the nursery age, we should stress most insistently what we grownups believe and feel and know. Children learn first from us, their parents or guardians and their teachers—those who are near to them and whom they love. Our faith in God and belief in his loving purpose, even in times of discouragement, will be reflected in the guidance of our children and in their own developing personalities; so will our understanding relationships with other people and our wholesome adjustment to life as individuals. In this chapter you will find a discussion of the faith and attitudes of all those who are guiding young children.

Also we should remember that God is at work in the life of each child in our midst. Let us approach the child as one whose life God has already begun to shape. We do not want to obstruct the child's growth by putting pressure upon it or by always directing it as we think best. Rather, let us provide the kind of nurture and environment that will help him develop as a child of God.

Christian believing

is not simply an intellectual acceptance of a set of statements concerning God, Christ, and the life of man; it is a personal response to a personal God. It is not something that a man does "on his own" or by force of sustained thinking; rather, we believe only when we hear in the gospel the good news that God has come near to us in Jesus Christ, humbling us in our sin but pardoning and redeeming us in his mercy. To believe is to rejoice that in Jesus Christ God has broken the power of evil over us and has opened to us a life of righteousness and purity and peace under his rule.

What, in brief, is the outline of this faith which Christians share when they have been brought by Christ under the gracious rule of God?

First is the confidence that, even though rainy days come for the just and the unjust alike, the world and all the events of our life in it are in the hands of a God who is almighty and who may be trusted to deal with us as a father with his children.

Second is the discovery, as we read the Gospels, that there is no other rightful Master and Lord for man than Jesus Christ. He is the light of the world, the truth, the way, the door to the Kingdom of Heaven, the good shepherd, the word of God in human flesh. Through him alone—his words, his life, his death, his resurrection—do we come truly into communion with God, and through him alone do we know the nature of our own true life.

Third, God is a Spirit, and when we repent and believe in Jesus Christ, God's Spirit becomes the very center and wellspring of our existence. We are no longer ruled by self but by the Spirit of the living God.

Such a faith as this brings us necessarily into the Church, for the Church is the fellowship of those who have been molded by God's Spirit into an instrument for carrying forward Christ's work of redemption. We are the body of Christ.

But we are able to open the way of redemption to others only because we know ourselves to be sinners to whom God's mercy and pardon have come through Christ. We believe in the forgiveness of sins because we have received it ourselves and because we are willing to give it unstintingly to others.

Finally, we believe in the life everlasting, knowing that the life with God into which Christ brings us triumphs over all darkness and evil and at last over death itself. We live, not as chips upon the stream of time, but as children of God with a destiny that reaches beyond the seen into the unseen.

—JAMES D. SMART,
Editor in Chief, Curriculum Materials, Board of Christian Education of the Presbyterian Church in the U. S. A.

OUR FAITH AND ATTITUDES

"I should prefer to take a group of the younger children," said a prospective teacher. "I know so little about the Bible and the doctrines of Christianity. If I teach the nursery or kindergarten children, that wouldn't make any difference."

Naturally we teachers and parents do not use long theological terms with little children, nor do we attempt to interpret to them fully the revelation of God through the Scriptures. But to think that what we believe or do not believe concerning Christian doctrine has no influence upon these children is indeed a serious error. For, as is pointed out repeatedly in this book, our own faith, which is the very core of our being, will affect our relationships with the children and will make a permanent impression on their lives. What is that faith to be for *your* children?

Let us consider the implications of the Christian faith as described on the opposite page, for those of us who teach and guide young children in our churches and our homes.

The Need of the Child for Security. We often speak so glibly about the importance of security in the life of the child. It *is* one of his greatest needs and is listed again as such in Chapter 3. But we seldom stop to think about how this security is to be gained. There is much fear and anxiety in our world today; many people feel that events have no meaning or purpose, that one must struggle against indifferent laws and forces. This attitude will produce fear and anxiety in the child. On the other hand, when those who live close to little children possess a real Christian faith in God, their Father, such confidence and trust will be passed on. This does not mean that there will not be days of sorrow or hardship, but security in God will make times of stress easier to bear. And young children often come through hardship or sorrow unharmed if they understand something of the nature of the difficulty and share in grievous experiences with those whom they love, who, in turn, are upheld by "the everlasting arms."

"He that dwelleth in the secret place of the Most High shall abide under the shadow of the Almighty.

"I will say of the Lord, He is my refuge and my fortress: my God; in him will I trust."

—*Psalm* 91: 1, 2.

The Child's Sense of God's Nearness. If God is not just some vague force who controls the universe, but is rather the One who is at the center of life for parents or a teacher, the child will find him near. Nor can God be far away to those who receive the indwelling of his Holy Spirit.

It is often through conversation or prayer in the home that the child, when he is old enough to understand, can sense this nearness of God to his parents. In the bedtime incident in the nursery book, *I'm Growing,* Timothy's daddy speaks of God and his loving care, as the family are gathered together in a feeling of oneness and comradeship. In *The Little Seeds That Grew,* Jerry's mother includes God's part in the growing process of the flower seeds as she talks about "the surprise," and his father offers thanks to Him for food as one who has felt his day-by-day partnership in the provision for man's needs.

The Child's Response to Jesus Christ. "Master," the disciples called him long ago, but he is Master through the ages to all those who give allegiance to him. Nursery children, at home and church school, will be unconsciously affected by the response of parents and teachers, who will either consult their own desires only or guide their actions by their Christian discipleship. We wonder how much the principle that encourages unlimited freedom for the child affects the ability of the individual to make right decisions later in life.

We shall talk to nursery children about Jesus too, but during the early years even this teaching will not be as influential as the practice of Christianity by their parents and teachers.

The Child's Attitude to the Church. The little child soon comes to learn what the Church means to his parents, and to his teacher when he starts to nursery class. Our whole faith in God is expressed as we enter into the fellowship of the Church for worship and for work. There is a further presentation of this subject in Chapter 5, "They Go to Church."

The Attitude Toward Wrongdoing. Those adults who themselves are humbled as they confess their sins to God can deal more understandingly with wrongdoing in their children. Gentleness and forgiveness will be present in a home where the mother or father prays:

"Have mercy upon me, O God, according to thy loving-kindness: according unto the multitude of thy tender mercies blot out my transgressions.

"Wash me thoroughly from mine iniquity, and cleanse me from my sin. . . .
"Create in me a clean heart, O God; and renew a right spirit within me.
"Cast me not away from thy presence; and take not thy Holy Spirit from me.
"Restore unto me the joy of thy salvation; and uphold me with thy free Spirit."

—Psalm 51: 1, 2, 10-12.

Why do we grownups so often try to hide the fact that we ourselves need to be forgiven by God, and why do we hesitate to say, "I'm sorry," to a child if we have misjudged him in some way?

Also parents and teachers who have known the loving reproof of the Father will hold a child in love and forgiveness even as they show him the error of his action.

The Perspective for Life. If we look at life in the perspective of the life everlasting, it will make a difference as we think about the future of our children. Not that we shall spend our time "getting ready for heaven" and ignore the realities of present-day living, but our values will be judged differently. What *are* the important goals to be achieved in our temporal life—success, money, fame, to be got at the expense of friendship, honesty, and good health perhaps? Or are there more deeply satisfying gains?

This does not mean that man should not feel that life is good—physical comforts and a sense of achievement are necessary and wholesome. But the Kingdom of Heaven is *now* as well as in the future. Jesus wanted all life to be worthy and directed by God. If that is true, we should examine our temporal activities and relationships with such standards in mind. What, then, will be our concept of love and marriage, of vocation, of leisure time, of death itself?

A Knowledge of the Bible. It is only as we adults find God's revelation of himself to man through the Scriptures, and of Jesus Christ as the Word, that we are able to communicate the spirit of the Bible and the very first teaching of it to our children of nursery age. A workable knowledge of the Bible does not come early or casually. We need to read and study the Bible for ourselves, taking time to do so, even when we are busiest. Reference to it, dependence upon it, must become a natural and a constant part of life. Suggested books to guide us in our own Bible study and enrichment are listed in the bibliography, pages 241-245.

Children, even three-year-olds, are amazingly sensitive to the

attitudes and feelings of grownups

around them. Parents who are irritated but try to cover it up rarely succeed with the young child. Grownups who are ill at ease with "young fry" may smile brightly and put on other airs of confidence. Seldom, though, does this keep youngsters from seeing through the façade. They know whether we really like them or are pretending to, whether we're comfortable and relaxed or only desperately trying.

Those of us privileged to live with three-year-olds, at home, in nursery school, or in church school, do well to take stock of ourselves. Indeed, we should know what to expect of these lively on-their-toes boys and girls. We shall want to be prepared to provide them with materials and activity suited to their developmental level. As important, though, is that which we bring of ourselves. Our feelings about ourselves, our self-concept, the nature of satisfactions we find in living with others are awarenesses we need to cultivate. Here are a few questions that may help in the building of important self-understandings:

Am I convinced that I know the one "right" way of doing things? Do I have a strong feeling of responsibility to see that children fit into this "right" way? Or do I recognize that children are different, that what works well for one may not be suitable for another? Can I be comfortable with children who move more slowly than I feel they should, or push others around, or act in ways that don't seem quite right? Is there real satisfaction in seeing children make strides of their own? Am I happy to see them begin to think and explore for themselves?

Do I "love little children" to the extent that most of my fun and satisfaction is found in them? Do I expect children, in turn, to show constantly their affection for me? Or do I have friends and relatives of my own age who mean a great deal, in whose companionship deep emotional satisfactions are to be found?

Is my whole life given to children? Do I find I have little interest or time for anything else? Or do I have interests outside the ones that are centered in being a parent or teacher? Do I enjoy reading, sports, hobbies, conversations about matters other than those concerning children?

The role of parent or teacher is not most desirably that of a trellis on which children are to be trained or a traffic officer controlling a "Stop and Go" sign. We are persons with feelings, human beings whose lives should include deep self-satisfactions, if we are to live most effectively with children. Only when our personal lives are growing, expanding ones, can we give most to the youngsters with whom we live and work.

—ERNEST OSBORNE,

Professor of Education,
Teachers College, Columbia University.

OUR SATISFACTIONS

"When children don't got mothers, they have to have somebody else be like their mothers, don't they?" said young Theodore. That was a very profound and true pronouncement. Little children must be sure of the love of their parents or other adults near to them—it is one of their greatest needs. They must feel at times a physical closeness and warmth of affection. However, as Dr. Osborne suggests in his statement, grownups can give such a wholesome love to their children or they can smother and stifle them in a possessive way. The latter will leave neither the adult nor the child free to grow as an individual, to expand his own circle of acquaintants, and to broaden his field of interests. As we have heard so often, it is good to "mother" our children but unwise to "smother" them.

There is a temptation for both parents and teachers to appeal to a child to do things "for me." Within reason, that is right. When Alice said, "I *eat* for Mommie," there was a pride in her voice that showed that she was genuinely pleased to be able to make happy someone she loved. Knowing Alice's mother, one was aware that she was not constantly making such demands on her child; with another parent, however, there might have been danger that this kind of relationship was being established. As we teach and guide young children, our true affection can be expressed as we say, "Let's do this together," or, "Because it's the right thing to do," rather than, "Do this for me," or, "Do this because I say so."

We are all human enough to want and to appreciate evidence of a child's affection for us. This too is right if it is not carried to an extreme or if it is properly channeled. Edward, age four, had been attending a day nursery where the teacher was quite stern and where he had never felt at ease. Then he was enrolled in another weekday nursery school. During the first days at the new school, he would jump up and hug his mother tightly when he said good-by and when he greeted her at the end of each session. During the morning he frequently rushed up to his new teacher and threw his arms around her. He wanted to be sure that he was loved and that all was well.

Then, as Edward began to "absorb" this friendly atmosphere where he could count on a constant love and respect from the teacher, he gradually stopped bestowing this demonstrative affection upon her.

Finally one day he approached the teacher, face alight and eyes shining. Without even touching her, he looked up and said, "I'm happy here," and skipped back to the sand table. The teacher smiled—actually she offered a little prayer of thanks. Edward was at home, and the teacher knew that his affection for her had outgrown a purely personal phase and was transformed into a quality of living.

Dr. Osborne directs our thinking also toward other interests that those who are concerned with children ought to have for a richer, fuller existence. We need to discuss the idea at greater length, as there are many factors to be considered.

Church school teachers, unlike parents and weekday teachers, often do not have enough time to give to children. Many of them are busy with their careers. They should be encouraged to do *more* reading and talking about children, to observe them whenever possible, to take leadership training courses and attend laboratory schools.

Parents and teachers can find satisfaction in engaging in activities, on an adult level, which their children also enjoy. Workshops, where only adults are present, are fun. There they can work with clay, poster paint, finger paint, hammers, nails, and wood. Such workshops serve a dual purpose. The grownups experiment with materials and have the joy of creating without worrying about the results of their varied attempts. And in addition they can better understand the feelings of their children, who are using these work and play materials at school and church school and in the home.

A group of nursery parents and the teachers spent a delightful evening finger painting. Most of the parents had not tried this medium before. In the beginning they were rather tense and would say, "Oh, *I* can't make anything." Then, as they began to sweep out in broad strokes, with paint up to their elbows, they forgot both their embarrassment and the passing of time. One mother, who had come to America from a mid-European country, looked with incredulity at what she had painted—a church done in orange and browns, with an atmosphere about it of old-worldliness and strength and beauty. "But I never *knew* I could do anything with my hands," she said.

In many modern families there is a need to do more things together. This is especially true in the cities. Since the days of the industrial revolution, family members are less interdependent for survival, and the breadwinner has gone outside of the home to earn the living. A pastor said recently that one of the most difficult jobs in his ministry was to get fathers to spend fifteen minutes a day with their children.

Family worship has been neglected because it seems impossible for all the family to assemble at the same time. Yet, isn't some plan for a project as important as this worth the working out? Perhaps grace at Sunday or evening dinner could be extended into a longer worship period. Songs, stories, and prayers with which the child has become familiar in church school can serve to create a bond between the church and the home. The use of such materials will also provide an opportunity for sharing in families where there is more than one child. Those of us who have grown up in homes with a family altar have felt its sustaining strength and have been thankful for it.

Everyone who guides and teaches little children should have companionship and satisfying relationships with other adults. Parents need to regard each other as comrades and as husband and wife, rather than always as the mother and the father of the family. In fact, each member of the family, adult and child, brings enrichment to the others when he has acquaintances of his own age. Teachers, in addition to enjoying personal friendships, will maintain good relationships with their colleagues, with the assistant teachers or the department head, and with the parents of the children.

Parents and teachers will be more interesting people if they pursue hobbies and other activities as individuals. Even a nursery child is aware of the glow and aliveness of a mother or teacher who has herself investigated and thought about some of the ramifications of life. There are the more serious things—world affairs and housing and prison reform. There are the marvelous things—astronomy and standing at the top of the Grand Canyon, or reading about the latest wonder drug. There are the beautiful things—gardening and collecting blue plates and listening to a symphony. There are the things for fun—tennis and a hay ride and eating pink cotton candy at the circus. There are the things to create—oil painting and designing hats and carving a piece of wood. There are the things to study—theology and Latin and French and geometry. There are the spiritual things—communing with God and learning about the message of the Bible and loving our fellow men.

These are some of the satisfactions that we bring as we live with our little children at home and in the church.

"Your Body Is a Temple of the Holy Spirit"

From I Corinthians 6: 19 (R.S.V.)

When your youngster was newborn, the little body seemed perfect, even to the miniature fingernails, yet it was unfinished. The proportions of head, trunk, and extremities, right for a baby, were different from those of later life. The eyes, destined to become marvelously keen, registered only a hazy picture. A thoughtful physician, even the thousandth time he witnesses this wonder, feels awed and humbled, knowing a little about the subtle processes by which the body grew in the womb and is now developing.

Parents and doctors help the Creator by providing loving protection and the proper food and environment, so that the natural processes which he has ordained can bring about orderly, harmonious growth and development and unfolding of the personality. Even a body with the limitation of a serious physical handicap is a home for the human spirit and the "temple of God."

During the first three years you have assisted and enjoyed a rapid and fascinating phase. Now you are guiding wisely the important transition from complete dependence to a period where the child is adjusting to a more challenging environment and an ever-widening circle of human beings. Here are a few points to remember as applied to three-year-olds:

A child loves to explore. If accidents are to be prevented, combine physical safeguards with guidance in this learning process. Have on hand, and learn how to use, a good first-aid book and kit.

Establish regular, but not rigid, schedules. A healthy child, given sufficient scope, will himself regulate the amount of exercise he requires. Rare, unavoidable interferences with routines, accepted calmly, and occasional optional exceptions for *good* reasons, do not harm.

A checkup every six months by a dentist and a doctor is desirable. Supposedly minor defects should not be neglected.

Inoculations against smallpox and diphtheria should already have been given. Avoid exposure to serious *contagious diseases*. Take your doctor's advice about injections against whooping cough, common colds, and other illnesses.

The three-year-old will learn wholesome health habits and a respect for his body as a gift of God, not so much by words as by the attitude and example of his parents.

—MARGARET DANN, M.D.,
Assistant Professor of Pediatrics,
Cornell University Medical College,
and Associate Attending Physician, New York Hospital.

HEALTHFUL LIVING

Many modern young parents are anxious to follow health rules for their children—they provide adequate food and protection from disease; they read books on child care. And yet they sometimes fail to realize that it is just as important to instill in their children a wholesome attitude toward health, for the children will be growing up and will then be responsible for looking after their own physical well-being. It is necessary, therefore, that parents, and teachers too, indicate in even more fundamental ways that they believe the body is a temple of the Holy Spirit.

Adults will seek to keep their own bodies and minds in good health. In our world today social pace and economic rush hold many people in their grasp. We like to entertain guests; we must earn a living; we take pride in achievement. But we are not to be enslaved even by these, so that nerves are on edge and bodies too tired as we live with our children at home or in nursery class on Sunday morning. Parents and teachers will try to live calmly and moderately, avoiding excesses of all kinds and eliminating harmful influences.

They will respect medical research and have their own regular checkups with the doctor. This will not make them overconcerned about their health, but rather it will free their minds from needless worry and give a practical and sensible direction to any care or precautions they need to take. Closely related to this is the attitude of grownups toward handicapped bodies—either their own or their children's. As Dr. Dann points out, we have an obligation to make the most of this "temple of God," for it houses the human spirit implanted by God; also it is wise to emphasize the normal qualities. Recently a group of religious workers visited a public school for deaf children, observing from the nursery school through the high-school classes. It was amazing to see how naturally the program, in addition to actual treatment and therapy, fell into the pattern of a good school anywhere. And members of the graduating class told the visitors—haltingly sometimes, it is true—about plans for their careers in college or in business.

Parents and teachers should be at ease with their children where bodily functions are concerned. It is best to avoid embarrassment and prudery and yet to respect good taste. There ought to be the same naturalness in the attitude of adults toward physical handicaps.

Adults will enjoy simple amusements with their children and will see to it that they have an opportunity to contact earthy things. Ground, water, sunshine, and air are elements to be explored and felt. Country children are fortunate in having an abundant provision of hills and soil and rocks. They walk through fields of wheat, smelling the goodness of each shaft as it brushes against their faces. They help gather warm eggs from the nests of the hens. Occasionally they sit in the evening twilight with their parents and see the stars turned on, one by one, in an expanse of sky.

We must see to it that city children have substitute experiences of this kind—a bit of earth in a window box, a sandbox, a dishpan full of water to splash in, a family picnic away from the city. Henry had been on such a picnic with his mother and father. One day he dictated a letter about it to his teacher:

> "I wented to the country all day. They had a sand pile and a nice young girl five years old and a big, quiet, black dog called Lily. They had flying rings and I hanged from them and Mommy pushed me and I swinged like a big clock.
>
> "I climbed a tree and I said shouldn't we have a picnic, that would be nice all right. So we ate outdoors in the gardnin and Daddy ate about a hundred pounds and fell asleep in the gardnin chair. . . .
>
> "I do not like roses to pick them, they have splinters on them."

Adults will be interested in the physical needs of others. In *The Little Seeds That Grew,* Timothy's family appreciate God's plan for things to grow, so that their own needs may be cared for. But an even deeper meaning is implicit in the book. Those of us who are blessed with adequate food and clothing must share with others in our world and see to it that all people are given an opportunity to earn their bread. Such was the teaching of Jesus.

Some of the most beautiful and significant verses in the Psalter are found in the Eighth Psalm:

> "When I consider thy heavens, the work of thy fingers, the moon and the stars, which thou hast ordained;
>
> "What is man, that thou art mindful of him? and the son of man, that thou visitest him?
>
> "For thou hast made him a little lower than the angels, and hast crowned him with glory and honor."
>
> —*Psalm* 8: 3-5.

This is a tribute to the esteem in which God holds man whom he has created—not only the spirit of man but his physical body as well.

CHAPTER 2

They Grow Toward God

"At the same time came the disciples unto Jesus, saying, Who is the greatest in the kingdom of heaven?

"And Jesus called a little child unto him, and set him in the midst of them,

"And said, Verily I say unto you, Except ye be converted, and become as little children, ye shall not enter into the kingdom of heaven.

"Whosoever therefore shall humble himself as this little child, the same is greatest in the kingdom of heaven.

"And whoso shall receive one such little child in my name receiveth me."

—Matthew 18: 1-5.

Mummie, I want to say thank you to God the way we do in nursery class."

Donny's mother was tucking him in bed. She was ready for the good-night hug and kiss when Donny's statement came so unexpectedly. She was not prepared for it—actually she felt a twinge of fear. She had supposed that Donny would ask "religious" questions someday. But she did have hopes that Donny's "religious training" would be adequately cared for by his attendance at church school each Sunday morning. She and Donny's father had decided several weeks before that with Donny enrolled in the church nursery class, it would be more convenient for them to attend the church service occasionally. But they *were* looking forward to the time when Donny would say a Bible verse or sing a little hymn or recite a prayer that he had learned in nursery class. They would be proud, and glad that their son's spiritual growth was progressing as it should in all nice families. *Now* Donny was not going to "recite" a prayer—he was going to "say" a prayer, and he looked up in wide-eyed expectancy, waiting for his mother to guide him.

23

What a pity that even one mother or father must feel fright or confusion or resignation when confronted by the possibility of sharing with a little child one of the most compensating experiences of parenthood!

Sue's mother was not so taken unawares. She knew that at church school the children had planted seeds as they observed and talked about God's plan for growth. One day when she was busy in the kitchen, three-year-old Sue ran in from the garden and said: "Mother, I think you should stop what you're doing right now and come outdoors. We can say thank you to God for the flowers and the rain that makes them grow." Sue's mother was not "too busy" to leave her work. She and Sue together, among the tall-stemmed iris, thanked God for the beauties of his world. And Sue's mother, from the fullness of her heart, added, "And thank you, God, for giving us such a nice little girl."

As we think especially about the "religious" education of three-year-olds, we must keep in mind several important ideas.

First, the spiritual growth and guidance of children, or adults for that matter, really can't be dissociated from their emotional, social, and even physical development. People's lives cannot be divided into compartments. Jesus realized the importance of the *whole* personality, and in both his healing and teaching that realization is very much in evidence. So often the healing of a man's body was the direct consequence of Jesus' forgiving him and cleansing his spirit:

> "And, behold, they brought to him a man sick of the palsy, lying on a bed: and Jesus seeing their faith said unto the sick of the palsy; Son, be of good cheer; thy sins be forgiven thee."—*Matthew 9: 2.*

If, for instance, Johnny has been up late on Saturday night and is tired in nursery class on Sunday morning, he may stage a nice healthy temper tantrum or push everyone away who comes near him. Or there is Judy, who feels alone and unhappy because her daddy left her in nursery class and hurried away before she said good-by. She mopes in a corner most of the morning. She does not listen to the story about Jesus or observe with other children a "wonder of God," the golden powdery wings of a butterfly. And her association with the church is a very unhappy one.

Second, no one actually knows the one answer to give to the question, "What is the best way to teach religion to the youngest children?" There are various "methods" in use. Some educators, unfortunately, would not even mention the name of God to this age group. At the other extreme are those who, failing to recognize Paul's belief that there is milk for the babes and strong meat for them that are of full age, insist upon an abundance of Biblical learning for three-year-olds.

We do not need to follow either of these extremes. We can take the Christian faith thoroughly in earnest in our nursery work, while at the same time we use the best methods of child guidance. This means that all of us, as teachers and parents, must keep seeking and learning and growing. The suggestions in this book about the spiritual guidance of the little child are being offered, not because they are absolutely final, but because *they have proved again and again to produce in even nursery children truly Christian experiences on their age level.* The example of Sue is only one of hundreds of such incidents.

Third, we should recognize that there are differences in children and in situations. Thus, if there are older children in the family, "theological" discussions will naturally become more involved. Some three-year-olds, whose language ability is advanced, will be asking profound

—and sometimes embarrassing!—questions of grownups. "Why does God have bugs that sting?" "Is God inside of me?" and so on.

Fourth, just because we are adults, it does not mean that we are walking books of knowledge and that we must give information for every question asked, even by a child. We should not be afraid to say, "I don't know," or, "Perhaps we can find out," or, "Maybe someday we'll know the answer." In this way misinformation will never have to be unlearned and, most important of all, respect for the word of the parents and teachers, and for truth itself, will become part of the character of the child.

No question is too minor for consideration. Thus, Tommy, deeply absorbed in looking into the aquarium, asked his weekday nursery teacher, "Do turtles have teeth?" The teacher didn't know and said so. Later in the morning Tommy accompanied her to the library where there was an encyclopedia. (Incidentally, turtles *don't* have teeth!)

Fifth, growing toward God takes place in many ways in the life of childhood. This discussion, therefore, will not be limited to the present chapter, where an over-all presentation is made, but will be continued at many points in the book. The purpose of our Christian guidance and education is that as the individual grows as a person, and as he becomes aware of other people and the world in which he lives, the works and working of God will become manifest to him.

Sixth, parents and teachers should be co-workers; they should understand each other's problems and needs, both in the home and in church school situations. They are concerned with making religion an integral part of the little child's life, with laying the foundation for a real and working faith.

And so, to summarize, we recognize that religion is part of all of life; even little children can have Christian experiences on their own age level; adults need to be aware of differences in the maturity of children who question; adults are wise to admit any lack of knowledge; children come to understand God as they grow within themselves and in relation to people and to the world around them; parents and teachers must work together.

GROWING TOWARD GOD

In the first chapter emphasis was placed on the idea that the atmosphere in a home first prepares the child for an understanding of God, the God whom Jesus Christ revealed. As parents express love and thoughtfulness and forgiveness, these qualities will become a part of the child's very existence.

When the child matures, he hears the word "God," and gradually, at two or three years of age, he begins to associate God with someone "special." We are often responsible for helping him to conceive of God as an old man with a long beard sitting on a cloud in the sky; as a kind of bogeyman who has an eye on "bad" children; as a magician (sometimes confused with Santa Claus) who grants or refuses requests at will; *or* as the Creator of the world, the God who is the maker of laws we must learn to know and obey, but who loves and is concerned with those whom he has created.

One has only to listen to the discussions of preschool children to realize that their idea of God is quite generally limited to a belief that his physical size is of first importance. Thus Bobby was overheard to remark to a circle of his contemporaries: "God is the tallest man in the world. His feet are even longer than my daddy's."

A three-year-old was among a group who engaged in the following conversation:

RONNY (age 5): "When I grow up, I'll be up a million miles as high as the moon—I'll be all over the place."
ANDY (age 4): "I'll be as high as over to the next town."
JUNE (age 5): "I'll be as big as lots of mountains."
LARRY (age 3): "I be big up to the sky tomorrow."
PEGGY (age 5): "You'll be big as you are now tomorrow."
JUNE: "I'll be the fattest."
RONNY: "No, God's the fattest—God's bigger than anyone."
ANDY (with finality): "God's the biggest."

All parents and teachers could repeat many similar conversations. It is natural, at this stage of development, for the child to think of God as a kind of magnified human person. This phase will pass as he grows in understanding. However, we do not want him to lose the personal feeling of God—the knowledge that God is one who thinks and feels and loves. "If a man love me, he will keep my words: and my Father will love him" (John 14: 23). At least the child should picture God as the right kind of person; and at the same time we can introduce the idea of God as a Spirit by speaking of what he *does* in connection with the child's own experiences.

We shall start, then, in teaching little children about God, with these three basic ideas:

1. God plans for things to grow.
2. God plans for people to live in homes and families.
3. God plans for people to live in communities and to help one another.

Two of the children's books, which accompany the nursery course, *The Little Seeds That Grew* and *I'm Growing*, are based on these concepts.

The following conversation indicates how a teacher had helped Mary come through a "theological experience" and to grow in the process.

The children were drinking their fruit juice after saying a simple grace:

MARY: "God's in the sky, isn't he?"
TEACHER: "God is everywhere."
MARY: "Is that God?" (Pointing to a picture of a peasant mother and her children.)
TEACHER: "No, that is a picture of a mother and her children."
MARY: "But God plans for children to have mothers and fathers and live in homes, doesn't he?"

Who will not believe that depth of understanding, which is related to living, can be achieved in the early years? Mary was four, but even when she was in nursery class, her teacher had discussed God's plan for families as Mary and the other children played in the doll corner or built houses of blocks.

Several principles apparent in the conversation above are useful to grownups as they respond to children's questions about God:

First, the teacher answered one question at a time and answered it simply; she did not offer long explanations which were not required.

Second, she explained, "God is everywhere." She did not leave Mary with the impression that God is "in the sky" only. It is true, of course, that when we tell children of God's omnipresence, they may ask if he is in their cereal or in their toy chest. But it is often our own attitude at times like these that determines how constructive the result will be. We may find that it is difficult not to be amused by such questions; but the child is serious, and we should answer as truly as we know how and in a matter-of-fact way.

Perhaps the best approach to such an inquiry as "Is God in my cereal?" is to give a positive statement like, "God planned for us to have good cereal to eat." Or, in regard to the toy chest: "God wants us to be happy and enjoy things to work and play with."

When the question is asked, "Does God walk?" or, "Does God have hands?" we can answer, "We can't see God, you know." One may then continue to discuss further the evidences of his existence in his creative and loving care.

LEARNING TO PRAY

As nursery children become acquainted with God's love and care for us, it is very natural that they should want to thank him. And so prayer has its origin. For some time they have heard, and will continue to hear, Mother and Daddy praying to God; often they do not comprehend the words, but they catch the spirit of prayer and fellowship with God.

However, even the youngest need prayer experiences on their own level. These are usually very short. They may come spontaneously on the part of the child or they may be prompted by the teacher or parent who has prepared for "the worship moment." Both Donny and Sue, to whom reference was made at the beginning of the chapter, were the initiators, although actually this was due to the fact that they had engaged in conversation and activities along a similar line in the home or church school. In the book *In Our Church*, Miss Anderson suggests thanking God for food and for the church, *while the children are ready and interested*. In the book *I'm Growing*, Timothy's daddy takes advantage of a happy family day to speak of God's plan for families to love and help one another. And so Timothy adds, "Thank you, God."

A good foundation is laid for a satisfactory prayer life if most three-year-olds can first say, "Thank you, God," with sincerity and a degree of understanding. Thus at bedtime Freddie, who has felt love and happiness during the day, prays, "Thank you, God, for our house and for the beautiful world." Later the child will come to understand that he can look for God's help and forgiveness in prayer.

Before Thanksgiving, a little group of three-year-olds in a nursery class were talking together with the teacher about special things for which they wanted to say thank you. The list included rain, babies, "us," Mommy and Daddy, milk, crackers, and macaroni. After the contributions were made, the teacher explained that God plans for wheat to grow, so that we can have crackers and macaroni, and for cows on the earth, to give us milk to drink. Again we see an example of how even young children can see God working through laws rather than as a magician.

Many parents and teachers believe, too, that it is best for nursery children to address prayers to "God" rather than to "Father," or "God, our Father." When, at a later stage in their development, they are able to discern the difference between an earthly father and God, their Father, the right words will follow. Three-year-olds are still accepting everything in its literal sense. Obviously, of course, all fathers cannot begin too soon to examine their own lives and help prepare their children for the comparison when it comes.

An example of a short grace for memorizing is the following:

"Dear God, thank you today
For food and rest and play."

BECOMING ACQUAINTED WITH JESUS

One of the children's books is entitled *His Name Is Jesus*. It includes two stories that are the foundation on which an acquaintance with Jesus is made. The Nativity is printed first, and the story of Jesus and the children second. Actually, however, especially in the church school where this is more practical, it usually is best to introduce nursery children to Jesus the man first. Then at Christmas time we speak about "when Jesus was a baby." There is probably less confusion in the minds of the youngest children with this approach. Four- and five-year-old kindergarten children are ready to add discussions of Jesus as a boy, with the implication that they can follow the same pattern of growth.

What, then, do we want our nursery children to learn about Jesus? Let us admit first that there exists in the minds of many of them a rather hazy mixture of ideas. Shortly after Halloween, at the time when the wedding of Princess Elizabeth of England was in the news, Tommy visited a department store Santa Claus with his mother. The following day he reported to several children in his nursery class, "I went to see Santa Claus; he said Halloween is coming and Jesus is going to be married."

During a session in a rural group, a little while after a child had suddenly died, Jean and Betty, both age three, talked to each other quietly at rest time. When the teacher started to listen, the conversation was as follows:

BETTY: ". . . if I don't die."

JEAN: "When you die, you go up there [pointing] where Jesus is at."

BETTY: "When Mother dies, she'll go up to live with God—she was at church."

JEAN: "I want to go where Jesus lives."

BETTY: "I do too. He lives way up there where the light is. I like Jesus."

JEAN: "I do too. I'm going to live with God and Mother and Daddy and Ruthie [sister]."

BETTY: "And Teddy [Jean's brother]."

JEAN: "Yes."

BETTY: "My mother and my daddy and Frank [brother] and Anne [sister]— we're going in the sky."

JEAN: "My mother and daddy and Ruthie and Teddy are going in the sky. We'll be buried [seriously], then we're going to the sky."

BETTY: "The bad man isn't up in the sky. When I see Jesus, I'm going to

play with dolls."
JEAN: "Will you play with Jesus too? I am."
BETTY: "Yes, I'll play with dolls too."
JEAN: "When Jesus is away."
BETTY: (Sings a song about Jesus, pointing upward.)

Actually there was a basically good and friendly attitude toward Jesus expressed by these children. But how will we teach about Jesus to three-year-olds in order to encourage more intelligent understanding and to avoid as much confusion as possible?

Their first stories of Jesus are of one who loved the children and whom children love. When they are a few years older, and can understand the resurrection, belief in the living Christ will mean a great step forward in their religious growth. Again it needs to be emphasized that the adults who guide little children should themselves believe with Peter, and express in their own lives, "Thou art the Christ, the Son of the living God." Also, in the home, where there are older people present, young children will hear the name of Jesus in various connections as the Bible is read or at other times.

However, as we introduce the nursery child to Jesus, we are providing the first steps in his life for an acquaintance with and love for Him whose disciples they will later become and in whose Church they will take an active part.

By means of the adults' attitude toward Jesus and through the use of several stories, nursery children will begin to learn that he was someone special, who loved and taught about God and whom God loved. In both stories in *His Name Is Jesus* this is evident.

In "Let the Children Come," Jesus is telling the people about God's love for them. In "A Baby Is Born," the message to the shepherds and Mary's song about God's sending Jesus and Jesus' bringing "love to all the earth" actually are beyond the understanding of three-year-olds, but these ideas, introduced into the realism of the rest of the story, give an impression of the wonderment connected with Jesus' birth.

The best stories about Jesus the man to be used with three-year-olds, in addition to that about Jesus and the children, are Jesus teaching about birds and "Jesus and the Flowers." (See page 227.) This last story is an appropriate sequel to the stories in *The Little Seeds That Grew,* for here Jesus too is leading people from an appreciation of things that grow to an understanding of God's love.

Some parents and teachers tell nursery children incidents about Jesus' healing, such as the story of Peter's wife's mother. *If* this kind of situation is referred to, it is best to speak of Jesus' "making her well" and not to include explanations about doctors' being unable to do so. In such an instance, Jesus will be thought of as a doctor by the young child, as was Dr. Brown by Timothy in *I'm Growing.* Jimmy greeted his mother at church school one day, after hearing the story of the nobleman's son, and said with enthusiasm, "Mother, did you know that Jesus was a very good doctor?" We will have to be careful, however, that the child does not think of Jesus as one who was concerned only with men's sickness. Since three-year-olds are just learning about the very "here and now," it is probably best to postpone the healing incidents to a little later time when they can understand somewhat their deeper significance.

The story of the children who went to see Jesus contains the most important teaching for three-year-olds. Through it they become acquainted with Jesus, who loved the children of his land and who had time to talk to them about God. In this way they are taking the first step toward a later comprehension that Jesus loves all children and a future acknowledgment of Christ as the Son of God and Master of their lives. Again and again teachers see three-year-olds approach the picture of Jesus and the children (see No. 5 in the picture set) and observe it quietly. Joe was thus deeply absorbed when the teacher told him about Jesus' love for the children. "And he didn't spank them, did he?" remarked Joe, smiling and returning to his block house.

And so we teach our children about Jesus—Jesus who loved little children, who helped people, and who was liked and known as a friend; and we tell them about Jesus the baby, whose birthday we celebrate at Christmas.

We have only to see the look on the faces of nursery children as we read, "Jesus held out his arms and said: 'Let the children come to me,'" to know that he is already occupying a place in their lives.

LEARNING ABOUT THE BIBLE

"We search the world for truth. We cull
The good, the true, the beautiful,
From graven stone and written scroll,
And all old flower-fields of the soul;
And, weary seekers of the best,

> We come back laden from our quest,
> To find that all the sages said
> Is in the Book our mothers read."
> —*John Greenleaf Whittier.**

Hearing great passages read from "the Book" by a father or mother, absorbing unconsciously the majesty of Psalm 19 or the rhythm and feeling of the Beatitudes—this is probably the first introduction to the Bible for the little child. But soon he is to become aware of the book itself as part of his own experience. Parents and teachers, therefore, need to consider ways of introducing the Bible to him.

In both the nursery class and the home it is wise to keep a copy of the Bible in evidence so that it can be referred to at convenient times. Often a child will approach and touch the Bible. The adult can then say, "In the Bible we read about God," or, as Miss Anderson said in the book *In Our Church*, "In the Bible we read about Jesus." So the child, guided by an adult whom he loves, first learns to handle and talk about the Bible. Occasionally, too, the teacher or parent can tell a story like that of Jesus and the children with the open Bible in hand.

Bible Verses: It is best to choose only a few Bible verses for the nursery child, and to use these over and over. They may sometimes be read from the Bible, but it is even more important that the child have an opportunity to experience their meaning. The teacher says quietly, "Be kind," as George and Louise and Doris all try to pick up a kitten at the same time. Daddy says, "Think of the wonders of God," as the family, sitting on a hilltop, observe the shining, changing clouds in a sunset sky.

The following verses are most appropriately used with nursery children:

> "You shall call his name Jesus."—*Matthew 1: 21 (R.S.V.).*
> "Let the children come."—*Mark 10: 14 (R.S.V.).*
> "Love one another."—*I John 4: 7.*
> "Be kind."—*Ephesians 4: 32 (R.S.V.).*
> "Think of the wonders of God."—*Job 37: 14 (Moffatt).*
> "The flowers appear on the earth."—*Song of Solomon 2: 12.*
> "The time of the singing of birds is come."—*Song of Solomon 2: 12.*
> "Be gentle towards all."—*II Timothy 2: 24 (A.S.V.).*

---

* Reprinted by permission of and arrangement with Houghton Mifflin Company, the authorized publishers.

Bible Stories: Three-year-old children are still closely bound to the familiar, so most of their stories, if they are to have any meaning for them, should be based on themes of contemporary life. There are a few Bible stories, however, which, because they deal with subjects of interest to children of all times, are suitable. Little children are interested in the story of Baby Samuel (see page 230), but even here the narrative should stop before Samuel goes away from his mother to the Tabernacle. They like to hear about David caring for his sheep (see page 228). And, of course, there are the stories about Jesus mentioned above.

In order to avoid including ideas that are too mature for three-year-olds, or "frightening incidents," such as concern lest Baby Moses be found by soldiers, some teachers and parents dilute great Bible stories so that they can use them with nursery children. Is it not better to wait until the children have grown spiritually, mentally, and emotionally, in order that they may understand the true meaning of such incidents? We do not expect a child to skip before he can walk! But it *is* important that each teacher and parent of the youngest age group know toward what the child is growing in his knowledge of the Bible, and what is to be added in each department—kindergarten, primary, and junior.

It has been pointed out that Jesus, in his own teaching, used many illustrations from contemporary life—the lost coin, the sower, the prodigal son. He did not always go to "the Scriptures" to emphasize a principle, but often referred to situations that men of his day understood and could feel. All who work with little children would do well to follow this example.

Most important of all is the fact that the nursery course, both the teaching plans and the children's books, and guidance in the home are based on Biblical *ideas* which are to become a part of the very life of three-year-olds.

"And one of the scribes came up and . . . asked him, 'Which commandment is the first of all?' Jesus answered, 'The first is, "Hear, O Israel: The Lord our God, the Lord is one; and you shall love the Lord your God with all your heart, and with all your soul, and with all your mind, and with all your strength." The second is this, "You shall love your neighbor as yourself." There is no other commandment greater than these.' "—*Mark 12: 28-31 (R.S.V.).*

Preparation is being made during nursery years for obedience to the two greatest Christian commandments. The little child comes to love God as he sees him in all areas of life; he is learning to love his neighbor as he begins to grow in independence, in sharing and respecting the rights of others, in both the home and the church school. He is learning too to comprehend the meaning of "neighbor" in a broader sense as he becomes acquainted with his doctor—"he that showeth mercy, with cheerfulness"—and with other friends in the community.

It can be said that even for the nursery child there is truth in the statement, "Thy word is a lamp unto my feet."

CHAPTER 3

They Grow as *Persons*

"And Jesus increased in wisdom and stature, and in favor with God and man."—*Luke* 2: 52.

ROWTH is part of God's plan for the grain in the fields, for mountain forests and flowering shrubs. But even more wonderful is his provision for the ongoing development of a human being. To prepare an atmosphere in which our children can best increase "in wisdom and stature, and in favor with God and man" is the responsibility of the home, the church, and the community.

In this chapter we shall see a picture of the nursery child—of his physical, emotional, and social abilities. We shall see him as a *person* as he adjusts to situations around him and to the people who are closest to him.

One of the newest trends in early childhood education is to think of the first years, through the age of eight, as one continuous growing period. If parents and teachers are acquainted with the facts of development concerning these years, they can better understand their own child or the children whom they are teaching. Also, activities will be planned accordingly in the home and in the church nursery, kindergarten, and primary groups. Every effort has been made to use these facts as a guide in the discussion of the program for three-year-olds and in the teaching plans for the year. (See pages 67–212.)

We should know something about the directions in which the body grows. As we observe a newborn baby, we notice that his head is large and that his legs are comparatively small. The large muscles in the upper part of his body are developing first—neck, shoulders, and arms—to be followed by development of the legs and then the fingers. Therefore most of the toys and materials for two- and three-year-olds and many of those for ages four and five will be of the big variety:

37

building blocks, paintbrushes, doll furniture. All children need to climb and lift and run to exercise their shoulders, backs, and legs. Older kindergarten and primary children, because their hand and finger co-ordination is further advanced, usually can sew, do more cutting with scissors, and engage in a few other small activities. The average three-year-old benefits from riding a tricycle, for his ankle and foot muscles are now mature enough to turn the pedals.

The little child does need large pieces of equipment and work materials. But have you noticed how much he enjoys holding a small object in his hand? He picks up a stone in the park and clutches it tightly in his fist. He drives one of his little trucks up and down the back of the upholstered seat in the family car. Since this kind of activity seems to give him satisfaction, and perhaps a sense of power or control, we'll want to include among the big toys in the nursery class a few smaller cubes and cars and dolls.

If parents and teachers are aware of the directions of bodily growth and the emotional, mental, social, and spiritual abilities of their children, they will know when not to expect too much by way of behavior or sustained interest in a story or the manipulation of fork and spoon. On the other hand, they will encourage their children toward increased independence and other new accomplishments when they are ready for them. Later in the chapter we shall look at the characteristics of the child of each age group. Here we want to recall several preliminary facts:

There are individual differences in the rate of growth of children. A three-year-old may still be quite "twoish" in his inability to share his wagon and yet be "fourish" in the length of attention he can give to building a rather complicated house of blocks. Each child has his own pattern; he will be slow in some things and advanced in others. When parents realize this, they will not become panicky if their child does not fit exactly into the standard mold set up for his age. While it is true that children pass through certain *stages* of development—they usually creep before they walk, they babble before they say words, and so on—they will not all pass through each stage *at the same time*. This is a reason why some children are ready to attend nursery class before others. The reluctant ones will enter gradually into this kind of experience under the loving guidance of their parents and the teacher.

Children may vary from the average too when they are temporarily affected by circumstances. Being below par physically often makes children seem dull or cross and restless. On some days Tony may be just "too tired" to put more than one toy back on the shelf. If Mary is catching cold, she will probably dawdle in eating the food on her plate or need Mother to help occasionally in the feeding process. In the preceding chapter reference was made to Judy, who moped all morning in nursery class because her daddy left before she said good-by. Shocks like this will certainly affect the way children act.

Because children do not grow at the same rate of speed, it is best not to compare one with another. In a three-year-old nursery group, we see children who are small and dainty and others who are tall and quite solidly built. When we speak about growing, we refer to the child's own rate of progress. This is true in *I'm Growing* where Dr. Brown measures Timothy during his checkup. And, of course, as far as physical development is concerned, heredity has already predetermined, to quite an extent, both height and bone structure.

It is so hard to find out what really goes on in the minds of little children before they can clearly express themselves in language. We may learn about a child's thoughts through his activities. Such was the case with Ernie, age four. Ernie seemed to be a problem in nursery school. Sometimes he would knock over the other children's towers; often he would retreat under the supply shelves. One day he was drawing with a large crayon on a piece of paper. He called the teacher over to him.

"See what I made," he said. "I'm taller than Molly."

On the paper were two "figures," one taller than the other. The teacher suddenly realized why Ernie wanted attention so badly. He was small for his age; his five-and-a-half-year-old sister was much taller than he. But in the picture *Ernie* was taller. When his mother and teacher talked it over, his mother said that at home they frequently told Ernie that he was "little" and that it would take him a long time to grow up. After this conference when, both at home and nursery school, Ernie was praised for things he could do well, he found more constructive uses for his time. Ernie was a four-year-old, but the trouble started long before he could express what was disturbing him.

It was important to Ernie to be told often that he was "big." However, the strain of having to live up constantly to the reminder, "You are a big boy," can be severe for many little children.

When children are quite young, comparisons are made in regard to their motor or language skills: "Mrs. Jones's Margaret can walk and my Beth is still creeping," or, in the nursery class, "Lucy can talk so well and Philip won't say a word." If only we would remember that time will unravel, at different tempos, the threads of growth and weave them into a pattern for each individual! We are apt to compare children in other ways too—their skill in painting, singing, and climbing, or in their ability to be friendly and helpful. We do not realize the unnecessary harm we may be doing by such comparisons.

A LOOK AT THE CHILD

Following is a brief picture of the child from two through five. Because all the preschool years make up a growth period, it will be easier to understand the three-year-old in relation to the children younger and older than himself—what he is growing *from* and what he is growing *toward*. For he does not completely change on his birthday!

The Two-year-old. He still walks rather stiffly, with his head forward, his feet pointing out, and his arms thrown back. His large muscles are used for lifting and dragging and hauling dolls and big blocks. He tries to give some help in dressing and undressing himself and in washing his hands. He needs a great deal of *time*. He often says, "No," or has a temper tantrum in rebellion against people's doing things for him in this period of new-found (though somewhat unreliable!) independence. He may have a vocabulary of three hundred words. A typical two-year-old sentence is, "Wook, big block on my truck." One must speak slowly and clearly to him, or repeat, for he does not always understand.

The two-year-old is not yet ready to share—he's just learning that objects belong to *him*. He likes the company of a few other children, but continues to play mostly by himself. His attention span is very short, so he flits from one interest to another, and his curiosity continually gets him into trouble in Grandmother's living room!

The Three-year-old. He is gradually assuming a more mature posture and walk. He can hop but will be unable to skip for another year or so. He still needs to exercise his large muscles, but he can put together wooden puzzles with ease, string big wooden beads, and use "jumbo" crayons. Saying "No" and temper tantrums will probably continue for a while as the new-found independence grows. The three-year-old takes a fair amount of responsibility in routines: he can wash his hands, unbutton and button large buttons, dress and undress himself with some help. He is beginning to take turns and put a few toys away and assist in other ways.

His vocabulary may consist of approximately nine hundred words; he uses more complete sentences and is starting to ask questions. We can often talk things over with him, as his reasoning processes are developing. Janie remarked, "When we spill the sand, we clean it up." The teacher can say, "If we rest well, we won't be tired when we go outdoors." Because of the three-year-old's lack of experience, there is a great deal that he does not yet understand. His concepts of time and distance are quite hazy. John remarked, "I went to the park tomorrow." It is because of such limitations that we use expressions like "before rest" or "after you eat your lunch." Also, talk about children far away across the sea and people who lived long ago is beyond the understanding of three-year-olds. A child of this age lives very much in the present and is becoming familiar with his closest surroundings. He loves to hear the same few stories and to sing several chosen songs again and again. He cannot remember over too long a period of time.

While he still likes to play by himself, he is usually happy in a group and is beginning to play with a few children. He does not remain with the same children very long, as do the four- and five-year-olds. He continues to hit out and bite at times in his early efforts to get along with others. In the eighteenth century it was common to moralize about this subject! Isaac Watts wrote:

> "Let dogs delight to bark and bite,
> For God hath made them so;
> Let bears and lions growl and fight,
> For 'tis their nature to.

> "But, children, you should never let
> Your angry passions rise;
> Your little hands were never made
> To tear each other's eyes."

We are are not going to encourage tearing one another's eyes, but some self-defense is desirable. And so often what appears to be a quarrel is quickly settled if the grownup doesn't interfere. However, the three-year-old is beginning to learn to take his turn and to share; he is finding out too that it really pays, for others will take their turn and share with him. He engages in dramatic play, often inaccurate, but with a reflection of the life around him. If there are several "mothers" or "fathers" in the doll corner, that will make no difference. During short periods a doll becomes a patient and he, himself, a fireman.

The attention span of the three-year-old is still short, and, in the nursery class, the teacher doesn't expect him to stay in a large group for stories or worship. Generally his creative efforts in painting, drawing, and clay-modeling, while they bring satisfaction to him, are not identifiable by adults.

The Four-year-old. One is much more "aware" of the four-year-old, for he is active and enthusiastic. He no longer expresses his anger as frequently by kicking out. But he tends to talk about his accomplishments. He is generally independent in the dressing and undressing processes and in the hand-washing routine. He can use scissors fairly well, although he often cannot follow a line. As he paints and draws, his ideas change from one moment to the next. He must continue to use large equipment for running and climbing.

The reasoning and thinking ability of the four-year-old is maturing. He tries out new experiences and finds new uses, more realistically and purposefully organized, for most of the same play equipment used by three-year-olds. He likes to talk and he may have a vocabulary of about fifteen hundred words. He enjoys the sound of new words, especially silly words. He is asking many questions about the world around him. His interests are similar to those of the three-year-old although they are not as fleeting.

The four-year-old likes to be with other children and stays with the same play group for a longer period. Discussions about co-operating and sharing and respecting people's rights have more meaning for him. He continues to discover that things work out better this way for everyone concerned. He often tries to direct the activities of others; but he is beginning to understand such a question as, "Is it fair?" He can usually be expected to listen to a story as part of a group. His increased interest span permits him to listen to a longer story.

The Five-year-old. He looks different as a rule—his body is taller and thinner than the three- or four-year-old's. Although he is able to do some finer types of work with his hands, he must have also an opportunity to exercise arms and back and legs, and to use big pieces of paper and paintbrushes. He is quite independent in many ways.

The five-year-old has a delightful sense of humor; he likes funny touches introduced into his stories. He wants information books too, about things that go and about people with whom he is familiar in the community. His vocabulary continues to increase and his sentences are longer. Bobby remarked, "I imagine little mice were in the stable where Jesus was." The five-year-old is still primarily concerned with here and now.

He is more aware that there are girls and boys in his dramatic play and this dramatic play is highly organized—blocks, dolls, boards, boxes, and cars are put to new and rather involved uses. He begins to choose certain friends with whom to play and does not always accept strange children in the kindergarten. He likes to have the approval of grown-ups.

The five-year-old can sit in a group for discussion and singing or to listen to a more complicated story. It has been discovered that when he paints or draws, he is now able to put on paper an idea which he has previously conceived. He is usually interested in carrying through a project to completion. Some group planning has a real place in the kindergarten.

THE NURSERY CHILD'S NEEDS

Our children need to be loved. This will not be a sentimental affection, but a deep, abiding love which does not change from day to day in the home or from Sunday to Sunday in the church school. Especially when children are disciplined, it is important that they can count on the constant love of those dear to them. They should feel wanted and safe as they become part of a group, in the family or in the nursery class. Doctors have learned that infants in foundling homes may die unless they prescribe for them a certain amount of "loving" and fondling daily.

In the children's psychiatric ward of a large city hospital, a very little boy greeted the visitors by picking up blocks, throwing them against the wall, then looking up for the attentive reaction of the grownups. He did not have a subnormal intelligence; he had been completely deserted by his family and he was longing for smiles and fondling and approval that were meant for him alone. What chance has such a child to understand the love of our Father—God?

In contrast, note the attitude of Miss Anderson in the book *In Our*

Church, and that of Timothy's parents in *I'm Growing*. In the two situations both wholesome love and respect are constantly and understandingly given and, we might add, are returned as well.

Our children must grow and feel important as persons. They should be in an atmosphere where they are at ease and where they are not pushed ahead or held back, so that they can develop at their own rate of speed. They should have an opportunity to express ideas and emotions by the use of play and work materials and through conversation and other experiences.

It is interesting to notice that the nursery group referred to in the preceding chapter wanted to thank God for "us." At this age—and perhaps we don't outgrow it!—the self is quite important. The three-year-old is growing in independence. So we encourage, but do not force him, to hang up his clothes, as does Billy in the church book, or to dress himself as does Timothy in *I'm Growing*, or to care for growing plants as does Jerry in *The Little Seeds That Grew*. Calm, unhurried surroundings are best in these early attempts at taking responsibility. Dressing himself, washing his hands, and feeding himself are still important activities as such for a child of this age. He is interested in the soapy water as he washes his hands, in making a depression with his spoon in the mashed potatoes on his plate. So there is often a great deal of dawdling which will be outgrown later as the child's interests broaden. Then he will hurry with routines so that he can get on to more challenging activity!

Not too long ago routines were overemphasized in nursery school programs and by parents too. Of course when these routines are regularly established, a child will have something firm to hold onto. The world won't fall to pieces if routines are varied, or if Anne or Paul occasionally needs more than usual of Mother's or Daddy's or the teacher's assistance.

Our children must feel pride in accomplishment and in being needed. The behavior of Ernie, the child who was "little," improved as those around him heard the teacher make such remarks as, "Ernie is a good block builder—he'd work well on that road you are building." Sometimes, too, parents and teachers will step in and help a child meet a problem if he finds he cannot solve it successfully.

But grownups can make even three-year-olds feel that they are capable of contributing to living. In *I'm Growing*, "Timothy helped make the bed in Grandmother's room. He smoothed the covers very carefully." Also, "Susan helped sweep away the fresh green grass from the sidewalk and pile it into a basket." In *The Little Seeds That Grew,* Jerry helped his daddy plant string bean seeds, and in the book *In Our Church,* Billy and the other children helped put the toys on the shelves. "Oh, dear," we say to ourselves sometimes, "we could do it so much faster and better alone." Of course that's true. There were probably grimy finger marks and wrinkles on the corner of the spread where Timothy patted it, and blades of grass dotting the sidewalk after Susan's cleaning up! No doubt some string bean vines appeared outside the straight rows after Jerry's planting, and the blocks on the nursery shelves looked like leaning towers! But something was happening inside these children, not so obvious at the moment, which was of greater value than cleanliness and neatness. And what fun it was for their parents and their teacher! We must be realistic in a busy world, but let's take time to work together whenever it's possible.

Our children need to grow in relation to others. They find that in God's plan for people to live in homes, churches, and communities, it is best to share and take turns and respect the rights of those around them. It is not always easy, for the young three-year-old, especially, still goes back to the two-year-old, "It's mine." So we must patiently guide and often *wait.*

Young Johnnie, however, is an example of a three-year-old who blossomed like a rose during a short period of time. When he was enrolled in the summer church laboratory school, he was uneasy about leaving his mother. After several days, when he felt at home with the teacher, his mother did not have to remain during the sessions. But he followed the teacher about, happily enough, engaging silently in a few activities, now and then touching the teacher's skirt. The teacher, of course, patted him occasionally; she and Johnnie looked at books and puzzles together or built a block tower. On the seventh day she took Johnnie's hand and joined in a game of "ring-around-a-rosy" with several children. Johnnie would laugh joyously as he fell down to the ground. Suddenly he left the group and approached George, sitting alone and still feeling a bit forlorn and forsaken. He touched George, smiled, and asked, "Play 'ring rosy'?"

Johnnie, having "found" himself, sensed a need in someone else. Jesus said, "Thou shalt love thy neighbor."

Why, we ask, did this change take place in Johnnie? First of all, his mother co-operated by staying for several days until he became acquainted with this new situation. Gradually, he felt completely at ease with the teacher, as he had been with his mother while she was there. As Johnnie followed the teacher about, her own attitude of calm enjoyment influenced him. Sometimes, using indirect suggestion, she would sing very casually, "I like our nursery class; we have such happy times here," or she would say, "We love our church; it belongs to children and mothers and daddies too." There was more direct action also. She often smiled at Johnnie or patted him to reassure him. He sat on her lap as they looked at books or worked on a puzzle. Then when several children were gathered in the doll corner or at the clay table, she and Johnnie, together, began to enter into their play. It was after one of these experiences, such as playing the game of "ring-around-a-rosy" mentioned above, that Johnnie was ready to venture out *alone* in seeking the fellowship of another person.

LABELS AREN'T FOR CHILDREN

We are told that our tendency in the past to speak of the "timid" child or the "aggressive" child is neither fair nor accurate. Children have difficulties along these and other lines, it is true, but if we place children in categories, we often concentrate so hard on eliminating what we think is a problem that we forget to see the whole child and his growth in relation to it! When these disturbances do arise, our main job will be to find out the *cause*. If we know our facts of growth, we shall discover that some of this behavior is just temporary anyway. But we do want to help children become well adjusted, so that their lives will be as happy as possible.

We shall consider a few of the most common "problems" that arise at home or in the nursery class, remembering, however, that if the needs of children discussed above are really met, if there is love and satisfaction in their lives, such difficulties will be more easily handled and less severe.

It does happen that some children who seem to be "good" are trying to gain the approval of the grownups or are restraining their emotions. Roger, a young three-year-old, apparently did not object to letting his mother go when she brought him to nursery class—he did not cry or kick and scream. But several weeks later he developed hives; the doctor said it was because he was feeling insecure about leaving his mother. Also expression of anger in a temper tantrum is more healthy than a less obvious smoldering resentment. This does not mean that we are going to suspect all the contented children who find life good!

The arrival of a new baby brother or sister is frequently upsetting. Not long ago, a speaker reported the following incident:

> A mother and her little girl were looking at the baby brother.
> CHILD: "I hate him."
> MOTHER: "You're a bad wicked girl. Say, 'I love him.'"
> CHILD: "I love him."

Obviously that was not only the least effective way of changing the child's attitude but it was actually harmful, for she was made to speak untruthfully about her real feelings. Letting her do things for the baby, giving her *extra* love, would be far more helpful and *Christian,* although, in spite of all the parents do to prevent it, some jealousy may remain for a time. In such a situation, the mother might even have talked over the problem with her little daughter saying, "You think Mother and Daddy don't love you any more but [holding her close] we do. We love you *very, very* much." Since there are new babies in many of the nursery children's homes, discussion about them and doll corner play in the nursery class will help in eliminating some of this uneasiness.

The overaggressive tendencies are certainly in evidence in most nursery groups. Charles would come in each Sunday roaring like a lion or kicking up his heels like a horse; once he terrified two angelic little girls sitting peacefully dressing dolls in the doll corner. Charles's mother told the teacher (nursery parents and teachers simply must work together!) that during the week Charles was completely dominated by a group of older children with whom he played. So the teacher did two things: when Charles had to be a horse, she "sent him out to pasture" in another room, and, in his quieter moments, she would ask questions such as, "Are you going to build a house or look at the new book I brought this morning?" He began to feel important as he made decisions. He had never been asked to do so when he played with the older children.

Jill, on the other hand, would sit quietly in a chair, watching the other children at work. She would say, "Thank you," and, "You're welcome," to the teacher in a very "proper" manner. She never wrinkled her starched expensive dress. Jill's very charming but Mid-Victorian grandmother lived at her house, and Jill was fast becoming "a little lady." The family, including the grandmother of course, hadn't realized what was happening. At the suggestion of the teacher, Jill wore more practical clothes to nursery class, and as she began to feel at ease, she entered wholeheartedly into activities, splashing paint about in big, bold strokes at the easel and being the first to kneel on the earth outside the church to examine a purple crocus and to thank God for it.

Fears are a natural part of our make-up, so we will not want our children to feel ashamed if they are afraid. A mother was getting ready to remove a splinter from her little boy's finger. His eyes were full of tears and, stiffening his body, he said, "Soldiers don't cry, do they?"

The wise mother answered: "Of course they cry. Everybody cries sometimes."

Discussions or stories about the dark, animals, thunderstorms, or firsthand experiences will help eliminate any fear connected with them. Naturally if her mother or teacher is afraid during a storm, it is more likely that Nancy will be too! Real security does not mean over-protection. It's a good idea to help a child face a fearful situation and learn to control it. If he has a low light near his bed, he can turn it on or off at will. If he is taught *how* to hold onto a slide, there is less chance of his falling. Even in a nursery school for blind children, independence and some rough-and-tumble play are encouraged.

Three-year-olds, however, do need supervision. For example, they cannot be counted on not to run into the street.

A child must give affection as well as receive it. If he seems to express too much, if he too frequently runs to his teacher or parents and throws his arms around them, it may be that he feels their lack of attention to him and is seeking reassurance.

DISCIPLINE—WITH LOVE

Our most important job, where discipline is concerned, is to help our children develop self-confidence. We will provide them with opportunities to explore and to experiment, but expect them to meet some difficulty along the way. The child will discover that certain actions bring unhappiness to himself and to others. He needs the guidance of adults who give him love, understanding, and respect, taking time to talk about and explain why "we do" or "we don't do" certain things.

For nursery children there are not very many hard-and-fast rules to be obeyed. The ones concerning the health and safety of themselves and others are *musts*. In addition there might be rules about taking reasonable care of their toys, about not touching anything on Daddy's desk without permission, or not climbing up on a special antique sofa which is Mother's pride and joy. However, in such cases we grownups should respect the child's own possessions and provide a place where he can legitimately climb!

It may be necessary to make use of punishment occasionally, but parents especially would do well to remember that when their child is being corrected, he must not feel that he has lost their love. If a child believes that he is rejected and that he has no worth, he will become anxious and insecure. In nursery class, the teacher will be careful not to admonish a child in front of the others or make him sit on a chair and refer to him as a "bad boy." He may have to be isolated from the children until he can "remember," but he knows that the teacher still loves and respects him. If the child has a temper tantrum, removing him to a quiet place where he can give vent to his feeling is a wise procedure. At such times an adult stays calmly nearby, often ignoring him until he is ready for reassurance; the child may have one toy or book.

Of course it is normal for parents and teachers to show some anger at times, but there *must* be a good basic relationship between them and the child. It often seems so much easier for us to scold, to use punishment or rewards and authoritarian control, rather than to guide our children toward the goal of self-discipline. If we find ourselves tempted to punish frequently, we might consider the following questions:

Do we grownups ever make mistakes?

Are we aware of the fact that it is healthy for a child to express his emotions (within reason)?

Are we acquainted with the child's stage of growth, recognizing some behavior as only temporary?

Do we say, "Don't," until it loses all meaning?

Are we consistent? Do we sometimes approve and sometimes disapprove of the same action, confusing the child?

Is the child tired or becoming ill?

Are we slow in using praise (wisely, of course) and quick to condemn or discourage?

Do we try to *prevent* unacceptable behavior by suggesting something positive that the child can do?

Do we give assistance in working through a problem?

Do we help the child co-operate by taking for granted in a matter-of-fact way that certain things are done?

Do we call a child "naughty" because of negligence on our part? Is he cross because he was put to bed late? Is he restless because he is made to sit still so long? Is he running around the room because there is not enough proper equipment to engage his interest?

With all our reading and studying about ways of being good parents and teachers we want to keep in mind two important facts:

First, that the best way to know our children is to live and play and work with them. Children do learn from us—our faith, our attitudes, our wholesome or unhappy approach to life. But we learn from them too, and as we observe their growth and reaction to things and people in their environment, we can better understand how to guide them.

Second, psychologists are now pointing out that techniques in child training can even be harmful if the grownups themselves are so worried about doing the right thing that they are always under tension. The current phrase, "Enjoy your children," is a popular one with both parents and teachers. A sense of humor is invaluable, and courtesy and consideration will work wonders.

It is rather confusing to parents when the methods of child guidance recommended to them suddenly "about-face." It was not too long ago that babies were fed only when the schedule rather than their own need demanded it, and children were treated more like guinea pigs than like human beings. Now many of the experts insist on having schedules adjusted to the physical and emotional needs of the child. But such changes should be expected in a young science like child psychology. Also it is sensible to keep the best of the old while accepting the new as it proves to be workable and helpful.

And so, with our faith in God, and with love and understanding, we shall guide the little children in their development as persons—our children whose growing bodies, minds, and spirits are committed to our care and keeping.

CHAPTER 4

They Become Aware
of Their World

"Drop a pebble in the water: just a splash, and it is gone;
But there's half-a-hundred ripples circling on and on and on,
Spreading, spreading from the center, flowing on out to the
sea.
And there is no way of telling where the end is going to be." *

IT'S A BIG WORLD in which the three-year-old lives, but he's not
concerned with a very large part of it as yet. When he drops his
pebble in the water, he looks down and sees only the few deep
ripples near "the splash." Grandfather, standing beside him, is the
one who looks up and out and wonders where the end is going to be.

The world for preschool children is bounded by their homes and
their immediate surroundings. For some, there will be air and light and
quiet beauty; for others, crowded darkness and grinding noise. For
some, there will be fields to roam and mountains in the spring—hills
white and pink with dogwood and azalea in bloom. For others, there
will be a narrow courtyard for their play, or a little square of stony
earth. For many, there will be a home of reasonable comfort and an out-
of-doors with exciting things for exploring and for learning. And in the
church materials will be introduced and experiences provided to help
these growing children find out about the wonders of God's world.

As the little child learns about his environment, he makes good use
of his mind. His mental growth is rapid during the early years. He
wants to know about things; he is curious. Reasoning and judgment
have gone a long way by the time he is ready for first grade. Note the
following questions and statements of two- to six-year-olds:

* From "Drop a Pebble in the Water," by James W. Foley.

"Can we eat the sand?" (Most two-year-olds would just go ahead and *eat* it!)

"Has dolls got real eyes?"

"A house doesn't have no tail."

"Houses have roofs, all buildings have roofs."

"The doll's clothes need to be ironed because they're wrinkled."

"The big soap—you know what happened to it? It got small."

"A zoo is where you put animals."

"Soldiers get killed, don't they? They keep on getting killed."

"I can carry two; I'm stout, you know."

"That's not the way to hold a baby."

"Nobody can go through there because we blocked the road."

For the two- and three-year-olds a great deal of learning takes place through trial and error, because they do not yet have the benefit of previous experience on which to act. We watch a child of two try to pull his wagon through a narrow space—he pulls and tugs and pulls and tugs; finally he backs it up and takes a different route. The three-year-old experiments with a large wooden puzzle, turning and fitting the pieces into place.

The attention span of the younger children is limited, but increases fairly rapidly during the fourth and fifth years. Stories told in the nursery class should be short, and the children should be free to change their activities quite frequently.

Sometimes, however, we take too much for granted where the memory ability of young children is concerned. For instance, if a child is punished quite a while after an action, he may not even connect the punishment with his misbehavior. And real memory training for nursery children is not to teach them long poems or passages, but to give them opportunities to explore and find things out. Little verses and songs and stories will be remembered best as they are frequently repeated in connection with an activity.

It is often through his senses, which are highly developed, that the preschool child discovers his world. The following comments are typical:

"My shoestrings are as slick as roller skates."

"In the spring the sun is so warm you can wear a bathing suit and ride on the warm shoot-de-shoots."

"My turtle's back is just as smooth as a piece of sandpaper can make a piece of wood."

"The flowers [paper ones] feel like potato chips."

"I have some unsticky clay."

When Jonathan came to school, he lifted up his foot, and, touching his shiny brown shoe, said proudly to the teacher, "Smell it; it's polish." And of course all parents have been just as excited as Junior about the hair-tonic aroma after his haircut! In the book *In Our Church*, Billy made a yellow-and-blue picture for his mother, he heard the bell sounds of the organ music, and touched the smooth gold edges of the Bible. In *The Little Seeds That Grew*, Jerry dropped the slippery bean seeds along the rows, and in *I'm Growing*, Timothy enjoyed his big red truck.

Imagination, "the picturing power or act of the mind," is very evident in the play of little children. It is important that parents and teachers understand why it is necessary to provide play opportunities and equipment. Play is really work for the child, and in the doll corner or with his blocks and trucks he is learning relationships or reproducing experiences about both people and things. In the doll corner "doctors" and "nurses" care for sick babies (somewhat roughly it seems to adult observers!) and a group of three-year-olds discuss God's plan for families after they have watched a neighbor baby through a porch window. Houses are built out of blocks and home play is enacted.

Before discussing what little children learn about their world, we should consider several facts:

Children are imitators of the grownups around them. Are we eager to see and find out things, are we aware of opportunities for enjoyment and for learning, for ourselves as well as for our children? Are we too old or too sophisticated or too worldly-wise to express wonder as we observe an ant carrying a mammoth crumb of bread, or as we watch the giant jaws of a steam shovel champing at the earth? Are we too embarrassed to say, "Thank you, God," as we touch the velvet softness of a pansy face or see rain soaking down into a dry, parched field?

Children learn better under certain circumstances. There are three laws or principles that especially concern us in our work with little children:

1. The law of readiness. It is necessary for the children to be interested in what we are teaching. This applies to the "worship moments" we talk so much about. When the little child experiences the need to thank God, he should do so at that moment if possible rather than wait

until later during a regular time for worship. Or, if the teacher wishes to point up a special idea during a session, such as sharing, she will watch for a chance to talk about it as two children are working happily together. She will be very casual, of course, and not spoil the play by making a long speech! (See pages 122, 129, 131.)

2. The law of exercise. Children will learn best through activity and repetition. Both at home and in the church school they will have an opportunity to *live* the Christian way of life and to develop their minds, bodies, and spirits, not just by listening, but by *doing*.

3. The law of effect. When pleasant results develop from an experience, the child will be more likely to repeat such an experience. He will want to return to nursery class if the parents and teachers have met his needs so that he feels at home there. He will want to dry the spoons again if Mother praised that effort and didn't scold because he dropped water on the floor.

What are some of the activities and materials we should provide if we are to help our children become aware of the world in which they live, so that reasoning and the senses and the imagination will be encouraged to develop?

The very first contacts with new things are in the home. The child follows Mother about, observing her cleaning and cooking or accompanying her to the store. And mother and child chat together, the child asking "why" and "where" and "what" and Mother, we hope, taking time to answer. According to one of our newspaper columnists, the modern kitchen is responsible for discouraging this kind of fellowship. She writes:

"There's no place there for the youngsters to play while Mother peels potatoes or bakes a pie. Dad, who loves to loaf about and chat with the family during that cozy hour just before dinner, is shooed out, or stands around miserably because a stool is the only sitting convenience. He feels much in the way.

"When will women demand something different? All the conveniences could be there, but why not a kitchen big enough to be a sitting room too, with comfortable chairs, growing plants, magazines, books, and games, where the family could visit together while meals are cooking?

"We've substituted a laboratory for the big, cluttered kitchen which used to be the heart of the home, when the home was a place everybody loved." *

---

* From "Home's Where the Kitchen Is," by Mrs. Walter Ferguson, in *The Pittsburgh Press*, April 28, 1948. Used by permission.

Talking with grownups, taking walks with them, examining and comparing objects, looking at books, making use of play materials like dolls and blocks and clay and paint, all these experiences will be valuable in learning.

CHILDREN LEARN ABOUT GROWING THINGS

In Chapter 2 reference was made to God's laws which govern the universe. We teach little children that God does not just *give* us flowers and grain; rain and sunshine and care by people are necessary for their growth. Jerry, in *The Little Seeds That Grew*, began to understand this principle as he planted and cared for his flower seeds and as his daddy talked with him about the rain and sunshine.

Another evidence of pattern in the world is found in the change of seasons and in night following day. "God plans for" is an expression that many parents and teachers find useful. Such an approach eliminates the danger of seeing God in nature rather than as Creator of nature. Children learn about other natural phenomena too—that ice and snow melt in the sun and that rocks are hard.

All those who have worked with little children could recount many incidents of their interest in the elements and the live things around them. One day Carolyn, age five, discovered "a baby fern" in the window box. "I like God," she said. "He's awfully good." And on another occasion, out-of-doors, she sang as she twirled around:

> "The wind is blowing
> Around and around,
> This is how the wind blows,
> Around and around."

Chris, age three, looking up at the old oak tree, chanted:

> "Little birds up in the tree
> Little birds up in the tree
> Little birds are singing."

And after a thunderstorm Vickie remarked, "The rain is leaking off the leaves."

A group of country children, ages three to five, went for a walk in the springtime. When they returned, they talked about what they had seen. Their report was as follows:

"In the spring God gives us food to eat.
Crops grow—we have cabbages, radishes, and
　　cucumbers.
The breeze makes you warm.
When the breeze is cold, it blows you around.

"In the spring flowers grow up pretty—lilies and
　　sweet peas and tulips.
There are cherry blossoms and peach blossoms.
Birds come out—bluebirds and robins and whip-
　　poorwills.
Baby birds are in the nests.

"God made the world!"

Little children living in a crowded city came back gaily from the
park bearing a real treasure—a bag of half-dried leaves and stones (including a few tiny loose pieces of sidewalk cement!).

Insects, fish, and animals are interesting to watch and care for. But
they can be a bit confusing. Charlotte, a young three-year-old, was
much intrigued by a discussion of birds and the fact that they could
fly. When she saw goldfish for the first time, she asked, "Can *they* fly?"

It is good when even city children have a chance to become acquainted with animals. After a trip to the pets' corner in the zoo, one
group of four-year-olds said: "We saw the animals. We saw a monkey
swinging so fast that we laughed. We touched a goat and a new piggy.
We looked at the piggy's eyes and they were open. The goat and the
piggy didn't say anything but the crow did—he said, 'Caw, caw, caw.'
The piggy and the lambs felt soft."

So children learn about growth and the beauties of the world, but
they learn also that because there are laws, flowers and animals—and
people—die; that hail sometimes destroys grain in the fields. If children
ask, we adults should interpret simply and positively these apparent
tragedies. When leaves lie dry and crisp upon the ground, we speak
of new buds in the spring. When wheat has been beaten to the earth,
we explain that the farmer will plant more seeds. It is not so easy
when a person dies. A typical conversation is as follows:

"Where is Grandmother?"
"Grandmother has gone away for a while."
"Will she come back?"
"Not for a long, long time. She is tired and she's going to rest."

We note that in the answers given above, there are one or two stock phrases that are frequently used to reply to the question about death. Actually these are at variance with what we really want the child to know. If we say that Grandmother has gone away for a while and is resting, the child will expect to see her again. Also this builds up an unhappy association with rest.

Sometimes one hears a discussion like this:

"Where is Grandmother?"
"Grandmother has gone to heaven."
"Where is heaven?"
"Heaven is where God is."

If we make such replies, saying, "Grandmother has gone to heaven," and, "Heaven is where God is," we must be sure not to imply that "God *took* Grandmother." And we should think about how we are going to respond to further questions, which are bound to come, concerning what heaven looks like. To say, "I don't know—no one has seen heaven," is probably satisfactory.

It is difficult to suggest exactly what to say or do, for circumstances vary. The attitude of the adults is always important. Even though they do display quiet, natural grief, there will be a serenity apparent that only those who trust in God can possess. And if the one who has died was a parent, it is necessary that a loving, close relationship be immediately emphasized between another member of the family and the little child.

When the situation arises, each individual must decide whether or not so young a child should see the body of a loved one. And many people have found that if a child asks, "Where is Daddy?" or, "Where is Toby [a playmate]?" the best answer is simply to say, "Daddy [or Toby] has died." To the next question, "What is 'died'?" they would add, "It means that he did not need his body anymore." Any answer that we give about life's mysteries will not be entirely understood by the young child, but at least we will be sincere and truthful and say what we believe. If a child has occasionally become acquainted with the word "death," through experiences with animals or people with whom he has no emotional ties, it will make explanation somewhat easier when he must face a personal loss. But most important always will be the faith of those who are round about the child, and their strong assurance that Jesus has overcome for us all fear of death.

The three-year-old will begin also to ask questions about birth. "Mommie, where did I come from?" The first, simple truthful answer to give is, "You grew inside of my body." Usually that will satisfy the very little child. We need to answer only one question at a time. If the child is still quite young and asks, "How?" the answer might be, "God planned for mothers and daddies to have babies." Generally the three-year-old is content with this response. Whatever answer we give, we should be truthful, matter-of-fact, and free from embarrassment. Wholesome attitudes toward sex and marriage are implanted early. Caring for pets will help teach naturally some of the facts about birth and death.

CHILDREN LEARN ABOUT THINGS THAT GO

"We walked this morning because we were out of gas," said Danny. It doesn't take long for a preschool child to become acquainted with this kind of situation in our modern world. Tops, hourglasses, thermometers, trailers, cars, engines, steam shovels, airplanes—things that go and things that "work"—are of intense interest to young children and, we might add, to their daddies too! This is recognized by construction companies, who cut out several niches in fences where excavation or building is in progress. Some of these observation niches are low and are marked "Junior Sidewalk Superintendent"; others are high and are marked "Sidewalk Superintendent."

A weekday group of four-year-old children visited the construction site of a new apartment house. They were fascinated by the fact that "the steam shovels were digging the dirt up" and a "machine was picking up beams with a pulley." So they went to a nearby hardware store, bought a pulley, and rigged it up in their nursery room. The teacher had to learn with the children how to make it work!

Things that go seem to encourage spontaneous rhythm and song—the "tick tock, tick tock" of the clock, the "whir, whir, whir," of the top, the "chug, chug, chug" of the engine. Barry chanted, as he pushed his wooden boat:

> "Steam, steam, steam
> Here goes the boat down the stream."

We'll want to take time whenever we can to observe machinery and smaller scientific gadgets in action and to answer a child's questions about them, or find out what the answers should be. We'll see to it that he has sturdy wooden toys and blocks with which to reproduce his experiences. For actually man's use of his brain and brawn to build houses and to provide for his other physical needs in a community is part of God's plan for living.

CHILDREN LEARN ABOUT PEOPLE

The first people whom the young child knows, of course, are his parents or other grownups who care for him, and his brothers and sisters. Gradually relatives and visiting friends and neighbors who live close by enlarge his circle of acquaintances. But even in the life of the three-year-old another group of people begin to be important to him— these are the community helpers. He is beginning to learn that God's plan for people to help one another extends beyond the boundary of his family ties. And yet most of these people—the doctor, the postman, the minister, and, in some cases, the farmer—come directly into contact with his home. This interest in outside helpers is much more developed in four- and five-year-old children, but we do well to introduce the threes to them and to their work. Sessions in Units 2, 3, and 4 in the teaching plans, pages 149–209, include this discussion.

One of the first "outsiders" to become a friend is the doctor. The story, "Our Doctor," in *I'm Growing*, can be used as one means of building up confidence in the doctor, who, because he must often of necessity inflict pain, may seem to be a frightening monster. Recently a little child was sitting in a doctor's waiting room with his mother. The child announced, "I'm going to bash that doctor's head in," and when his turn came to go into the doctor's office, he screamed and kicked. It is quite likely that if the child had been taken for regular checkups when there was no pain, such a situation would have been eased. Also, when it *is* going to hurt, we should say so in advance rather than tell an untruth.

When children pray, and at other times, we have an opportunity to speak of the way God works through people. They say, for instance, "Thank you, God, for chairs and tables." We then explain: "Yes, we are glad for chairs and tables. We are glad that God planned for trees to grow; wood comes from trees. We are glad too that men made the chairs and tables for us out of the wood." And, by our own attitude, let us build up in the children an appreciation for all kinds of work, not just that which is professional or highly skilled.

The older preschool children, especially, can begin to see that man is often responsible for catastrophe. If a fire sweeps through a tenement house and people suffer, the question is not, "Why did God let it happen?" but rather, "Why hadn't the owners repaired the building so it wouldn't be a fire hazard?" And, of course, even the children themselves or the parents of younger ones must take responsibility in watching traffic lights and in not dashing out into the street.

The nursery child is rarely aware of racial or economic differences in his playmates, but it isn't long before his attention is called to them. We must begin to teach the child to value people as individuals, and, when groups or classes become recognized, to direct his attention to both their contributions and their needs.

Raymond, a Japanese-American child, was three and a half when he attended the first session of a Bible school where most of the children were older than he. After he returned home, his mother asked, "Did you have a good time, Raymond?"

"Yes," replied Raymond, then added thoughtfully, "they called me Japanese." The mother said, "Well, you are Japanese-American." "No," answered Raymond, "I'm not Japanese—I'm Raymond."

Thus the children grow and become aware of the world around them—the world which contains so much of wonder and of gladness and yet is so perplexing with its mystery and sorrow. But it is our Father's world: we grownups and our children will learn confidently together; we will enjoy the happy times which come and meet the sober ones with courage and serenity.

CHAPTER 5

They Go to Church

"Rise up, O men of God!
    Have done with lesser things;
    Give heart and soul and mind and
        strength
    To serve the King of kings.

. . . .

"Rise up, O men of God!
    The Church for you doth wait,
    Her strength unequal to her task;
    Rise up, and make her great!

"Lift high the cross of Christ!
    Tread where His feet have trod;
    As brothers of the Son of Man,
    Rise up, O men of God!" *

ONE of the first ventures away from home for the little child is his attendance at the nursery class of the church school. Whether or not this is to be a satisfying experience that will lay the foundation for future participation and membership in the church depends to a great extent on our attitudes as parents and teachers, and on the kind of program we plan.

The Church is waiting for every one of us to rise up and give of our time and our interest and our resources. We must continue to strengthen this fellowship of Christian believers which has contributed so much to us.

"Before I was born my church gave to my parents ideals of life and love that made my home a place of strength and beauty.

"In helpless infancy my church joined my parents in consecrating me to Christ and in baptizing me in his name.

---

* William Pierson Merrill, in *The Hymnal* (1933). The Westminster Press. Used by permission of The Presbyterian Tribune.

"My church enriched my childhood with the romance and religion and the lessons of life that have been woven into the texture of my soul. . . .

"When first my heart knew the strange awakenings of love my church taught me to chasten and spiritualize my affections; she sanctioned my marriage and blessed my home.

"When my heart was seamed with sorrow, and I thought the sun could never shine again, my church drew me to the Friend of all the weary and whispered to me the hope of another morning, eternal and tearless.

"When my steps have slipped and I have known the bitterness of sin, my church has believed in me and . . . she has called me back to live within the heights of myself.

"Now have come the children dearer to me than life itself and my church is helping me to train them for all joyous and clean and Christly living.

"My church . . . asks my service and my loyalty. She has a right to ask it! I will help her do for others what she has done for me. In this place in which I live, I will help her keep aflame and aloft the torch of a living faith." *

We will give our loyalty and our service. Our spirit of joy will be caught by the little child as we sincerely feel, "Lord, I have loved the habitation of thy house, and the place where thine honor dwelleth" (Ps. 26: 8), and, "I was glad when they said unto me, Let us go into the house of the Lord" (Ps. 122: 1). On the contrary, if we act impatiently as we rush about to get ready for church school or make hurried preparations to teach after the children have come, we shall not be providing the calm atmosphere which they need.

Children will be quick to perceive our attitude toward other people in the church—those who appear to be congenial and those who, for various reasons, seem to be "different." They will unconsciously absorb our desire to reach out to strangers and invite them into the church fellowship and to know and serve Jesus Christ. They will begin to notice whether we give grudgingly of our substance or whether the right of stewardship is held by us as a privilege.

We shall see to it too that this church, of which our children are to be a part, is interested in both the souls and the affairs of men. Its voice will be heard in community and national concerns: relationships between industry and labor, maternal and child welfare laws, preservation of a peaceful and a truly democratic way of life. It will be active

* From "My Church," by William Henry Boddy, D.D. Department of Evangelism, Board of National Missions of the Presbyterian Church in the U. S. A. Used by permission.

in the enterprise of missions so that men everywhere may hear and benefit by the "good news."

How, then, can we teachers and parents make the first contact with the church itself a happy one for the children? This is an initial step away from the completely ingrown unit of their own family toward a larger fellowship.

In the home there is often a discussion of *our* church; the young child must feel that his parents are entering into such an experience *with* him. Belonging to a church gives a feeling of stability, especially to a family that must move often from place to place. The parents and the child might take time during the week to walk or drive by the church or to discuss church activities at mealtime. The minister will be invited as a friend who is interested in talking with the little child as well as with his parents. The child will first be taken to the nursery class to visit and will then attend regularly, unless he has a cold or is not emotionally ready. He will know, while he is there, that his parents are in another class or in the church service. All these activities are related to the vows taken by parents at their child's baptism, when they promised to bring him up "in the nurture and admonition of the Lord."

The teacher will try to make the nursery class experience as home-like as possible. She will not call the church "God's house." Rather, the church is where "we hear about God." The child takes a very literal interest in the church building—it is *his*. One day, during a summer laboratory school, several three-year-olds were busy washing the stone around the church entrance with big paintbrushes and water. An observer asked Harry, "Why are you cleaning the church?"

Harry replied, "Because it's dirty."

The observer was somewhat taken aback, for she had expected an answer that would imply that God's house must be kept clean. One might add that an activity like that above can build up a feeling of friendship and appreciation for the sexton.

Real living goes on in the church nursery class—there are activities for learning the Christian way of life. And it is another home for the child—his church home. Read the story "The Nursery Class," in the book *In Our Church*. There you will find crayons and blocks and balls and dolls in use. There you will see the attitude of the teacher—her warmth of affection and courtesy as she becomes the mother substitute. You will see the thoughtfulness of Billy's parents; they do not rush away, but wait to say good-by and to tell him that they will be back.

There are other rooms in the church that because of their homelike-ness appeal especially to preschool children. Excursions to visit them are usually not too difficult to arrange. The dishes in the kitchen, the cupboards in the dining room, the books in the minister's study will appeal to the interests of the little child. If classes are meeting in these various rooms, it is possible to forewarn the members, so they will expect the children and talk with them "as friends" rather than be amused by them.

Nursery children are learning about the larger church building too. In the story "The Big Church," in the book *In Our Church*, Miss Anderson takes the group on a visit to the sanctuary. Sometimes this must be a slow process, especially where dark or large interiors may be frightening to the children. On one occasion a teacher and her three-year-olds were sitting calmly in a pew when Richard suddenly went rushing out the back, crying, "Let's get out of here!" In preparation we may want to read the story many times or take the children only as far as the door at first. And before entering the sanctuary, we will say to the children, "We walk slowly in church, for there are many things to see." To say that we do not run because God is there or for a similar reason is building up a frightening relationship with God. The children will soon assume a reverent attitude if we walk and talk softly; and we do say, "Our mothers and daddies come into the big church to hear about God."

During the past several years ministers and other religious workers have been especially interested in the program for children under the age of six. An increasing number of churches are discovering the value of conducting weekday morning nursery schools. Various kinds are being established. There is the regular five-mornings-a-week nursery school which is usually found in large city and suburban churches. In some communities play groups are organized. These are held two or three days a week under the supervision of mothers, who take turns staying with the children. Recently, in several industrial sections where downtown churches once had closed doors, day nurseries have been set up to meet the needs of working parents. And, incidentally, as a result Sunday church congregations are beginning to appear.

It is not easy to establish schools for preschool children. State and city health rules are usually very strict—as they ought to be. The program should be supervised by a trained teacher. Equipment can become expensive. But churches *are* finding ways of tackling the prob-

lem. Contributions of service and money by church and community members, making one's own equipment, working out a tuition system to take care of expenses—these are some of the methods that have been tried and found helpful.

If it *is* possible for a church to organize a weekday preschool program, there will be an opportunity to continue activities begun in the Sunday nursery or kindergarten classes and to give a day-by-day guidance which is more effective. Parents in this way will have frequent contacts with the church too. However, not all young children are ready for daily separation from home ties. Parents and the teacher should talk over the advisability of enrolling each child or of waiting to send him later or only occasionally.

You will find that many suggestions offered in this nursery course can be applied to the weekday program.

Recently a seminar was held on "The Nursery Child in the Church and the Community." Pastors, religious education directors, and teachers were there. Their backgrounds and their parishes were varied—the large city, the suburb, and the rural area were represented; so were the advantages and the problems peculiar to each situation. Yet all the workers seemed to have one common goal—to return to their fields determined to improve as far as possible the program for the youngest children under their guidance. A pastor remarked that he would put more time on visiting the parents of babies. Another said that his congregation was preparing to build a new church—he would see to it that a large, light room was included for the three-year-olds. The teacher in a one-room church school thought that by using folding screens inside and by holding classes outdoors in good weather, she would be able to separate the preschool from the primary children. A director of religious education from an industrial section realized more fully her obligation to take part in investigating certain community conditions which affected the lives of little children and would undoubtedly contribute to delinquency.

These are important years—the early years. Children are learning from us our faith and our attitudes. They are growing toward God, they are developing as persons, they are becoming aware of their world, they are going to church. Are we ready to guide them?

IN THE
NURSERY CLASS

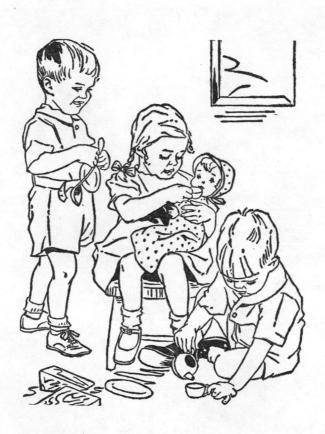

CHAPTER 6

The Nursery Class
in the Nursery Department

THE NURSERY CLASS for three-year-olds in the church school and activities related to it are a vital part of the total program of the nursery department.

WHAT IS THE NURSERY DEPARTMENT?

The nursery department is the organization in the church that is concerned with children from birth through three years of age, and with their parents. The department reaches the parents and homes of *all* these babies and children. Names of babies and children under the age of three constitute *the nursery roll*. (If there is not a nursery class, the nursery roll includes the three-year-olds as well.) There should be classes and forums for the parents, and usually groups for the children within the church.

THE NURSERY COMMITTEE

In the average church, the nursery committee may consist of the nursery department superintendent, the nursery roll supervisor, the teacher and assistants of any nursery groups, and a parent couple from each of these groups. At certain times the committee should call into consultation the minister, the general church school superintendent, an elder, a trustee, and a deacon. Because church officers and leaders often know so little about work with younger children, it is advisable to acquaint them with this phase of the program. And the nursery department will become a more integral part of the Sunday church school. A director of Christian education or a home visitor would be a member of the committee.

In the small church those responsible for nursery work may be the nursery teacher and her assistant and several parents. But at times they too would call in the minister and church officers.

The nursery committee will recognize the arrival of a new baby in the church family. The announcement is usually printed in the church bulletin or made orally by the minister from the pulpit. Flowers may be placed in the front of the church on Sunday and then may be taken to the mother in the hospital. The home visitor or nursery roll supervisor will call in several weeks to ask that the infant's name be written on the church's nursery roll, and will present the father and mother with a certificate of membership. The infant's name will be inscribed in a book or on a nursery roll chart (sometimes referred to as a cradle roll chart) in the church school. At fairly frequent intervals announcements of meetings will be sent and visits made. Religious and secular literature on child guidance may be given or recommended. (See bibliography for suggestions, pages 241–245.) Records are kept in the general files of the department. Cards will contain the names of the babies and children on the nursery roll, the names and church affiliation of their parents, dates of visits to the homes, and a short statement concerning each visit.

The pastor has a fine opportunity to challenge parents with their responsibility for the early Christian education of their children as he discusses the sacrament of Baptism. Parents are not to take the vow lightly. Confessing their own faith, they will agree to provide an atmosphere in the home in which an acquaintance with God and Christian practice may continue to develop. They should co-operate with the church program too, and enroll their children in the church nursery class when they are ready to enter.

Every member of the nursery committee ought to appoint himself an evangelist. The names of new families and new babies in the community will be secured, and a visit will be made in those homes. If there is already a church affiliation, no harm is done and the warm gesture is appreciated. But what tragedy there would be in leaving untouched by the church a home in which a young child might have been guided toward God in the earliest years and was not! Churches are finding that the parent members of the committee, with babies and preschool children of their own, do an especially good job at getting in touch with strangers.

NURSERY GROUPS IN THE CHURCH

In many churches there are three nursery groups—one for babies, another for two-year-olds, and a third for three-year-olds. The first two are "care groups," while the class for three-year-olds has a more organized and directed program.

When the nursery sessions are held during the church hour, it gives parents an opportunity to attend the morning service. In some churches a longer session is held for the three-year-olds. In this case the class begins at the same time as the rest of the church school and extends through the church hour, and includes a lunch of milk or fruit juice and a longer rest period for the children. The parents can be present at a parents' class and then go to church. In other churches, owing to an increased enrollment of young children, two nursery sessions are held, one group of children coming during the regular church school hour and another during the church service.

When it is absolutely necessary for nursery and older children to be in a care group in the same room, an adequate number of assistant teachers and the use of screens will help relieve this situation.

Group for Babies. If there is a warm, clean room available, and competent supervision, a nursery for crib babies and the smallest toddlers is a means of bringing young parents to church. Cribs and "first toys" should be kept sanitary, and any signs of illness checked. A trained nurse in the congregation, assisted by parents, may volunteer her time. It is very important that care groups be handled by mature and experienced people.

Group for Two-year-olds. If the babies' room is quite large, screens for dividing it will provide a place for the two-year-olds. But whether the room is shared in this way or whether a separate room is used, the needs of two-year-olds should be met. There will be a variety of appropriate toys—trucks and pull toys, big blocks, soft dolls and blankets and a sturdy doll bed; also washable books to be looked at *and* carried around. Clay and large crayons and good-sized sheets of paper are valuable. Two pieces of some of the equipment are necessary—we remember that the two-year-old is still not ready to do much sharing. He likes the company of other children, but engages mostly in individual play. In a calm and quiet atmosphere he will explore many interests, spending a very limited time with each. There will be short and incidental music and story and worship experiences with individual children, or with a group of two or three.

Two-year-olds should not be crowded together; nor does the good teacher hurry them in any way. It is quite probable that a few of the children will be uneasy about leaving their mothers. Parents should be invited to stay in the room as long as this is necessary, or to sit for several Sundays in a rear pew in the church service, where they can be on call if their children are unhappy without them.

If there is an extended session, hand-washing, drinking milk or juice, and a longer rest on mats will be included in the program.

Class for Three-year-olds. There is a big increase in the number of churches that are forming a class for three-year-olds, thus separating them from both the younger two-year-olds and the kindergarten (or beginners) group. Recalling the facts of growth in the first section of this handbook, we recognize that three-year-olds need a program to fit their needs. They are more mature than the twos—more steady on their feet, more ready for entering into a group experience in which they can begin to co-operate and to take turns. Creative play and language are developing, and many questions are asked. The children of this age are growing in independence and in assuming responsibility.

On the other hand, their attention span is still quite short, and they cannot be expected to stay in a large group for stories or worship, as do most of the four-year-olds and the fives. They become tired easily and are overstimulated by the outgoing energy and more highly organized play of older children. Socially they can cope with their equals—there will be a certain amount of hitting and conflict—but not with older children, who naturally often take advantage. And, because growth in children takes place in the large muscles first, three-year-olds are not yet ready to participate in the few activities demanding finer hand co-ordinations which are beginning to find a place in the kindergarten program.

WHAT IS THE PURPOSE OF THE NURSERY CLASS FOR THREE-YEAR-OLDS?

There is a directed program for this age group. Teaching plans for a year in the nursery class are found on pages 111–212. Throughout these sessions, the purpose will be reiterated, but we shall summarize here as well.

1. In the nursery class for three-year-olds there is real religious development on the part of the children, but it is expressed in simple terms. They begin to know more about God—about God's plan for growth and for people to live in homes and in communities and to help one another. Worship is deeply rooted within them, for it is an integral part of many experiences. They hear stories of Jesus—when he was a baby, and how, when he was a man, the children came to him. They begin to understand that he too loved God, and appreciated God's world. They see and talk about the Bible. They absorb the atmosphere resulting from the Christian faith and love of the teacher.

2. They gain in independence and security. They have opportunity to plan, to work out problems, to hang up wraps, to put toys away, and gradually to assume other responsibilities. They are at ease because they can go along at their individual rate of speed—they are not forced ahead or held back. Their emotional horizons are widening—here is another place outside the home where they are *wanted* and feel as though they belong.

3. They practice Christian attitudes toward others. Through play they begin to share, to co-operate, and to consider other people.

4. They become increasingly aware of their environment. Through activities and the use of their senses, they learn about nature, and about institutions close to them.

5. They grow physically. There is equipment that promotes physical development. The program alternates between activity and rest. There is protection against colds and contagious diseases.

6. They receive early a joyous, satisfying association with the church.

7. The nursery class draws parents and teachers together. It is an instrument for more thorough and concrete Christian guidance on the part of the church in influencing the homes of young children.

A discussion of the organization, guidance, room, equipment, and activities for the class for three-year-olds is included in the chapters " 'At Home in Church' " and "Three-year-olds at Work."

PARENTS' CLASS

A parents' class, held during the church school hour, provides a convenient time for a study of Christian beliefs and practices and their application to the lives of the parents and their children. A lending library, containing books and pamphlets on spiritual growth and child guidance, may be housed in this classroom. A bulletin board, with announcements, newspaper articles, and other clippings, encourages interest.

PROMOTION

In the first section of this book, the fact was emphasized that children develop at different rates of speed. Therefore it is important for the nursery and kindergarten teachers or superintendents to keep in close touch. It is preferable not to set a hard-and-fast rule of promotion but to move the children from one class to another as they are ready for it—physically, emotionally, and socially. It is not a question of intelligence—parents, please note!—but of placing the child where he can best grow and yet feel at ease.

In some weekday experimental nursery schools the program is so organized that children are free to wander at will between an "older" and a "younger" room. It may not always be practical for us to follow this kind of arrangement. However, we *should* prepare children for promotion by letting them visit the new group in advance, to become acquainted with the teacher and the room; and after a child is promoted, we should allow him to return to his own group for a while if he seems happier there.

CHAPTER 7

"At Home in Church"

IT WAS a very hot midsummer Sunday morning. Only six three-
year-olds and the teacher were present at nursery class. The children lay down on the rug to relax and the teacher sat beside them.
The weather made the children very restless. In a few minutes Kenny
got up, walked to the shelf, chose a block, and carried it back to his
place. He enjoyed holding the block as he settled down to rest. One
by one the other five children followed his example. Somehow sens-
ing the contentment which this brought, Kenny returned to the shelf,
chose another block, and, smiling, gave it to the teacher! She was both
amused (not obviously) and touched. But this incident also represented one of those very special moments which come in our teaching.
For the teacher, as she accepted the block from Kenny, thought of the
words, "Here, in the nursery class, is another place outside the home
where children are *wanted* and feel as though they belong." Truly,
it could be said that Kenny was "at home in church."

Now obviously it is not always easy to provide quite so informal an
atmosphere, for in many churches attendance is large or somewhat
crowded conditions exist. However, *the spirit can be the same,* and
through careful planning, and dividing children into smaller groups,
it is possible to create a more homelike situation. As an introduction to
the following discussion, review Chapter 5, "They Go to Church," in
the preceding section.

A ROOM FOR LIVING

The physical environment for the nursery children will not be the
same in every church, but there are several types of situations which
are most often found (pages 76-78). Even these would include
adaptations and individual touches necessary to meet the needs of each
group and to make the most of the room or space provided.

1. The ideal nursery room. The room has been designed for fifteen three-year-olds. It is of adequate size and attractively painted in soft greens and beige. In addition to the basic furnishings, vines and pieces of brass and a permanent picture of Jesus and the children add a home-like atmosphere. Interest centers, the tools for learning in the nursery class, are grouped informally about the room. Open *shelves for blocks* and toys to accompany block play face on a cleared area of the floor space. This is covered by a large rug. In one corner of the room, *the doll corner,* we find a bed (big and sturdy), a stove, a table, a chest of drawers, dolls, and housekeeping equipment. *Bookshelves* and a book table stand near the windows; also a painting easel. A *nature center* contains all kinds of objects—a goldfish bowl, a pine cone, a magnifying glass, growing seeds. A phonograph and a basket of *musical instruments* are in readiness. The chairs and tables (not one long table) are to the side rather than in the middle of the room. On these are found several wooden puzzles, large crayons, and drawing paper. Hanging above a simple *worship* or *special table* is a picture of a family working in a garden, the theme picture to which the teacher wishes to call special attention. Low hooks for hats and coats are located in the hall outside the door. (See Diagram A below.)

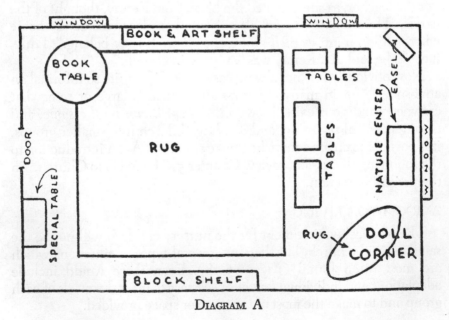

DIAGRAM A

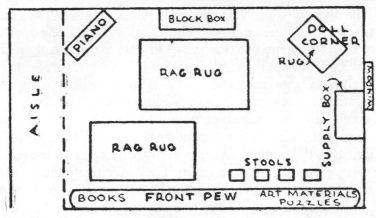

DIAGRAM B

2. A corner of a room. In the small church, it is often necessary for the nursery class to meet in one corner or section of a room. Even this setup and the use of the outdoors in comfortable weather can work out satisfactorily for good teaching. Above there is a diagram of such a room section, set up in the front part of a small church sanctuary between the platform and the first pew. (Diagram B.) The back of the piano partially encloses the fourth side. Beaverboard covers the pew seat to protect it, for this is used as a work and book table. Footstools, kept under the pew when they aren't needed, serve as chairs. A supply box, on casters, is nearby. A block box, also on casters (see page 95), stands against the platform, and a few trucks and cars are ready for the children. Two or three pieces of doll equipment are found in one corner. Special pictures hang low on the back of the piano. Ivy, growing in water, decorates the window sill. These plants do not have to be watered daily and therefore are an excellent addition to a church school room. Heavy rag rugs are placed in the interest centers. A warm floor covering is essential, for the floor, rather than chairs, is used almost entirely. If the corner is very small, it will not be possible for the children to engage in many activities at the same time. The teaching plans on pages 111–212 are easily adapted for use by a small church. Only those experiences which deal more specifically with the theme for each Sunday need be stressed. It is better not to limit three-year-olds too severely in their choice of things to do, so one should try to secure as large a space as possible and to meet frequently outdoors.

3. The divided room. Nursery class enrollments are on the increase everywhere. Many medium-sized churches, with an average attendance of sixty to seventy-five three-year-olds, are facing a real problem. It is thrilling to accept this challenge, but it is not always easy to plan adequately for a large group and to provide the homelike feeling which is so essential. Three-year-olds feel uneasy and become tired when they are "herded" together in such numbers in a big room. And they must have space in which to move around as they "learn through doing." For this reason the nursery department superintendent or the teachers make every effort to divide the group. They investigate the possibility of finding another room—in the church itself or in a house nearby. If this fails, they separate a large room by means of curtains, or they divide it into units of interest (block building, books, doll equipment), by using folding screens, or low open shelves which serve also as a storage space for the various materials. And, of course, in a great number of churches, double sessions, one held during the church school hour and another held during the church hour, alleviate the difficulty.

4. The shared room. Sometimes the room allotted to the nursery class is needed by other groups during the week. Although it means extra work for the teacher and her assistants on Sunday morning, it is worth setting up the interest centers and putting the equipment away again. Junior high and senior young people may volunteer such service. Several large cabinets with doors may be used to good advantage. Supplies are stored on the top shelves, and the blocks and toys on the lower ones, ready for the Sunday session.

Another kind of room-sharing may have to take place. Sometimes the enrollment of children under six is very small and the three-year-olds and kindergarten children must meet together. In this case the teachers will be aware of the needs of the various ages and will arrange to separate the older children at times by meeting with them in a different part of the room, especially for stories or worship. Folding screens are valuable for this purpose also.

A detailed list of furnishings and equipment for the nursery class, with sizes and dimensions included, appears on pages 92–95. Turn to pages 95–102 to see patterns for the construction of homemade equipment.

There are certain *safety measures* to be taken, both in preparing a room for nursery children and during the session itself. They are as follows:

Do not crowd too many children into one room. An allowance of 25 square feet per child is given as a minimum figure.

Place covers or bars around radiators.

Be sure the windows are screened or barred if they are low, especially if the room is on the second floor or higher.

Cover the floor with heavy unpolished linoleum or warm rugs.

Attach locks high on doors and gates leading to the street.

See that hooks on which the children hang their coats and hats do not jut out into the room, endangering children's eyes.

Eliminate rough edges from furniture and toys.

Avoid the use of toys covered with poisonous paint.

Guard against the common childish habit of putting beads or other small objects into the mouth.

Keep the room and equipment clean and sanitary.

Maintain the temperature of the room between 68° and 72°. Hang a thermometer three feet from the floor. Be sure the floor is not drafty. (See page 102 for a screen pattern.)

Have some isolation spot available in case a child shows signs of illness. *It is important* that parents and teachers co-operate in not sending or accepting a child when he has a cold.

Know first aid and have on hand the name and telephone number of a doctor close by. Making preparations for emergencies does not mean that they will occur. But it is only sensible for us to take precautions where a group of young children is assembled.

A PROGRAM TO FIT THE CHILDREN

Into such an environment as one of those described above come the three-year-olds every Sunday. Read "The Nursery Class" in the nursery book *In Our Church*, reprinted on pages 215, 216 of this handbook. The story partially describes a typical hour-length nursery class session. After each child arrives, he is greeted cordially by the teacher. He takes off his wraps, with occasional assistance, and hangs them on his own hook or hanger, placed low enough for him to reach and identifiable to him by an object picture above it. If he has an offering, the teacher lets him drop it into a basket or other receptacle; she then replaces the basket on a shelf out of reach of the children.

The child then enters into one of the activities or watches the others in the group for a few minutes. In an hour session most of the time is spent with the play and work materials. During this period the teacher, alert to teaching opportunities, introduces to individuals or small groups of children, music and stories and worship and conversation. Guided by the teaching plans, she may stress God's plan for homes on one Sunday and so encourage doll play; or she may wish to stimulate an interest in the church on another Sunday and so display pictures of churches near the blocks, to suggest church-building and to "set the stage" for a story on the subject. But she is always ready to change her plan. If Pammie brings a bird's nest to nursery class, that becomes a main interest of the morning.

Even during an hour session there is time for the children to assist with putting their "work" away—it is too tiring for them to do it all. A few minutes before the materials are to be returned to their place, the teacher approaches each child or group and says, "In a few minutes it will be time to put our work away, so finish what you are doing." Even younger three-year-olds gradually understand this request, although one can't always expect nursery children to comply.

After a few minutes' rest or relaxation, some effort may be made to bring the group together, on the rug or chairs, for a special discussion or activity. Generally, however, only a few children will stay long— unless the interest is something special like a visiting turtle! Most of them will come to see what's happening and then return to individual activities. A short walk, or play outdoors, or an excursion in the building, or an occasional special music time will usually be an experience for the whole group.

When there is an extended session of two or three hours, hand-washing, a midmorning snack, and rest on mats become part of the regular program.

Following are suggested schedules for both a one-hour and an extended session. Note the alternation of activity and rest.

One-hour session:

10 minutes—greeting, and removing wraps.
25 minutes—free of work materials, including some directed activity by teacher in play, music, story, and worship experiences.
5 minutes—assisting with putting materials away.
5 minutes—rest or relaxation.
10 minutes—special activity in which a few or all the children take part.
5 minutes—dressing to go home.

Extended two-and-one-half-hour session:

10 minutes—greeting, and removing wraps.

45 minutes—free use of work materials as above.

10 minutes—assisting with putting materials away.

20 minutes—preparation for midmorning lunch (toileting and hand-washing), and lunch.

15 minutes—rest.

20 minutes—introduction of new material, such as clay, and special activity (discussion, making gifts, music, story) in which a few or all the children take part.

5 minutes—relaxation (finger play, etc.).

10 minutes—dressing to go outdoors.

15 minutes—walk or play outdoors or excursion inside building. (In the latter case, of course, dressing to go home would come last.)

In some churches that conduct an extended session the program is so arranged that individual children can come for either the first or the second hour only. This is not very desirable, but if it is necessary, the first group leaves after materials are put away, and the second group arrives in time to prepare for lunch.

TEACHERS WHO UNDERSTAND

A comfortable and attractive room cannot alone produce a warm and friendly atmosphere in the nursery class. The adults who are there to guide the children must themselves be prepared as individuals and as teachers to give wholesome affection and understanding to their three-year-olds. Review Chapter 1, "They Learn from Us," as you consider this discussion. Each teacher, continually growing in her own spiritual life, makes every effort to gain knowledge and training in the nursery field. She reads, takes courses, attends laboratory schools, and observes in weekday nursery schools whenever this is possible. She takes an active interest in various other subjects as well, to enrich her thinking and enlarge her world.

The teacher is friendly yet sincere; there is a feeling of fellowship as she and her assistants, together, provide for the growth of the children in this happy, homelike environment. She knows how to put assistants at ease, as well as the children. A few years ago, two young student teachers reported for duty in a nursery demonstration center of a well-known university. As they entered the door, a worried-looking teacher rushed up to them and whispered, "Go over in the corner and make yourselves as inconspicuous as possible." How fortunate that ideas have changed, so that both parents and teachers can now act like human beings even in a scientific laboratory school!

Each assistant in the nursery class will have a special job to do—to observe one child through the morning or to supervise the block or art center. (There should be a helper for every six or eight children, and always at least one, no matter how small the group.) The assistants will help plan and evaluate sessions; they will not be made to feel embarrassed when they make mistakes. The head teacher does and should take the lead, however, for children are less confused when one adult seems to stand out in a situation. But when it is necessary to divide a large class into smaller groups for walks or other special activities, the same assistant may always be assigned to certain children.

The teacher has an understanding relationship with the children as well as with the adults. Possessing a quiet manner combined with a radiance of personality, she gives to them—and they return to her—both affection and respect. She helps each child grow in self-confidence and makes him feel necessary to the group. She sees to it that he finds security, but at the same time is careful not to overprotect him. She meets the needs of individual children; she notices if they are outgoing and active or restrained and tense. She provides materials for vigorous dramatic play for the former; she does not hurry the latter, but guides them slowly to the place where they are ready to take their own initiative.

She tries to handle most problems that arise in a positive manner so that the child "comes out" with a satisfying experience. One morning Jack threw blocks on the floor, laughing and saying, "I'm making a banging noise."

The teacher approached and said: "It's fun to hear banging noises, isn't it? But we don't make them that way. There is a pounding board over on the shelf."

Jack brought the pounding board back to the teacher. As he hit the pegs with the wooden hammer, he smiled. He believed that the teacher too was enjoying (!) this delightful sound.

If the child must be isolated as a disciplinary measure, the teacher does not frighten him by leaving him alone in a strange room; neither does she show her disapproval of *him*, but only of *his action*. And the teacher realizes that she must look for the cause of misbehavior. She knows that by expecting good behavior and using praise, she encourages right actions. She often prevents negative response by making a positive statement in a matter-of-fact manner. She says, "It is time to wash our hands," not, "Do you want to wash your hands?" After having given the children a few minutes' warning about finishing their activities, she says, "We put our work away now," not, "Will you put your work away?" There are a few reasonable rules to be observed, especially where safety is concerned, so the teacher may have to tell Patsy, who is pushing the child in front of her, "We walk carefully going down the stairs—that is our rule."

Read over again carefully Chapter 2, "They Grow Toward God," and Chapter 3, "They Grow as *Persons*," as you think especially about the religious and emotional needs of the children in the church school.

As the teacher considers the teaching plans to be used in the nursery class, she will recall that three-year-olds must not be hurried, and that through just "living" in the nursery class they are building a happy association with the church. Therefore, although she *does* want them to absorb the ideas presented in the teaching plans, she may often find that the children cannot take too many planned experiences at one time. She will certainly introduce these experiences whenever she can do so wisely. It's a good idea to review occasionally the goals of the nursery class as they are listed on pages 72–74.

The principle discussed above suggests *how often* the teacher should join in the children's activities to direct their thinking toward a certain idea. In "The Nursery Class" in the book *In Our Church*, Miss Anderson gives definite guidance at several points. Yet during a good part of the session, not described in the story, the children would be occupied with their own activities while Miss Anderson was a passive observer. Of course the teacher will set the stage for her teaching, and actually, if she becomes one with the children themselves rather than being formal and unbending, she can live and work with them in a natural way and not worry about "technique."

A room for living, a program that fits the children, teachers who understand—these are important factors in making our three-year-olds feel "at home in church."

CHAPTER 8

Three-year-olds at Work

"I N NURSERY SCHOOL, we teach ourselves how to play," said Arthur. What a good description of the teaching method in a nursery program! To the young child, play is work. Toys and books, art, music, and science materials are the physical tools that he needs in order to grow toward God, to grow as *a person*, to become aware of his world, in the church school and in the home. Arthur's statement, "We teach ourselves how to play," implies too that the teacher was *guiding* but not *imposing* as she lived with the children.

In this chapter we shall discuss briefly most of the materials and processes that are the learning tools in the nursery group; a list of equipment follows on pages 92–95. All the principles involved will enter into the thinking and planning of every nursery teacher. Some of the more detailed suggestions offered will be omitted or adapted in individual programs, depending upon the situation. For instance, goldfish or turtles need daily care and are more practically kept in a weekday nursery school. Such pets may be brought to visit on Sunday by the teacher or the children. In like manner, outdoor climbing equipment is less appropriately used on Sunday morning than in sessions held during the week.

DRAMATIC PLAY

In the interest centers the three-year-old reproduces the life around him. In the block center, cars, trains, wooden people (see pages 97, 98), and animals will stimulate such play. So David said to Bonny, as they piled their trucks with blocks, "You and me can be farmers together." Thus Billy and the other children in the book *In Our Church* made "a church," and sang the church-bell song. It is important, for satisfying work, that there be a sufficient number of blocks and that they be built up accurately from the size of the basic unit (see page 96). The three-year-old does not usually produce complicated structures like those of the kindergarten children, so we'll accept his simple designs as they are.

In the doll corner, good use is made of dolls, furniture, dishes, and other housekeeping equipment. Imaginary food is cooked on the toy stove; as it is served, a blessing is asked. Doll babies are tenderly cared for, and there is deeper understanding of a parent's love as part of God's plan.

The furniture in the doll corner should be child-sized and sturdy. Furniture made from boxes (see page 99) is smaller, but will serve quite well. Sometimes, if a thirty-inch bed is not available, a mattress only is placed on the floor, for as part of their dramatic play, three-year-olds themselves enjoy taking the part of a baby.

There is dramatic and rhythmic play too, as children use arms and legs to imitate leaves falling or to pretend they are getting ready for church school. They can engage in all kinds of dramatic play outside as well as indoors. Large hollow blocks (see page 101), big balls, walking boards, packing boxes, and climbing equipment are valuable. These provide physical exercise also.

NATURAL SCIENCE

Review especially Chapter 4, "They Become Aware of Their World." We see that it is important to provide as many nature experiences and materials as possible in the nursery class. Care of goldfish or a turtle teaches that "we must be gentle with little things." Children look with a magnifying glass at a deserted hornets' nest, brought in by an older brother. They see and feel the little hard brown seeds in an apple. They watch the strange ways of a snail, enthusiastically contributed by a member of the group who has brought it from the fish market. They find a pink-brown earthworm wriggling among the roots of pansy plants in a box, and are fascinated by the discovery.

Three-year-olds are ready to do some planting, either indoors or in a garden. It is generally best to have all the children plant seeds in one large container, rather than in separate ones, as there will be individual disappointment if the seeds don't mature. Or, after the seedlings have come up above the ground, they could then be transplanted to paper cups or small flowerpots.

Several children and a teacher planted six string bean seeds in a window box—but they didn't grow. The teacher finally realized that the earth was too hard and not rich enough (it had come sterilized and packaged from the ten-cent store!). So she secured new earth, the children replanted the seeds, and six beautiful string bean plants developed. It may not have seemed to be worth the time and effort, but the teacher had said that God plans for things to grow—and the children were waiting. It was a good lesson to learn, for as she and the children replanted, the teacher explained that the earth was too hard for the seeds to push through, that we must do our part to help by taking care of the earth.

On the table or in the center set apart for nature materials, there should be one or two watering cans available to the children. It's a good idea also to encourage the children to bring objects of interest for the table. A teacher had not noticed a trusting child place a brown toad among some rocks in the nature center, when he first arrived at nursery class on a Sunday morning. A few minutes later, she was indeed startled to see one of the "rocks" leap across the table top!

As the children become acquainted with growing and alive things, they often lose self-consciousness and learn confidence in meeting new situations without fear; yet they observe caution too when this is necessary. Also they learn more about God's laws and his loving care. And the teacher, herself enthusiastic about the wonders of the world, will answer questions truthfully and simply; or when she doesn't know, she will say so and try to find the answers.

Easter, for the nursery child, comes to be associated with the reawakening of a sleeping world in springtime and with Jesus who expressed appreciation of the beauty and care provided by God.

ART

Provision is made for art expression—a painting easel, where there is room for it (see page 102), large paintbrushes, unprinted newspaper, and poster paint; clay for patting and pulling; big crayons and Manila drawing paper; and, if possible, finger paint. It is amazing how creating with art materials contributes to a child's becoming at ease in a situation. At this age he is still experimenting with the materials themselves. The feel of the clay or the brush or the crayon in his hand and the brightness of the color on the paper are intriguing.

The *process*, not the result, is the principal element in the artistic expression of three-year-olds. Often they do not identify their creations at all. Sometimes they do name the indefinite strokes or masses of paint on the paper, or an irregular lump of clay, but even such ideas change from one second to the next. It is best for us not to be too inquisitive about results. One day Mildred, who had covered a sheet of easel paper with paint, said to the teacher: "See what I made. It's a surprise." The teacher was not content to let well enough alone. She asked, "And what is the surprise, Mildred?" Mildred answered, "I don't know—it's a surprise to me too!"

The teacher could inquire occasionally of a child, about his artistic creation, "Would you like to tell me about it?" And of course we will not criticize or compare the children's efforts.

There has been some controversy recently about the advisability of including a sand table in the nursery classroom. Unfortunately in many nursery groups sand tables are practically the only equipment. However, if there is room—especially in the weekday nursery class— and if other play needs have been provided for, a sand table may be used at times to good advantage, for free play. Washed health sand should be secured, and ought to be kept sanitary by exposing it at intervals to the sun and air. Also the sand must be kept damp enough to prevent dust particles from arising. Psychologists tell us that sand and water play are valuable in helping a child to adjust and have more confidence. Such play and easel painting are sometimes difficult to carry on in a church school room, unless precautions can be taken to protect the carpet and the children. Large sheets of oilcloth will protect the floor; aprons for the children can be made from father's old shirts, by cutting off the sleeves and, perhaps, some of the length. And there are a few rules for children to try to observe—to "tap tap" the brush against the wide-topped glass of paint in the easel trough before lifting it to the paper, and to assist in sweeping up spilled sand. Lapboards make a good working surface for clay and may be used on a table, the floor, or outdoors in warm weather (see page 93).

As we know and teach little children, as we become more aware of their needs and capabilities, we understand why "handwork," as such, has a limited place in the nursery class. Cutting and coloring patterns are difficult for three-year-olds; their muscles and nerves are not ready for fine work of this type. There *are* a few special things they can make, and these are included in the teaching plans. Children like to give gifts occasionally—even at three they are finding out that it is "more blessed to give than to receive." A scribbled picture, like the one Billy made for his mother (see *In Our Church*), is quite an appropriate gift from a child of this age.

MUSIC

Joy comes to the three-year-old through rhythmic and musical expression. Group activity is encouraged by the use of wrist bells (bells sewed on elastic), cymbals (saucepan lids), box rattles (small cardboard boxes containing several wooden beads), or an oatmeal box drum and rhythm sticks (short lengths of window-shade sticks or Venetian-blind slats). (See page 100 for illustrations.) However, no child should be forced into taking part in group music or made to feel embarrassed because he hesitates.

The children sing or chant their own songs, or those they have learned, as they work with various materials. Frequently the teacher sings as she passes among the small groups of busy children. Even though some effort is made to sing certain songs with the children, the teacher will often find herself singing alone.

It is best to use a few well-chosen songs with three-year-olds, and to repeat them often. The melody should be simple and the words intelligible to this age group. Playing a piano to accompany the songs of three-year-olds is not necessary; in fact it often places a strain upon their voices. If a piano is used, it should not be played too loud. It is valuable for "listening music" or for quiet music at rest time, or for rhythms. But a phonograph, with good records, will serve just about as well and doesn't take up as much room. (See the songs on pages 231–234 and a list of selected music books and records on pages 95, 98.)

The teacher will find it interesting to jot down bits of creative music and language sung and spoken by the children during class. Examples of individual creative songs were given in Chapter 4. Sometimes this becomes a group experience also. One day several children were changing the water in the goldfish bowl. Jenny started to sing, "Baby black-eyed fish." Other children added bits such as: "Orange fish"; "He's swimming so fast"; "He's swimming in the water." The teacher put the phrases together and sang back to the children:

"Baby black-eyed fish,
Gold fish, orange fish,
Swimming in the water,
Swimming so fast."

The song became one of their favorites.

WORSHIP

Worship for the three-year-old is a vital experience. It is a natural part of many of the activities and so becomes real in the life of the child. It will last just a moment or two. Peter says, "I like God," as he observes the first daffodil in bloom. Miss Anderson says, "Thank you, God, for our church," in the book *In Our Church* as she and the children stand quietly in the sanctuary. Virginia contemplates the picture of Jesus and the children. The teacher comes near and talks of how Jesus loved them. Or when everyone is happily at work, the teacher sings a song of thanks to God for friends at church.

In some nursery classes there is a worship table, to which you will find reference in the teaching plans. The table is not used for formal worship, but as a special place to put objects that will direct the thinking of the children toward God. Individual children or small groups will come to it; a teacher will stay near to talk about the book, picture, or nature object that is found there.

STORIES AND PICTURES

Stories for the nursery child ought to have rhythm and repetition, and should primarily be based on happenings in his everyday life. Stories for telling are not as long as stories in books where each page of script is accompanied by a picture which the children can observe as a teacher reads. It will be noted that the stories in the four nursery books, pointing up religious concepts appropriate for the three-year-old, have been based on these principles. Also sentences and words tend not to be too short, as those making a study in the field find that young children need and can understand a flow of language and ideas in their literature. Stories, like other activities in the nursery class, should be told or read to individuals or small groups of children. They are especially interesting if names of characters and details are changed to suit each group or situation. (See the stories on pages 215–230 and a list of suggested books on page 94.)

Pictures, both those in books and large pictures for mounting, ought to be attractive and clear. It is best if there is a plain background against which one figure predominates; also an absence of confusing details is desirable. The pictures should be hung at the eye level of the children. A large permanent picture may be hung somewhat higher. (See page 93.)

We should check the subject matter of the pictures too, in order to avoid confusion. If, for instance, angels appear, or if the children see pictures of them elsewhere, we shall have to be prepared to answer when children ask about them. We might say: "They are angels. No one knows what they look like. The man who painted the picture thinks they look like that."

SPECIAL DAYS

The little child is easily overstimulated, so that any special event should be kept as simple as possible. To recognize a child's *birthday*, singing "Happy Birthday" or offering a little prayer for the child, is sufficient. The teacher may wish to send a card to his home. Rather than have three-year-olds "perform" at a large *Christmas entertainment* or on *Children's Day,* they may invite the parents into their room for a visit. Even such an event, if it is not carefully planned, will be exciting. In churches where nursery children must appear in the sanctuary on Children's Day, they could simply walk in, place flowers on the Communion table, then sit in the front pews for a short while.

EXCURSIONS

As three-year-olds tire easily, excursions will not take them far away. Walks around the church, a visit to the sanctuary or to see a baby or puppy that lives next door, are adequate adventures.

ROUTINES

Bathroom. There should be as much self-help as possible. A sturdy platform, with one step, or an apple box can be used to reach high fixtures. Hand-washing is unhurried. In an extended session, where bathroom activities are included in the routine, the nursery and kindergarten teachers should check the schedules, so the bathroom will be free for each group at a certain time.

Lunch and parties. In a longer session, eating a lunch of fruit juice (or milk or water) and a cracker will become part of the program. In the teaching plans the suggestion is made several times that the children have a "party." In general, this will be conducted exactly the same as a regular lunch time.

It is wise to check with the mothers about such menus. Also the expense should be cared for by the church school budget or the parents rather than by the teacher.

The teacher must decide whether her group are mature enough to wait for one another while hands are being washed, and have lunch together, or whether each child, as he comes from the bathroom, will have his lunch and then go to rest. There is value in the group experience of saying grace, especially when "a party" occurs only occasionally. But even when each child eats individually, the teacher, close by, may quietly say, "Dear God, thank you for this food."

Heavy paper cups—if the budget permits—and paper napkins, cut in quarters and used as plates, facilitate cleaning up. The children enjoy pouring their juice from little pitchers into their cups. After they have finished lunch, they drop the paper cups and napkins into the scrap basket.

Rest. During an hour session, the children may relax a few minutes on the rug, with paper towels serving as pillows, or rest their heads on their arms as they sit at a table. In an extended session, each child needs his own rest mat (a rag rug or a heavy bath towel, or part of a worn quilt). The rugs may be tagged for identification with pictures that are duplicates of those above the coat hooks. There should be adequate protection against a cold floor and drafts; light woolen covers will be needed at certain times of the year. The room is darkened and an atmosphere of quiet is provided.

Rest during an extended session should last about fifteen minutes. Too much is not to be expected by way of silence or "being still," as long as the children stay on their mats and do not run around the room, disturbing others. They may relax best by sitting up or changing position. They often engage in quiet conversations or sing. The teacher may read poetry or chant softly. Sometimes she sits beside a child who is having a difficult time to settle down. When rest is over, the children fold or roll up their mats and put them away.

SUGGESTED EQUIPMENT FOR THE NURSERY CLASS

Dagger (†) indicates the necessary equipment

Room Equipment

Chairs 8" and 10" high. Stools of comfortable height to fit pew or table.

Tables 10" higher than chairs. Square (30" x 30"), oblong (24" x 36").

Racks or hooks for wraps 36"—38" from floor.

† Floor covering (see page 79).

Low, open shelves for books, blocks, and toys (see page 101).

† Floor blocks. Quantities given below are a minimum for fifteen to twenty children.

40 units, 40 half units, 40 double units, 10 quadruple units, 10 cylinders, 10 half cylinders, 10 pillars, 10 cubes, 8 triangles (halves of units), 8 triangles (halves of half units), 8 triangles (halves of cubes), 8 curves (quarters of circles), 2 ramps (of half units).

See page 96 for patterns and dimensions of blocks, if they are to be home-made or constructed at a local lumber company.

Write to the following companies * for catalogues if blocks are to be purchased:

Educational Equipment Company, 69 West Twenty-third Street, New York 10, New York.

The Arts Co-operative Service, 340 Amsterdam Avenue, New York 24, New York.

Macedonia Co-op Community, Clarkesville, Georgia.

Educational Playthings, the American Crayon Company, Sandusky, Ohio.

Colored cube blocks 2" x 2" x 2".

Nests of blocks. May be made of boxes or tin cans, sandpapered or smoothed.

Several large wooden trucks with wheels.

† Smaller wooden trucks, cars, boats, trains (on wheels and interlocking).

† Wooden animals and play people (see pages 97, 98).

Pounding boards with wooden hammers.

Wooden puzzles in trays (4 to 6 large pieces).

† Doll furniture: bed (large and sturdy, 30" long), stove, table, cupboard. Sandpapered and painted or decorated wooden boxes can be used (see page 99).

† Dolls (washable) 10" to 16" long. Also blankets and doll clothes (open down back with large snaps or buttons so dolls can be easily dressed).

Attractive dolls of different races.

Soft stuffed animals (with painted or embroidered features).

† Doll dishes, telephones, iron, ironing board, clothespins, broom, dustpan.

---

* Write to these companies also for catalogues of science, music, or art materials, and for toys to accompany block play. (There is a charge for the catalogue in some instances.)

Painting easel (see page 102) and men's shirts, with sleeves removed, for smocks.

Big paintbrushes (brush ¾" to 1" wide, handle 12" long),† large non-poisonous crayons, water color and finger paint. Unprinted newspaper for easel (18" or 20" x 24"),† Manila drawing paper (12" x 18" and 18" x 24"), powdered clay for mixing. Plasticine is not very satisfactory for this age.

Musical instruments: phonograph and records, tambourine, tom-tom,† oatmeal-box drum,† bells,† cymbals,† rattles,† rhythm sticks (see page 100), and a xylophone for experimentation.

Natural materials: fish or turtle aquarium,† plants,† seeds, magnifying glass. Other science materials: egg timer, magnet.

† Rag rugs, heavy bath towels, or quilts for rest in extended session.

† First-aid kit and book.

Wall thermometer placed three feet from floor.

† Supplies such as paper cups, napkins, Scotch tape, Kleenex, clothespins (for fastening paper to easel and snapping galoshes together).

Screens 3' x 3' on stand, or triple folding screens (see page 102).

Pictures: † picture set that accompanies this course (see page 116). File of additional pictures on home, church, social science, nature, animal, and activity subjects, cut from magazines and mounted on large sheets of colored construction paper.

> Permanent picture (good color, artistic design), such as:
> *Jesus Blessing the Children,* by Plockhorst.
> *Feeding Her Birds,* by Millet.
> *All Things Bright and Beautiful,* by Tarrant.
> *Happy Hours,* by Pothast.

Write to the following companies for catalogues (or inquire through your denominational bookstores):

> Artex Prints, Inc., Westport, Connecticut.
> The Arts Co-operative Service (see address on page 92).

†Bulletin board or low picture rail (to be placed at the eye level of children).

Sand table 2½' x 4', 22" high (inquire at local contractor's or building company for washed health sand).

Lapboards (approximately 9" x 12") made of plywood or possibly of heavy cardboard.

Outdoor Equipment (primarily for weekday use)

Climbing platform 40" x 32", 24" high, with railing 28" high. Steps on one end, wide incline on the other.

Saw horses 12" high.

Planks 5' or 6' long, 10" or 12" wide.

Packing cases, sandpapered and varnished.

Large hollow blocks. Quantities given below are a minimum for fifteen to
twenty children.

(10) 8″ x 8″ x 8″   (6) 8″ x 4″ x 16″
(10) 8″ x 4″ x 8″   (6) 8″ x 8″ x 16″

See page 101 for pattern if blocks are to be homemade or carpenter-made.
Otherwise consult catalogues of equipment companies listed on page 92.

Swing, low slide, tricycles, large rubber ball, beanbags.
Sandbox with cover.

Books

† *The Holy Bible* (without pictures).

CHILDREN'S BOOKS

† The four basic books that accompany this course:
  In Our Church
  His Name Is Jesus
  The Little Seeds That Grew
  I'm Growing

The following additional books may be ordered through your denominational
bookstores:

Animals for Me, by Lois Lenski. Oxford University Press.
Anybody at Home?, by H. A. Rey. Houghton Mifflin Company.
Ask Mr. Bear, by Marjorie Flack. The Macmillan Company.
A Year on the Farm, by Lucy Sprague Mitchell. Simon and Schuster,
  Inc. (pictures only).
Bobbie and Donnie Were Twins, by Esther Brann. The Macmillan Com-
  pany.
From Crocus to Snowman, by Pearle Boyd Bascom. Abingdon-Cokesbury
  Press.
Just Like Me, by Ruth MacKay. Abingdon-Cokesbury Press.
My Bible Book: Verses Selected by Janie Walker. Rand McNally &
  Company.
My Prayer Book: Verses by Margaret Clemens. Rand McNally &
  Company.
Now It's Fall, by Lois Lenski. Oxford University Press.
Stop-Look-Listen, by Virginia Mathews. Hampton Publishing Company,
  Inc.
The Little Farm, by Lois Lenski. Oxford University Press.
The Little Family, by Lois Lenski. Doubleday & Company, Inc.
The Little Golden Book of Birds, by Hazel Lockwood. Simon and
  Schuster, Inc.
The Tale of Jeremy Gray, by Romney Gay. Grosset & Dunlap, Inc.
Time for Bed, by Inez Bertail. Doubleday & Company, Inc.
Toby's House, by Lois Maloy. Grosset & Dunlap, Inc.

Also see stories in this book on pages 215–230.

POETRY COLLECTION

Sung Under the Silver Umbrella, prepared by Association for Childhood Education. The Macmillan Company.

MUSIC BOOKS

A Little Book of Singing Graces, collected by Jeanette Perkins Brown. Abingdon-Cokesbury Press.

A Little Singing Time; Singing Time; and *Another Singing Time,* each by Satis N. Coleman and Alice G. Thorn. The John Day Company.

When the Little Child Wants to Sing. The Westminster Press. For the kindergarten. Some songs and selections suitable for nursery.

Songs for the Nursery School, by Laura Pendleton MacCarteney. The Willis Music Company, Cincinnati, Ohio.

Also see songs in this book on pages 231–234.

Phonograph Records. See list on page 98.

Block Box*

This block box has a removable top which extends 12 inches beyond the sides and ends when in place, thus serving as a table. The box is equipped with casters, and with rope handles at each end, so that without the top, it may be easily moved to or from the block center.

One of the fathers or a local carpenter could construct a box with materials available. The box proper, over all, might be approximately 24 inches high, 54 inches long, and 24 inches wide.

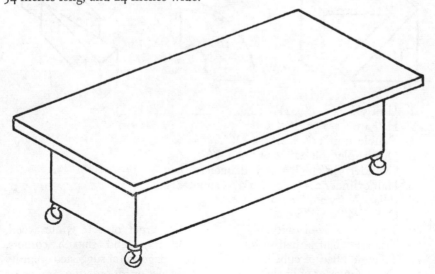

* Contributed by Helen Patterson.

Floor Blocks

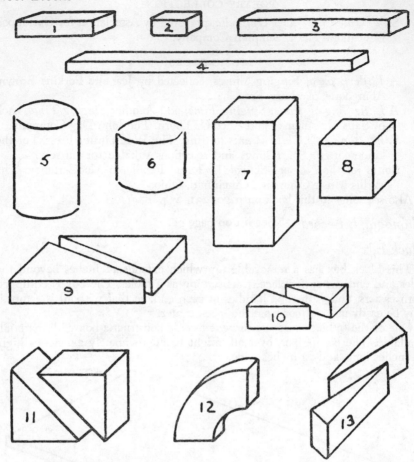

1. Unit 5½″ x 2¾″ x 1⅜″ (approximately brick size).
2. Half unit 2¾″ x 2¾″ x 1⅜″.
3. Double unit 11″ x 2¾″ x 1⅜″.
4. Quadruple unit 22″ x 2¾″ x 1⅜″.
5. Cylinder 5½″ high x 2¾″ diameter.
6. Half cylinder 2¾″ high x 2¾″ diameter.
7. Pillar 5½″ x 2¾″ x 2¾″.
8. Cube 2¾″ x 2¾″ x 2¾″.
9. Triangle (half of unit).
10. Triangle (half of half unit).
11. Triangle (half of cube).
12. Curve (quarter of circle).
13. Ramp (half of unit).

Construct of soft white wood, sandpaper, and smooth corners. (See page 92 for suggested quantity of blocks or for ordering, and pages 84, 85 for their use.)

Play People *

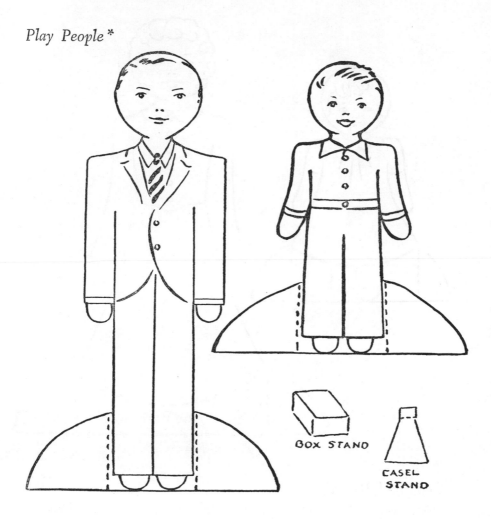

BOX STAND

CASEL
STAND

These play people, used to accompany block building, may be cut from plywood or mounted on heavy cardboard. It is best to construct them of wood, however, as flimsy toys are not practical for a group of three-year-olds.

* "Play People," reprinted from *A Treasury of Play Ideas for Tiny Tots,* by Caroline Horowitz. Hart Publishing Company. Used by permission.

Phonograph Records

(May be used in whole or in part for rhythms, appreciation, and rest).
"Tales from the Vienna Woods," by Strauss.
"March of the Toys," by Herbert.
"Flight of the Bumble Bee," by Rimski-Korsakov.
"Nutcracker Suite," by Tchaikovsky.
"Spring Song," by Mendelssohn.
"Cradle Song," by Schubert.
"Lullaby," by Brahms.

Doll Furniture

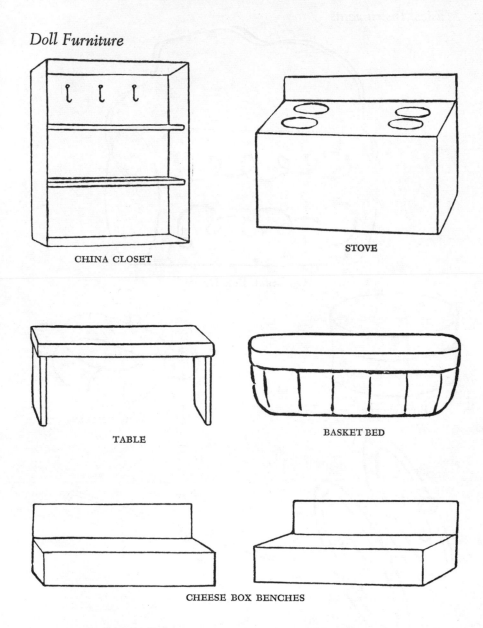

CHINA CLOSET

STOVE

TABLE

BASKET BED

CHEESE BOX BENCHES

The wooden boxes are sandpapered, painted, or otherwise decorated.

Musical Instruments

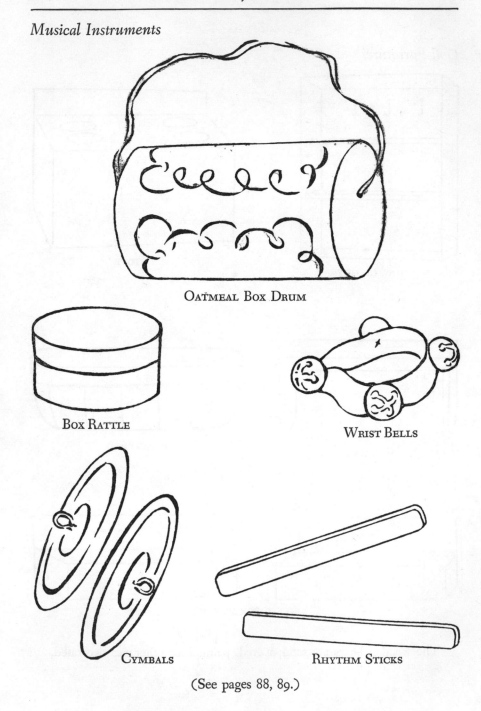

OATMEAL BOX DRUM

BOX RATTLE

WRIST BELLS

CYMBALS

RHYTHM STICKS

(See pages 88, 89.)

Shelf for Blocks and Other Materials *

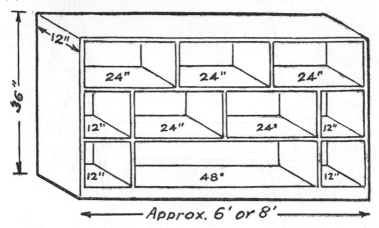

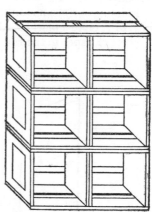

ORANGE CRATE SHELF

Fasten three crates together so that they don't tip over; sandpaper, and paint if desired. Similar units may be added, side by side.

HOLLOW BLOCKS

Use hard, but not too heavy, lumber or plywood and smooth all surfaces. The two opposite ends of each block are left open, or grooves are cut for lifting. Paint or varnish.

(See page 94 for dimensions and suggested quantity.)

---

* From bulletin *Suggested Equipment for Four- and Five-year-old Kindergarten Children*. Published by the State Education Department, Albany, New York.

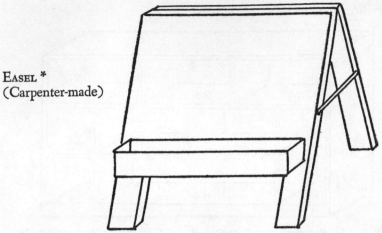

EASEL *
(Carpenter-made)

Wood—¾" thick x 3" or 4" wide for frame; ½" thick for box for paint jars. Painting surface masonite plywood or Celotex. Height of easel, 42".

NOTE: A child's blackboard may be used as an easel by thumbtacking a large sheet of paper to the frame at the top.

FOLDING SCREEN *

(Carpenter-made)

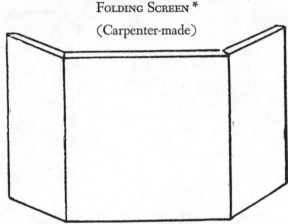

Material for panels: 2 plywood, 4-ply Celotex or masonite cut to outside dimensions. Panels are 3' squares.

Wood for frame: 2 inches wide. If frame is made double and panel material set in between, use wood ½" to ¾" thick.

If frame is made single and panel material nailed to back, use wood 1" to 1¼" thick.

---

* From *Children's Centers*, edited by Rose H. Alschuler, pages 131, 144. Issued by National Commission for Young Children. Reprinted by permission of William Morrow & Company. Copyright, 1942, by William Morrow & Company, Inc.

CHAPTER 9

Parents and Teachers
Know Their Job

TEACHERS and others in the church who plan for the guidance of the three-year-olds will want to review certain basic considerations.

First, it is only by receiving the co-operation of parents that any real nurture can be given to the young child, for he is in the home the greater part of the time. Parents and teachers must work together for his welfare and growth.

Second, it is not "parent education" that is to be stressed so much as the current more inclusive idea of "parent relationships" or "parent-teacher co-operation." So often fathers and mothers have been on the receiving end only. Their advice and experience will contribute to the program and to mutual respect and friendliness on the part of parents and teachers. Frequently, because parents are not consulted, they either become resentful or lose confidence in their own ability to be wise and helpful in the rearing of their children.

Of course, there is a definite place in the program of the church for offering suggestions and factual material. Parents *are* asking for counsel and specific suggestions as they meet problems or desire better ways of living in the family. They observe, too, in the nursery class and learn more about their children, or see principles and ideas in action that can be applied at home. One father remarked, after watching his three-year-old daughter take off her hat and coat and hang them on her own hook, "Soon she'll be smarter than her dad." Dickie's father met the teacher in a grocery store. He told her that at home Dickie wanted to thank God for his food, "as he does in nursery class," and then added, "You don't realize that these little ones notice so much."

Third, parents and teachers should become interested in each other as *people,* and not just as parents or teachers. They may belong to an adult group in the church where there is discussion of social and political issues, or to a hobby club where they share a common interest in collecting stamps or writing or painting. At a sewing meeting nursery mothers and the teacher spent most of the evening talking about working conditions in factories in which some of the mothers were employed. A group of rural parents discussed the crops and the proposed farmers' co-operative in the community.

Casual conversations often center around personal interests—the teacher's new dress, or her trip to another city where she gave a talk; a mother's purchase of chintz curtains for the living room, a father's promotion in business, or an attractive toy which he has designed. Parents and teachers enjoy sharing unusual or amusing comments made by the children, although naurally they do not refer to these within the hearing of the youngsters.

Fourth, because older people, especially grandparents, are so much a part of the family these days, they too are to be kept in mind in any parent program. They will be invited to some of the meetings, they will be referred to in discussions with the children. Also, because most grandparents of three-year-olds are still only middle-aged, and may have leisure time, they should be called to assist in the nursery class teaching or visitation programs.

An older friend of Sally's grandmother had died. Sally asked, "You won't die, will you, Grandmother?"

The grandmother answered: "Not for a long, long time. Mrs. Jones was very old."

"But you're still quite *new,* aren't you, Grandmother?" said Sally.

IN THE NURSERY CLASS

The chapter "They Go to Church" deals in part with home activities that help the child feel secure after he has been enrolled in the nursery class. Co-operation between the parents and the teacher is of great importance in introducing him to this experience. If parents speak at home about the church, if they invite the teacher to come to call so that the child can become acquainted with her, and take him to see the nursery class before he is actually enrolled, this rather serious step will be made easier for the three-year-old.

The teacher and the parents must work out the most satisfactory arrangements for the first several Sundays too, when children want their parents to stay with them. It is not always easy to decide what is the right thing to do. There was Eleanor who came to a vacation church school. The first two days she stayed close to her mother as the other children engaged in activities together. By the fourth day she played quite happily, returning occasionally to her mother, who was sitting in one corner of the room. The teacher suggested that the next morning the mother should say good-by and leave immediately. She followed this advice. Eleanor was fine for about fifteen minutes and then suddenly burst into tears. The teacher carried her around the rest of the morning—her mother had gone shopping and could not be found. Eleanor sobbed and felt miserable most of the time. The teacher had misjudged her readiness to stay alone. When the mother called for Eleanor, the teacher asked her to come the next morning prepared to stay. So for several days, Eleanor's mother sat outside the open nursery door and caught up on her mending.

Frank, on the other hand, would let out a lusty howl while his mother was leaving, but played happily and contentedly after she had gone. It seemed to be a habit pattern which wasn't really based on deep feeling, so the teacher and the mother decided that she needn't remain. When this was taken for granted, the howling ceased.

Parents and teachers both realize that if a mother or father "sneaks out" of the nursery room, it can be a real shock to a little child who is not at ease. Sometimes a father leaves his hat in the room, or a mother leaves her gloves, as they explain that they will come back later.

Parents will be welcome in the nursery rooms at all times, for going to church is a shared experience of the family, and the little child must feel that his father and mother are *with* him in a new venture. That is why the terms *our* church and *our* family and *our* doctor are used in the stories in the nursery books that accompany this handbook.

When parents do visit in the nursery class, they will be discreet about coming in large numbers or talking to one another. And they will be interested in quietly watching their children's behavior and activities as they work and play with children their own age.

There are many ways in which parents can serve in the nursery class itself. Some churches are pioneering in having a young couple take charge of this group, thereby adding to the homelike atmosphere. Per-

haps a mother who was a nursery school teacher before her marriage
would take the leadership. Mothers or grandmothers volunteer as
regular assistants or for special occasions, such as accompanying the
children when they visit in the church building or go for a walk outdoors. When parents serve as assistants, it is probably best for each to
volunteer for a block of time, as long as possible, before another takes
a turn. If there are different assistants each Sunday, it is apt to be more
confusing to the children.

In churches where the services of a caretaker are not available, parents often come in during the week to clean the nursery room and put
it in order for the Sunday session.

VISITATION IN THE HOME

Not only should the church visitor or the nursery department superintendent make regular home contacts, but also the teacher (and the
assistants, if possible) of the nursery class. She sees the child in his
family environment and is better able to understand him and to establish a friendly relationship with him. And the teacher, especially if
she does not have a family of her own, will be helped in her teaching if
she becomes acquainted with typical home situations or problems that
differ from those in a nursery class. The story is told of a child psycholo-
gist who was writing a book on the guidance of children. She was suddenly called to the home of her sister, who was ill, and cared for three
young children during a period of several weeks. After she returned
to her writing, she revised four chapters in the manuscript—working
with the child in the educational laboratory and guiding him in the
home were two rather different matters!

Local custom will dictate whether the teacher feels free to drop in
casually to visit or whether she should telephone first. In either case
the most successful calls are informal. The visitor may find herself
preparing vegetables in the kitchen or mending socks in the living
room or admiring a collection of antique demitasse cups in the dining
room or prize roses in the garden. If the three-year-old in the house has
not seen the teacher before, he will probably stay shyly beside his
mother or run out of the room. If he knows the teacher, he is likely to
bring to her for approval his favorite possessions—a rag doll, a truck, a
wooden mixing spoon. Calls should sometimes be made in the eve-
nings too, when both the father and the mother are at home.

PERSONAL CONFERENCES

Conferences between the parents and the teacher will contribute to more effective teaching and guidance of the young child. If the teacher asks a mother about having a conference (the mother may suggest it first), she does not give the impression that "something is wrong" or that she is going to tell the mother about mistakes made in the child's training at home. Frequently one hears a worried mother say very tensely at the beginning of such a conference, "I'm so afraid I'm not training my child in the right way."

Rather, the teacher's approach will be—and rightly so—that if they talk together about the child, she, as the teacher, can better understand him and thus give him more intelligent guidance in the church school. These chats often assist both the teacher and the parents to work out nursery children's problems—their insecurities, overdependence, and so on. Also, the teacher admits her own mistakes and speaks of her efforts to improve her teaching. However, conferences should be held when there are no difficulties to discuss. The teacher, of course, exercises professional ethics in receiving confidences and uses diplomacy in regard to referring to other people's children.

Conferences can be extremely informal. In a small rural church, the teacher and a mother cleaned the nursery room one afternoon during the week. As they mopped the floor and dusted, they discussed the nursery program and the child's interests and adjustment in the nursery class.

MEETINGS

Parent-teacher meetings may be large gatherings with an address delivered by an outside speaker. They may be discussion groups where parents, themselves, take the leadership. Sometimes they are held in the church building, on other occasions in one of the homes. An atmosphere of informality is best, and refreshments, served under the auspices of a parent-teacher committee, always add to the fellowship. Often an opening or closing period of worship is appropriate.

One of the questions asked most frequently by young fathers and mothers today is, "How can I teach my child religion?" When children first seek answers concerning God and life and death, some parents are confused and embarrassed. They then request the church to give all the religious training, believing that they themselves are excused from any responsibility. But other parents remark, as did a mother recently, "We need the church to *help* us with the religious education of our child." A parents' meeting on this subject is not the only means of giving such assistance. But a presentation by the pastor, or one of the nursery department staff, or another specialist in the field who understands how to teach *the young child* about religion, will open the way for the questions and suggestions of the parents.

A pediatrician, preferably a member of the church or from the local community, might discuss the physical and emotional health of the preschool child. One parent said, after such a meeting, "Dr. Smith knows our problems—he's from our own neighborhood." Additional resources for this kind of meeting can be used—securing speakers and films from public health, welfare, mental hygiene, and educational agencies.

Leaders and speakers should not always be brought in from the outside. There is a growing trend toward encouraging parents, teachers, and assistants to contribute to group thinking by means of their own reading, study, and discussion. This handbook, with the use of the study outline on pages 237–241, will serve as a basic guide for under-

standing nursery children and their needs. Talking over the teaching plans used in the church school will direct the parents' thinking toward what their part should be, to follow through, in the home during the week. There might be a smaller group, composed of the teacher, the assistants, and parent assistants, who meet to prepare for or evaluate the Sunday sessions.

Other kinds of get-togethers are valuable as well. A clay-modeling or finger-painting party, like that described earlier, is fun. Making equipment (see pages 92–102) and sewing curtains, or painting the walls and furniture, help parents feel that the nursery room belongs to them too.

RECORDS

In church schools where personal records of the children are kept, these will include the activities of each child, how he adjusts to new situations and to the other children. If it is possible, certain incidents can be jotted down by an assistant exactly as they occur. Such records are useful in parent-teacher conferences, not as a professional analysis of the child, but as an indication of his satisfactions and interests and needs.

When parents and teachers know their job, nursery children will be guided into a more abundant and Christian way of life.

TEACHING PLANS
FOR THE YEAR
IN THE NURSERY CLASS

Teaching Plans for the Year

FIRST QUARTER

Book: *In Our Church*

SECOND QUARTER

Book: *His Name Is Jesus*

THIRD QUARTER

Book: *The Little Seeds That Grew*

FOURTH QUARTER

Book: *I'm Growing*

TWELVE MONTHS, or fifty-two weeks, or three hundred and sixty-five days—what a long time in the experience of a little child who is passing from the age of three to four, and how important this year in our teaching plans! The suggested activities for the nursery class of the church and the weekly plans for guidance there may be adapted for use in the home. Parents and teachers should work closely together so that both home and church may be truly effective in helping little children to grow toward God. Parents too should become acquainted with the teaching plans. They will have a more thorough understanding of the program of the nursery class, and can follow through during the week, thus making the Sunday teaching more effective.

The year in the nursery class is divided into four quarters, and the teaching plans for each are based on one of the reading books prepared for three-year-old children. While these plans have one special emphasis during each quarter, it is recognized that many kinds of learning take place at the same time, and that the child in the nursery class is growing throughout the year, in relation to every element in his environment. Thus while the first quarter is concerned with his experiences in coming to church, related experiences will include hearing stories of Jesus, associating these stories with the Bible, feeling the beauty and wonder of God's plan for his world in autumn, learning to play happily with other children, growing in ability to do things, growing in appreciation of the child's home and his family as part of God's plan for his care, and becoming increasingly aware of God so that he wants to talk to him. Similarly, the activities suggested for every quarter will be found to provide experiences in all these areas, whatever the special emphasis.

If the teacher checks the index of teaching plans for the whole year (pages 113, 114), she can sometimes choose a session to fit a particular occasion, even though it does not follow the order of the outline. For example, if it is raining, she may use Session 4, Third Quarter; or, if a pet is brought to visit, she will probably refer for suggestions to Session 5, Fourth Quarter. The extra session, "The Friendly Dark," may be used in a special situation, or where there are fourteen sessions in a quarter. Throughout the year, the care of the teacher in preparing for each session from week to week, and her own growth in experience and understanding, will enable her to change her plans on any occasion according to the immediate experiences of the children.

For the convenience of the teacher who wishes to reorganize the order of the teaching plans in a completely different way, they have been reclassified in an index, found on pages 211, 212.

However you may use these teaching plans, it is important to remember that no one session is complete in itself. Three-year-old children like to do the same thing over and over again, thus offering us repeated opportunities for guiding toward a definite goal. Our special aim in any session will not be achieved in that session alone, but through continuing guidance of experiences and activities that may be related to it.

The nursery books *In Our Church, His Name Is Jesus, The Little Seeds That Grew,* and *I'm Growing* are for the children, and one is to be taken home each quarter. The eight stories from the books are reprinted in the back of this manual (pages 215–223) for ready reference by parents and teachers.

NURSERY TEACHING PICTURES

The set of twelve large teaching pictures, to accompany the course, is suggested for use in both the church school and the home. The pictures are enlargements made from illustrations in the children's books. They are as follows:

1. Saying grace in the doll corner in nursery class.
2. Going to see "the big church."
3. The church sanctuary.
4. Parents, children, and babies on their way to see Jesus.
5. Jesus and the children.
6. The Nativity.
7. Caring for seeds.
8. Helping a grownup and caring for a pet.
9. Saying grace at table in the home.
10. Sharing toys.
11. A family prayer at bedtime.
12. A checkup at the doctor's.

As teachers and parents prepare to guide their three-year-olds through the use of the following teaching plans, they will of course review the first sections of this handbook. They will do some thinking about their own faith and attitudes; they will observe their children developing religiously and as persons; they will be concerned with the expanding interests of three-year-olds as they provide an environment and activities, in both the church school and the home, that promote growth and happiness.

The teaching plans, as they are written, refer to a one-hour session. However, they are even more profitably used in a longer period, as there is additional time for free play, through which the ideas may be presented. If your church has an extended session, read especially pages 81, 90, 91 for a program schedule and routine suggestions.

FIRST QUARTER
Book: *In Our Church*

FOR THIS QUARTER, October to December, the activities in the nursery class will be closely related to the children's early experiences in coming to church. Before such experiences actually take place, the parents' part is to help their child anticipate them happily, and to prepare him as far as possible for new situations they know will arise. The teacher's part is to see that the church environment for nursery children is informal and homelike, with simple playthings and low furniture such as might be found in a playroom at home (see pages 92–94).

In the church as in the home, it is important to recognize that religious growth may be fostered through everyday experiences in living, and that Christian character may find its roots in desirable habits and attitudes. Learning to play happily with other children, to co-operate in simple routines, to do things for himself, to associate God as Creator with the wonders of nature and with provision for our care, are all experiences of definite religious value. It is important also to remember that the nursery room itself, its equipment and furnishings and activities, as well as plans for co-operation between home and church, are all a part of our teaching.

In addition to the many new experiences involved in coming to church, this autumn quarter brings the joys of Thanksgiving and Christmas, with the opportunities these festivals offer for helping the children to feel God's love and care. While our teaching plans are based on the first nursery book, *In Our Church,* the second book, *His*

Name Is Jesus, should be given to the children if possible in time for the story of the baby Jesus to become the center of their Christmas experiences.

SESSION 1. TIME FOR CHURCH

Thinking About the Children

This is the season of the year when many children are coming to the nursery class for the first time, and each session may bring newcomers who must be helped to feel at home. Their previous experiences with the church will have varied according to the attitude of their parents and the nature of the community in which they live. Care should be taken to provide for individual needs. The experiences to be considered in planning for this session may include the parents' part in helping a child to anticipate a new adventure, immediate preparation for coming to church, happenings on the way, observations on arrival, and first contacts with grown-up persons and children whom he meets there. In planning for new children, we are thinking also of the opportunities their coming offers to children who are already at home in the nursery class, and who will grow in friendliness as they learn to share this experience with others.

The informal, homelike atmosphere of the nursery room, or of the most suitable space available for three-year-old children in your church, is an important element in creating favorable first impressions. As you plan for this session, try to see your room through the eyes of a little child as he stands for the first time at the door and looks in. He should see familiar toys and playthings, also new ones that arouse his curiosity or suggest something to do. He should see pictures and picture books showing objects or situations he can recognize or will naturally ask about. He should see low chairs, and perhaps tables and other furniture of proportionate size. And in this attractive setting, he should see a grown-up person whose friendly greeting to children as they arrive, and whose sympathetic interest as they talk with her or proceed to activities of their own choosing, will help him feel that she is his friend. (Reread especially pages 75–83.)

Keep this picture in your mind from week to week, for any session in the year may be a first one for some little child coming to your nursery class. If your "room" be merely screened or curtained off from a larger one where other groups are meeting, extra care must be taken to preserve its homelike character, and to give the children a feeling of having a place of their own. Your special aim for this session should be to help the children feel that they *like* to come to church, and want to come again, and this aim should underlie your teaching throughout the year.

Getting Ready for the Session

Make sure that toys and work materials most likely to appeal to new children are laid out where they will see them as soon as they arrive. If your room lends itself to an arrangement of "centers" or "corners" for various activities, plan these carefully, so that materials in cupboards and on shelves may be conveniently near the part of the room where they are to be used.

Low, open shelves or a large box of blocks may indicate a *block center*, where a few blocks may be laid on the floor in readiness for use (see pages 95, 96, 101). Small cars and trains, boats, and figures of people should be close at hand, for these are always in demand in play with blocks (see pages 97, 98). For this session, the first nursery book, *In Our Church*, opened at the picture of Billy's church (page 7), or a picture of your own church might be placed near the blocks as a suggestion to the children to build a church as Billy did in nursery class. A few small bells would add to the interest in this play.

Be prepared to sing "Church Bells" (page 231), as you ring real or imaginary bells:

> " 'Ding dong, ding dong, the church bells ring;
> Ding dong, ding dong, come to church.' "

A doll or two and a few articles of toy furniture and housekeeping equipment are sufficient to set up a *doll corner* (see pages 85, 99).

In any play of putting a baby to sleep, be prepared to sing softly "Lullaby" (page 231):

> " 'Lullaby, lullaby; sleep, dear baby, sleep.
> Lullaby, lullaby; sleep, dear baby, sleep.' "

A small rocking chair is conducive to such play. Be sure that toy dishes are of heavy plastic and that there are no sharp edges that will cut or scratch. Such dishes may be used this session to suggest having breakfast, as Billy and Mother and Daddy did before going to church, or to prepare breakfast, as Billy did for the doll family in the nursery class. (See "The Nursery Class" in the first nursery book, *In Our Church*.)

The *book center* may consist of a few low chairs and a table, preferably round, placed near a shelf from which the children may choose their own books. If you haven't room for a book table, stand the books against the wall, on the floor, or place them on a chair or pew. While there are certain books that will always be available to the children, guidance may be given from week to week through your selection of books to be found on the bookshelf or perhaps on the table. Several copies of *In Our Church* should have a prominent place in the book center this session, and teachers should be prepared to look at the pictures with the children, to comment and answer questions about them, and to read or tell the story "The Nursery Class." Other books on the bookshelf might be: *My Bible Book, Just Like Me, The Little Family, Now It's Fall*. (A list of all suggested books, with the names of authors and publishers, will be found on page 94.)

Materials for painting, coloring with crayons, pasting, modeling with clay, or for other artistic expression, may be assigned to one part of the room, which may be regarded as an *art center* (see pages 86–88). Here also there might be large wooden beads, peg boards, color cones, nested blocks, very simple inlay puzzles, and other manipulative playthings. If all such materials are kept on low shelves, the children will learn where to find them when they want to use them, and where to put them when they are through. If your space is limited, it will be necessary to choose a few of the above materials from your supply box, or let the children do so. For this session, sheets of newsprint paper, laid out with large crayons conveniently at hand, may suggest that the children make a simple picture such as Billy made for his mother. (See "The Nursery Class" in the first nursery book, *In Our Church*.)

Autumn flowers or leaves arranged in a low bowl will add much to the attractiveness of the nursery room. These could be placed on a special low table. Pictures are also important, and Nursery Pictures 1 and 5 would have value for this session. Children who come early may be asked to help arrange flowers and hang pictures. This may be one way to make children feel at home.

With the Children in Church

The session begins as soon as the first child arrives. Children who are at home in the nursery class, and familiar with its procedure, will know where to hang outdoor clothing and where to find materials with which to play. They will respond to your friendly greeting, and may proceed directly with some activity of their own choosing, or may imitate what other children are doing or join with them in doing it.

A new child may feel the friendliness of the nursery class, and be quite happy in watching the other children, or exploring the room, or engaging in some activity; he may cling to his mother's hand, afraid to venture without her into this new environment. In the latter case, you may offer him a toy or suggest something he might like to do, and you might invite his mother to stay in the nursery class for a while and share in its activities. The mere fact that she is welcome there may help him feel that he is among friends, and he may be willing to stay without her. If his mother seems reluctant to leave him, and you feel that her presence is hampering his adjustment to the nursery group, assure her of your concern for his happiness, and say, "If you sit near the back of the church, I will send for you if he isn't happy."

The session in the nursery class is a period of creative activities and simple routines (see pages 79–81). As the children arrive they will take off their outdoor clothing, and hang it on the hooks or rack provided. Give assistance where necessary in this routine, but allow time for the children to know the satisfaction of learning to accomplish it alone.

If a child has brought an offering, show him the little basket in which to put it, and remark casually: "When we bring money to church, we call it an offering. It helps buy coal or oil to keep our church warm, and to buy a picture or a new rug or curtains or something we need to make our church beautiful." Such a remark is sufficient to attach a true significance to money brought by the children, without overemphasizing an activity that can have little meaning for them.

Allow the children to choose their own activities, and to turn quite freely from one to another. Be sure to share their interest and be prepared to give guidance where necessary to encourage constructive play or desirable social attitudes. If you have one or two assistant teachers, plan with them so that each one may be observing, and giving guidance to a small group of children or individual children.

Such remarks as: "This is the place where we build with blocks"; "We keep crayons on the table"; "You may look at a picture book when you put the beads away"; "Here is a wastebasket for your scraps"; or, "If you wheel the doll carriage along this side of the room, you won't bump into anyone," may be sufficient to foster a sense of things belonging in certain places, thus keeping activities from conflicting with one another.

Friendly social attitudes may be encouraged as you say: "You can take turns in putting the baby to sleep, Margaret. Now you can sing while Barbara has her turn"; or: "Donald needs more blocks to build his church. You could let him have those you aren't using, Bobby"; or, "You and Jean could look at that picture book together, Allen"; or, "If you want a red crayon, Nancy, perhaps Joan will trade with you."

As you thus seek to guide the children's activities, keep in mind the importance of their finding satisfaction in these so that they may feel that they like to come to church and want to come again. To children playing with blocks, you might suggest that they build a church. This, no doubt, will be a high tower of blocks or merely a wall enclosing a space. When their church is built, talk with them for a few moments about their preparations for coming to church today. Show them the book *In Our Church*, and look with them at the pictures as you read or tell the story "The Nursery Class." Other children may gather around to look and listen. When the story is finished, they might play that they are ringing the church bells as they sing with you:

> "'Ding dong, ding dong, the church bells ring;
> Ding dong, ding dong, come to church.'"

Children playing with dolls and with housekeeping toys may be having an equally happy time, and their activities may be similarly directed so that they will associate these experiences with coming to church. You might suggest that they put their doll babies to sleep, and then sing for them:

> "'Lullaby, lullaby; sleep, dear baby, sleep.
> Lullaby, lullaby; sleep, dear baby, sleep.'"

Remark that while the babies are sleeping you will tell a story, then look with the children at the book *In Our Church* and read or tell the story "The Nursery Class," or merely comment on the pictures. As in the block center, other children will come to look and listen, perhaps for a second time, and may sing with you "Church Bells." After the story, they might play that they are having breakfast as Billy did, or are getting breakfast ready for the doll babies when they wake. This would give an opportunity to say the grace that the children offered: "Dear God, thank you for our good food."

Children coloring with crayons will readily respond to the suggestion that they make "a picture" of a church, and might then like to listen to the story "The Nursery Class," and look at the pictures. Other children might come to join them. After talking about Billy's experiences, suggest to the children that they make a picture as he did to take home to their mothers.

Children looking at picture books will also be interested to hear the story of Billy, and you may tell or read it again, or talk with them about the pictures. You might sing with these children as you did with those in other groups.

Most of the teaching in the nursery class is done in this informal manner, giving guidance in small groups or with individual children. Sometimes the children may come together in one group, but there should be no compulsion for everyone to join it. When there has been plenty of time for activities of the children's own choosing, then you might say, "When we put away all the things we have been using, we can have a little rest."

Most of the children will respond to this suggestion, and to your example of gathering up toys and other play materials and putting these in boxes or on low shelves where they belong (see page 80). The children may then lie down or sit quietly on the rug for a few minutes, or may sit at the tables with their heads resting on their hands while you sing "Lullaby." They may wake up as you ring imaginary church bells, and sing "Church Bells." (See page 91.)

You might then say: "We can play that it is time for church, and we are getting ready to come to nursery class. Let me see how carefully you can wash your hands." As the children play that they are washing their hands, sing for them to the tune of "Here We Go Round the Mulberry Bush":

" 'This is the way we wash our hands,
Wash our hands, wash our hands,
This is the way we wash our hands,
To come to our church on **Sunday.**' "

Repeat this play, adapting the words of the song as the children "brush our hair," or "put on our shoes," or "eat our breakfast," or make other preparations they may suggest. They might like to go "hop, hop, hop" and "jump, jump, jump," as Billy did. Then say, "We can say thank you to God for the happy time we've been having in our church today." Some of the children may offer this prayer with you.

You might remark: "When you go home, you can tell Mother and Daddy about all the things you have been doing in our church today. And you can have one of these books about Billy for your very own, so that Mother and Daddy can read it to you at home."

There may be time for each child to look at his own book *In Our Church* before putting on outdoor clothing to go home.

With the Children at Home

Through the children's interest in their new picture book, and their eagerness to talk about the pictures and to hear again the story about Billy going to nursery class, their parents may have a real share in their nursery class experiences. As you speak with parents a moment at the close of the session, perhaps you will have an opportunity to draw their attention to the message in the children's book that is specially for them, and to the songs their children are learning to sing in nursery class and can sing also at home.

If a new child has drawn a picture for his mother, try to speak with her a moment before he gives it to her. Help her recognize how her expression of interest and appreciation in such a gift, however crude it may seem, will bring her child's home and church experiences closer together.

SESSION 2. THE NURSERY ROOM

Thinking About the Children

Our plans for the last session were much concerned with helping new children to feel at home, and similar plans may be followed with newcomers this session. Care must be taken that children who are coming a second time may find the atmosphere of the nursery class just as friendly and homelike as they found it at first.

For this session, our special aim should be to foster in the children a feeling of confidence through assisting them to become familiar with the nursery room or corner and its equipment, and to know where to find toys and work materials they want to use.

Getting Ready for the Session

If you found your arrangement of the room satisfactory for the children's activities last session, arrange it the same way this week, making sure that toys and other equipment that proved of special interest to new children will be seen by them as soon as they arrive, or are where they expect to find them. Have the same pictures low on the wall. The picture of Jesus and the children (Nursery Picture 5) might be fastened above a low table on which autumn flowers or leaves, or other lovely things from outdoors, are placed. A book such as *My Bible Book* might also be placed on this table. From week to week, it may come to be a special place where the children will expect to find objects or pictures or stories that help them to know of God's world and of his plan for their care (see page 89). For this session, as the children look at the picture of Jesus and the children, you might plan to bring the Bible from the shelf or table where it is kept, and show it to them, as Miss Anderson did in the book *In Our Church*, and say, "We read about Jesus in the Bible."

In addition to having corners and centers conveniently arranged for varied activities, make sure that all toys and materials for the children's own use are readily available on low shelves or in suitable containers. This session, as new children explore the room and observe materials that are unfamiliar to them, help them name these, and perhaps discover how to use them. Plan to allow plenty of time near the close of the session for the children to experience satisfaction in putting toys away. Be prepared to sing with one or two children, or with a larger group, "Putting Our Toys Away" (page 232). This song is very simple, as the first line is sung going up the notes of the scale, and the second line coming down.

If possible, have several copies of *In Our Church* in the book center as suggested for last session, and have extra copies on hand to give to children who were not present then.

If you have not previously used a picture to mark each child's hook for outdoor clothing, this might be an activity in which the children could share. Have ready small colored pictures from advertisements in magazines, or simple outline figures cut from white paper, or gummed seals. Paste these on small pieces of colored cardboard of uniform size. A loop of yarn or wool added to this card will provide for hanging it over the hook so that each child will always recognize the place for his belongings. Such pictures might represent a star, snowflake, ball, bird, butterfly, airplane, car, cup, spoon, pitcher, shoe, mitten, leaf, flower, horn, drum, or any other object with which the children are familiar.

With the Children in Church

Always remember that the session begins as soon as the first child arrives. If he should be a newcomer or a child who came for the first time last Sunday, you should make an opportunity to talk with him quietly, to help him take off his outdoor clothing, and to show him where to hang it. Getting dressed to come to nursery class has probably been an important part of this new experience, and your interest in his coat or his hat, or some other article of clothing he is wearing, may help create a real bond of understanding between home and church. Not only this session, but from week to week, allow plenty of time for children to learn to take off outdoor clothing and to care for it according to the accommodation provided. At the end of the session, allow plenty of time for putting it on again. These simple routines are important in our teaching, for in learning to do these things for himself a child is acquiring skill and a feeling of responsibility that will make for happy co-operation in other routines of living.

A new child may be interested in choosing a picture to mark the hook for his clothes. (See preceding page.) If your nursery class must meet in the church sanctuary, and if there are one or two empty pews available, the children might place their hats and coats on the seats. Pictures, fastened with easily removable Scotch tape along the back of the pews, would indicate each child's section.

As the children proceed to work or play in the various corners or centers you have arranged (see Session 1), be prepared to share their interest or conversation. Watch for opportunities to guide new children in discovering where toys and work materials are kept, and encourage children who are familiar with the room and its equipment to help them. You might say: "I think Jimmy would like a small car to put in his garage. Could you show him where to find one, Douglas?"; or: "I think we have some bigger crayons, Anne. You could show Mary where they are kept"; or: "There is the box for the beads, Betty. This one is for the clothespins." Such guidance may be given to children individually or in small groups.

As children work at activities similar to those in which Billy engaged in the book *In Our Church,* you might help them recall the story, and might find occasion to sing "Lullaby" or "Church Bells" as you did last session. You might find opportunity to say, "We can say thank you to God for the happy time we are having in our church," and the children may listen or repeat this prayer with you.

Sit down on the rug or on one of the low chairs in the book center, and open the book *In Our Church.* Children are sure to gather around as you turn the pages and look at the pictures. Some of the children will want to tell you about Billy going to nursery class; then you might read or tell this story as you did last session.

Allow time for the children to put toys and work materials away without any feeling of hurry. Walk over to the blocks, and proceed to pick up any of them that are not in use as you sing softly:

> " 'We have had a happy play,
> Now we'll put our blocks away.' "

The children will probably join you in both singing and helping. Say, "That is a quiet way to put the blocks in the box," or, "That is a good way to pile the big blocks in the corner" or "on the shelf."

Similar help and suggestions may be given to children playing with dolls, or coloring with crayons, or engaged in other activities. Suit the words of the song to playthings or work materials to be put away, and help the children to find satisfaction in discovering where each belongs. With teachers helping, there should be time, even in a short session, for the children to rest or relax for a few moments after putting away their toys.

After a brief rest, the children could play that it is time for church, and that they are preparing to come to nursery class (see Session 1). As each child gets ready to go home, he will find the hook on which he put his outdoor clothing, and will enjoy naming the picture he chose to mark it. Give necessary assistance in dressing, but encourage the children's own efforts.

Give a copy of *In Our Church* to any children who did not receive one last session.

With the Children at Home

Plan to get in touch with the parents whose children have been away from nursery class for the past two sessions, so that these children may have a copy of *In Our Church* to enjoy at home. If a child is sick, let his parents feel your interest in him; but also stress the importance of his staying away until all danger of infection is over.

SESSION 3. FRIENDS IN CHURCH

Thinking About the Children

One of the greatest values of the nursery class lies in the opportunities it provides for bringing the three-year-old child into contact with other children of his own age, and with grown-up persons who are considerate and understanding of his needs. Even before he is ready to play with other children, he may like to play near them and to do the same things they are doing. Gradually, he will join in their play, and may have his first experiences in sharing and taking turns and respecting the rights of others.

The experiences included in this session may be related to the children's indoor and outdoor activities in autumn. Guidance may be given in associating these with God's plan for our care. With all seasonal emphases, however, adaptation will have to be made to fit various situations and climates.

Getting Ready for the Session

The teacher will follow from week to week the same general procedure as has been suggested for the two preceding sessions, keeping in mind the special aim for each session. Autumn leaves and flowers and nuts and pine cones, also fruits and vegetables and grain that ripen at this season, would be of special interest this week, and would suggest home and outdoor experiences the children have in common. Pictures of birds and squirrels might have a similar interest, while Nursery Pictures 1 and 2, fastened low on the wall, would suggest familiar church situations. *My Bible Book*, with a few shiny nuts or pine cones, might be used on the worship or special table that is set apart for objects or pictures or books that help us think of God's love and care. Although the pictures on the wall above this table will be changed occasionally, the one of Jesus and the children (Nursery Picture 5) will always be a favorite.

Have in readiness pieces of colored paper from which the children may tear colored leaves to paste on a sheet of drawing or wrapping paper.

With the Children in Church

Watch especially for situations in which children can share or take turns. Be prepared to encourage gestures of friendliness by such remarks as: "Bryan needs a crayon. Can you spare one, Gordon?"; or, "Has Betty had a turn yet?"; or, "It's fun to take turns like that."

If Billy knocks down Tommy's blocks, you might say: "Tommy doesn't want them like that. He wants them up high. Let's help him build them up again."

If Marian pushes Jane, you might say: "Jane doesn't want to be pushed. She might like to have a party with you."

Pictures and nature objects may suggest experiences the children can recall in their play. Blocks may be used to build a barn, a fence around the farmer's field, or a road along which he drives as he takes his potatoes or apples to market. Friendly play may be encouraged as children keep adding blocks to make the road longer, and run toy cars and trucks along it. As you share their interest, and talk with them, perhaps you will say, "I'm glad God planned for potatoes to grow for us to eat"; or: "I'm glad the farmer knew how to plant the potatoes and help them grow. That is part of God's plan." If children tell about their mothers and fathers putting fruits or vegetables away for the winter, help them feel that this also is part of God's plan for us to have food to eat.

A child playing in the doll corner might respond to the suggestion that he cook for dinner potatoes, or other vegetables that grow in the farmer's field. Other children could be invited to come for dinner, and may help set the table. They might say thank you to God as Billy did in the book *In Our Church*.

Children's interest in the colored leaves that you have brought into the nursery room, or that they have seen on their way to church, may be deepened as you sing (page 232):

> " 'Down, down, with rustling sound,
>   Leaves are falling, all around.' "

Some of the children will imitate you as you move your fingers to suggest the falling leaves, or they will play that they are leaves whirling and twisting in the wind; or they might tear pieces of colored paper to make leaves, and paste them on sheets of wrapping paper or drawing paper. In talking with one child or with several, you will probably find occasion to remark that leaves are part of God's plan for his world to be beautiful.

While children are engaged in any activity, you might recall with them similar things that Billy did in the book *In Our Church*. As children are looking at this book, sit with them for a few moments and talk about it.

Use the song "Putting Our Toys Away" (page 232) in time for this to be a friendly experience in working together. When the children have had a brief rest, look with them at Nursery Picture 2. Let them notice the children going to church. Sing with them "Church Bells" (page 231). Then look at Nursery Picture 1, and talk with the children about it. Comment on things they themselves have been doing in nursery class. You might tell the story "When Betty Went to Nursery Class" (page 223). Then say: "We are glad for the nursery class in our church. We hear about God, and we are happy with our friends."

With the Children at Home

The children would enjoy taking home the sheets of paper on which they have pasted the leaves torn from colored paper. Suggest to their parents that this is an activity they could repeat at home during the week.

SESSION 4. LEARNING TO SHARE

Thinking About the Children

Learning to share involves many experiences, both in giving and taking, and much individual guidance. Even where children have been encouraged in sharing with other members of their family, they may have had no experience in playing with children their own age who are likely to want the same things they do at the same time. Our observation of the children in the nursery class as they play alone or with one another should help us know where guidance is most needed.

For this session our special aim should be to help the children discover, through actual experience, the happiness that sharing can bring.

Getting Ready for the Session

Colored leaves, nuts, pine cones, fruits, and vegetables may still be a part of the children's outdoor experiences, and they will be interested to discover some of these in the nursery room. Use Nursery Pictures 1, 2, and 5 as suggested for the last session; also Nursery Picture 10, which shows children sharing toys at home. *My Bible Book* may be used on the special table, and the picture of Jesus and the children fastened above it. Have materials in readiness in case the children might like to repeat the activity suggested for last session of tearing colored leaves from paper and pasting these on sheets of wrapping paper or drawing paper.

With the Children in Church

Many of the experiences of last session will be repeated in this one as you watch especially for situations in which children can share and take turns. Your observation may lead you to say quietly to a child, "That is the kind of thing that friends do"; or, "You made Ann happy when you let her have the baby doll"; or, "Ronald might like to help you build the church"; or, "You might tell Nancy about the pictures in this book." Children who have been coming to nursery class for some time will probably respond readily to such suggestions, and their friendliness will encourage newer children in similar attitudes.

Opportunities for such guidance will come most naturally as the children work and play with materials of their own choosing, but you will find occasion to draw the attention of one or two children at a time to the pictures in *My Bible Book* or *My Prayer Book,* or to other pictures suggesting friendly ways of sharing. As you talk about these pictures, say, "In the Bible we read, 'Love one another,' and when we love someone, we like to share"; or, "In the Bible we read, 'Be kind,' and we know that sharing is a kind thing to do." You might show the children the Bible, and let them see the printing in it.

If you have a copy of the nursery book *I'm Growing,* look with the children at the pictures of Susan and Timothy sharing and taking turns, and tell them about this part of the story. The children might also like to hear again the story of Billy in the nursery class *In Our Church.* Comment on the way in which the children shared in building with blocks, and in getting breakfast ready for the doll family.

"Putting Our Toys Away" may be sung when it is time for doing so. Encourage the children in sharing in this procedure, and say: "It's fun putting our toys away when we all help. Then we'll have time for a story [or a game, or looking at pictures, or singing, or some other activity they have enjoyed together in preceding sessions]." The children may relax on the rug, or rest for a few moments with their heads on their hands, before this activity. When it is time for them to get ready to go home, you might say: "We are glad for the nursery class in our church. We hear about God, and we learn to share, and we are happy with our friends."

With the Children at Home

As you talk with parents for a moment or two at the door of the nursery room, you might remark: "Margaret has been learning to share today. Do you think you can give her opportunities to share with someone at home during the week?" In some cases you may plan to visit a home, or to talk with parents on the phone, in order to deepen your own understanding of their child or to enlist their co-operation.

SESSION 5. LEARNING TO HELP IN CHURCH

Thinking About the Children

During the past four weeks we have been concerned with leading new children into making happy associations with the church through a growing feeling of being at home in the nursery class and with friends whom they meet there. Through experiences in sharing and taking turns they are beginning to have a sense of belonging, and this sense may be deepened as they are led to recognize ways in which they can help in church. Such help may include learning how to use materials and where they are meant to be used, and putting them back where they belong; turning the pages of books so as not to tear them; picking up scraps of paper from the floor; helping to fill a vase with water for flowers; being careful not to knock down blocks when another child is building; observing routines in taking off and putting on outdoor clothing.

Our special aim for this session should be to guide the children into discovering ways in which they can help in the nursery class, and to have satisfying experiences in doing so.

Getting Ready for the Session

A toy broom and mop and carpet sweeper are popular equipment in the doll corner, and may encourage the children in picking up scraps of paper from the floor and in keeping their room neat and clean. A small corrugated carton about ten inches square makes a satisfactory "wastebasket" that can readily be replaced when it becomes soiled or worn. The children may help fold in the four flaps at the top, making firm, double sides, and decorate the carton with pictures you have previously cut out. If you have a collection of suitable pictures, let the children choose one for each side of the carton. Heavy cord could be fastened for handles in two opposite sides, if desired. The children might help in preparing similar cartons in various sizes for holding blocks or other equipment that has to be put away in cupboards.

If you have brought flowers or nuts or seeds or fruits or vegetables or other things from outdoors, plan to let children assist in arranging these.

With the Children in Church

As the children arrive, and proceed to take off and hang up their outdoor clothing, give any necessary assistance, meanwhile commenting encouragingly on the degree to which a child has learned to accomplish this routine for himself. You might remark that the sexton (or janitor) or a mother or father has made the room neat and clean, and that children help to keep it that way when their clothes are hung on the hooks or folded on the pews. You might remark also that flowers or other lovely things from outdoors make the nursery room beautiful; then ask the children to help you in arranging some of these. If there are any papers or scraps left on the floor after this is done, you might say: "We don't want our room to look untidy. Let's pick up these scraps and put them in the wastebasket." If there is no wastebasket, this will help the children feel the need of one. You might show them a small carton, and help them discover how to fold down the top flaps to make it strong. If you have pictures ready, some of the children will help decorate the carton, while others will choose materials with which to work or play.

Whatever the children's activities, you will find occasion to remark on ways in which they are helping, or to suggest ways in which they can help. Children playing with dolls will always enjoy various phases of housecleaning, and through this play you may guide them in discovering how they can assist in keeping the nursery room neat and clean. Watch for opportunities for the children to work with you as you fasten pictures on the wall or arrange materials on a shelf. Also, occasionally ask them to bring you things you need—such as a book or toy. When it is time for putting toys away, remark that this is one way in which we all help in church, and comment casually on individual efforts to do this quietly and neatly.

While the children have a brief rest, hum or sing very softly "Lullaby" (page 231). Suggest that they play they are helping in church, and sing with them to the tune of "Here We Go Round the Mulberry Bush":

> " 'This is the way we pick up our blocks,
> Pick up our blocks, pick up our blocks!
> This is the way we pick up our blocks,
> In church on Sunday morning.' "

Similarly, they may play that they hang up their clothes, or put away their toys, or pick up papers, or engage in other activities they may suggest.

At any time during the session, you may find occasion to say to one child or to several, "I'm glad we have a nursery class in our church, and I'm glad we can all help make it a happy place."

With the Children at Home

Remind the children that they can help at home as they help in church, and, if possible, ask their parents to provide special opportunities for them to do so.

SESSION 6. A STORY OF JESUS

Thinking About the Children

It is not too soon to begin to look forward to Christmas by telling the story of Jesus' love for little children. As this story is told this session, and recalled during the next few weeks, the children will begin to know Jesus as a kind and loving friend whom little children liked to be near, and who talked with them and told them stories. Thus they will be interested to hear about Jesus' birthday, as they are to hear about birthdays of people they love, and stories of "when Jesus was a baby" will gradually begin to have significance in relation to his life of love and service.

The story of Jesus and the children brings a timely message to parents and teachers, who are all too inclined to become rushed and hurried with Christmas plans and preparations. We need to remember that Jesus, whose days were crowded with teaching and helping and healing, was never too busy to talk with little children and tell them stories of God's love. It is only as we put the children first in all our plans, and take time to understand them and to share their interests as Jesus did, that we can help them know God.

Our special aim for this session should be to guide the children in thinking of Jesus as a kind and loving friend of little children.

Getting Ready for the Session

Read carefully the story "Let the Children Come" (pages 218, 219), and be prepared to tell it to the children. If you have a copy of the nursery book *His Name Is Jesus,* place this on the table above which the picture of Jesus and the children (Nursery Picture 5) is hung. Fasten the picture of parents, children, and babies on their way to see Jesus (Nursery Picture 4) on the wall nearby. Make sure there is a baby doll in the doll corner, so that the children's play there may include caring for a baby. Place books showing pictures of babies and families on the low table in the book center.

With the Children in Church

Keep in mind the experiences in sharing and helping that the children have been having during the past few weeks, and watch for opportunities for repeating these or leading the children to discover other ways of sharing and helping. As you observe children at play with the dolls, remark on the care with which they hold the doll baby in their arms, or rock it gently, or tuck it in bed. You might join in their play as you make "finger play" toys for the doll baby, and recite "Here's a Ball for Baby" (page 235). You might then sing "Lullaby" (page 231) as the children rock their baby to sleep.

Sit for a few moments with children in the book center, and look with them at pictures of babies and families. These pictures might suggest that you recite "Here's a Ball for Baby," or sing "Lullaby." If children in the block center are building a house, ask them about the people who live in it. You might repeat, as if part of your conversation, "This Is a Home" (page 235).

As the children look at the pictures of families going to see Jesus, sing softly "Jesus and the Children" (page 232). You may have to repeat your conversation and song several times, as other children come to look at the pictures. After the toys and play materials are put away, and the children have relaxed, they might sit down on the rug as you tell the story "Let the Children Come" (page 218).

If the nursery book *His Name Is Jesus* is used in this session, and the children ask about the pictures in the first story, you may say, "That was when Jesus was a baby."

With the Children at Home

Perhaps you can plan for a parent-teacher meeting this week or next, in order that home and church may co-operate in plans and preparations for Christmas.

SESSION 7. OUR BIG CHURCH

Thinking About the Children

In helping little children to feel at home in the nursery class, we are seeking to foster happy associations with the church. Gradually, as the children become familiar with other rooms in the building, and particularly with the part that is used for congregational worship, they will begin to think in terms of "our church," and to feel that their fathers and mothers share their experiences there.

For this session our special aim should be to familiarize the children with the church building, and to foster a feeling of sharing with their family in its fellowship.

Getting Ready for the Session

If your church sanctuary is not in use at the time of the nursery class session, you could plan a visit there as Miss Anderson did in the nursery book *In Our Church*, with experiences similar to those that Billy and the other children had. This would follow the rest time, as it did in the story. Otherwise, you might be able to plan for a visit some day during the week. In either case, your guidance during the first part of the session should help the children think of the nursery class as belonging to "our church" and to anticipate a visit to the part where their fathers and mothers meet.

If you can procure pictures of your church printed on the weekly bulletins or other leaflets, cut these out and paste them on colored mounting paper for the children to take home. Write "OUR CHURCH" in clear letters at the bottom of the picture.

Use Nursery Pictures 4 and 5 as suggested for last session. Have Pictures 1, 2, and 3 in readiness to look at with the children as you talk about Billy in nursery class and tell the story of his going to visit the big church.

With the Children in Church

As the children play with blocks or toys or dolls, or work with art materials, you will find many opportunities for relating their activities to experiences definitely associated with the church. You will suggest perhaps that the family who live in the house built with blocks would like to go to church, and the children may build a road or sidewalk on which they can drive or walk. Children playing with dolls will probably respond to your question, "Are you getting your children ready to go to church with you?" Similarly, children drawing with crayons might respond when you ask, "Would you like to make 'a picture' of a church?" In any of these groups, you may sing with the children "Church Bells" (page 231).

Sit with children in the book center, and look with them at the nursery book *In Our Church*. They will probably tell you all the things Billy is doing in nursery class; then you can tell them about his visit to the big church. They will thus be somewhat prepared for their own visit to the sanctuary, or will listen with greater interest if the story is told again to a larger group. You may find occasion to draw the attention of one child or several to Nursery Picture 5, and to recall this story as you sing softly "Jesus and the Children" (page 232).

If you are going into the sanctuary this session, allow time for this after the children have a rest. Otherwise, the play period may be a little longer. Then, after their rest, the children may sit with you on the rug, and sing "Church Bells," and look at the pictures and listen to the story "The Big Church," in the book *In Our Church*. At the end of the story, remark that we too can say, "Thank you, God, for our church," and the children may offer this prayer with you, or you may sing softly "At Church" (page 231). If any of the children are timid about entering the sanctuary, a helping teacher could stay with them outdoors.

With the Children at Home

When you are talking with parents on the phone, or in their home, or at a parent-teacher meeting, call their attention to the story "The Big Church." Help them recognize their part in making any experiences their children may have in the church sanctuary joyous and reverent, as in this story.

SESSION 8. WE SAY THANK YOU TO GOD AT HOME

Thinking About the Children

During these autumn days, at home and outdoors, the children are observing and sharing in preparations for winter, through which they may be led to feel God's wondrous provision for their care. Although their experiences will vary according to the part of the country in which they live, most children know something of the way in which the harvest is gathered, and how fruits and vegetables are stored in their homes. As days grow colder, they will know the comfort of a warm house and warm clothes, and woolly blankets to cover them at night. Through careful guidance, all these things may be recognized as part of God's plan for our care, and the children may be led to express this recognition in a simple prayer of thanks.

Such guidance will be our special aim this session, so that saying thank you to God may have real meaning for the children at Thanksgiving time and all through the year.

Getting Ready for the Session

Fruits and vegetables with which the children are familiar, also a glass jar of peaches or apricots or pears or other fruit that retains its shape when preserved, should be in sight. Fasten Nursery Pictures 9 and 11 low on the wall near the worship table above which is the picture of Jesus and the children. *My Prayer Book* might be placed on the table.

A "party" always suggests a happy time, and in this session could be related to the children's Thanksgiving experiences at home. A small glass of tomato or fruit juice and a cracker might be served (see pages 90, 91). Cut round pieces of paper for plates, or oblong ones for place mats, and let the children decorate these with seals or with pictures you have previously cut from seed catalogues or magazines.

With the Children in Church

The children's interest in the fruits and vegetables which have been brought will encourage conversation about God's plan for things to grow for food, and about preparations being made at home for winter. Such preparations may be reproduced in the doll corner. You might say to children building with blocks, "Are you building carefully so that your house will be warm in winter?"; or, "Are you putting in a furnace or a stove to keep the house warm?"; or, "Are you going to have a fruit cellar?" As you share the children's interest in various activities, you may find occasion to say: "God planned for us to have food to eat, and homes in which to live. He has helped our fathers and mothers know how to care for us. We can say thank you to him."

Call attention to the picture of a family saying grace at table. Look, with one child or with several, at *My Prayer Book*. Help the children think of things for which they say thank you to God at home. You might sing softly "Thank You" (page 231):

> "'Dear God, thank you today
> For food and rest and play.'"

Sing "Putting Our Toys Away" (page 232) when it is time for the children to do so. Remember to encourage sharing and helping in this activity. If you have planned for a "party," this may follow the rest time. Use "Thank You" as a grace.

With the Children at Home

Let the children take their paper plates or place mats home. It is important to children that the things they make in church school be noticed, admired, and used. An advance reminder to parents in such instances will insure their co-operation. Also suggest to their parents that they use at home the thank-you prayer sung in nursery class.

SESSION 9. WE SAY THANK YOU TO GOD IN OUR CHURCH

Thinking About the Children

This session will probably follow the children's Thanksgiving activities at home, and should provide happy experiences in saying thank you to God in church. While our teaching in any session should lead the children to associate God with their welfare and happiness so that they will naturally say thank you to him, our special aim this week is to make such expression of thanks a joyous part of their church experience. We shall help them recall their visit to the big church, or the story of Billy visiting there, in the book *In Our Church,* so that they may think of their fathers and mothers as saying thank you to God in church as they do.

Getting Ready for the Session

Use Nursery Pictures 1, 2, and 3 for this session, placing them low on the wall. Choose picture books carefully for the book center, including *In Our Church,* and such books as *My Bible Book* and *My Prayer Book,* or other books showing pictures of things for which we give thanks to God. *From Crocus to Snowman* would be a good addition to the bookshelves.

With the Children in Church

As the children arrive and proceed to take off their outdoor clothing, you might greet them with such comments as, "Aren't you glad your mother made you such a warm, woolly coat?"; or, "Isn't this a lovely day to come to our church!"; or: "The moon was beautiful in the sky last night. Did you see it?"; or, "We'll soon need to wear our mittens to keep our hands warm"; or, "I wonder what you had for breakfast this morning?" Such remarks will turn the children's thoughts to things that make them comfortable and happy, and they will recall these later as they sing or say thank you to God. As they work or play in the various "corners" or "centers," or look at pictures or picture books, you will find opportunities to make further remarks, such as, "Aren't you glad we have blocks to build with in our church?"; or, "Our church is a happy place to come with our friends"; or: "This picture helps us remember that Jesus said, 'Let the children come.' We're glad that we hear about Jesus in our church"; or: "The children in this picture are saying thank you to God in their church. We can say thank you to God in our church"; or: "Here is a picture of something for which we can say thank you to God. What is it?" Singing "Church Bells" (page 231) or "At Church" (page 231) may be a natural part of your conversation with the children, and may be followed by the prayer song "Thank You" (page 231).

When the toys are put away, and the children have had a brief rest, sit on the rug and encourage them to join you. Use pictures to help them recall things for which they would like to say thank you to God. They might play, as in the previous sessions, getting ready to go to church, naming each step in their preparations to the tune of "Here We Go Round the Mulberry Bush." Sing with them "Church Bells." Open the nursery book *In Our Church* and use the pictures to help the children recall that Billy said thank you to God in his church, and fathers and mothers said thank you too. Sing softly "At Church," then "Thank You."

With the Children at Home

Remind the children that they can say thank you to God at home just as they do in church.

SESSION 10. HOME FROM CHURCH

Thinking About the Children

One of the happy experiences in going to nursery class is returning home again, and the children's appreciation of their home should be deepened through this brief separation from it. The friendly attitudes that are being fostered in the nursery class ought to carry over to situations with their family. As children are learning to share and to take turns and to help in church, they should be led to find happiness in doing the same at home.

Our special aim for this session is to help the children to think of happy times at home, to recognize their part in contributing to these through readiness to share, and to take turns and help. Fostering such attitudes should lead to joyous Christmas experiences. The story of Jesus and the children may be used as you talk about happy times that all the family can share.

Getting Ready for the Session

Nursery Pictures 9, 10, and 11 suggest home situations that may be related to nursery class experiences, and Pictures 4 and 5 help recall the happiness of fathers and mothers and children who went to see Jesus. Use these pictures this session, fastening the one of Jesus and the children on the wall above the table on which the children expect to find things that help them think of God. Other pictures of families or of happy home experiences may be found in picture books, or may be cut from magazines and mounted on cardboard to be placed on the table in the book center. A book like *The Little Family* will be useful.

You might copy the words of "The Family" (page 234) on slips of paper for the children to take home.

With the Children in Church

Observe the children as they choose materials with which to work or play, and be prepared to guide them in friendly ways of sharing, taking turns, and helping. You might say, "That is the way Ruth shares with her little brother at home"; or, "You could help your mother like that, couldn't you, Frank?"; or, "I saw Tommy rolling his ball to his little brother yesterday and letting him have a turn." With children in the doll corner, you might recite "Here's a Ball for Baby" (page 235) as you develop this finger play. With children building with blocks or drawing with crayons, you might suggest that they make a home, then recite "This Is a Home" (page 235). With children looking at pictures, you might sing "The Family." With children looking at Nursery Pictures, sing softly "Jesus and the Children" (page 232). In all such guidance, help the children feel their fathers' and mothers' part in making happy times at home, and their own part too.

When it is time for the children to have a brief rest, sing "Putting Our Toys Away" (page 232). As they put everything in its proper place (more or less!), suggest that they help in this way at home.

When the children are ready to rest, remark that Mother sings a lullaby when she puts the baby to sleep, and that you will sing a lullaby for them. Sing softly "Lullaby" (page 231). After their rest, look with them at the pictures chosen for this session, and note what the different members of the families are doing. Sing or recite again any of the songs or verses used with small groups in the earlier part of the session.

You might say: "In the Bible we read, 'Love one another.' We can love one another at home by sharing and taking turns and helping."

With the Children at Home

Before the children go home, sing with them "The Family." If you have copied the words of the song for them to take home, suggest that they ask Daddy or Mother to sing it with them there.

SESSION 11. WHEN JESUS WAS BORN

Thinking About the Children

The Christmas sessions in the nursery class should be planned with the happiness of little children clearly in mind. Play activities will differ little from those of other sessions, for with all the rush and excitement that characterize Christmas preparations in many homes, children need the security of an accepted routine. While they will enjoy making simple decorations for a Christmas tree, and "surprises" for Daddy and Mother, be sure to allow time for familiar playthings and activities and for repeated experiences in listening to the story and looking at the pictures that tell of the night when Jesus was born. This story, "A Baby Is Born," with the pictures, is in the nursery book *His Name Is Jesus,* and should be related to the story of Jesus and the children that is also found there. (See pages 217–219.) Always refer to Jesus as a baby by saying, "When Jesus was a baby," thus avoiding the term "the baby Jesus," which might suggest a different person from the Jesus who said, "Let the children come."

Our special aim for this session is to tell the Christmas story so simply that every child may feel its joy and wonder, and may think of Christmas as a happy day because it is the birthday of Jesus.

Getting Ready for the Session

Fasten the picture of the Nativity, Nursery Picture 6, above the special table reserved for things that help us think about God, and plan to leave this picture there for the Christmas season. Place a few evergreen sprays on this table, also the nursery book *His Name Is Jesus,* if you have received it by this time. Fasten the picture of Jesus and the children, Nursery Picture 5, on the wall nearby. Use pictures of home situations as suggested for last session.

If possible, have a small Christmas tree or an evergreen branch set up for the children to decorate, and simple materials that they can use for this purpose. Large, colored price tags, with cords attached, require only a Christmas seal on each side to make attractive decorations. A big, round wooden bead, tied at each end of a short length of string, makes an ornament that is easily hung in place. Stars or bells you have cut from colored cardboard may be attached to string in the same way. Strips of colored cellophane, crepe paper or tin foil, and pieces of absorbent cotton, will adhere to branches and are always effective.

Have materials in readiness also for a simple gift that the children can make. A large Christmas tree previously cut from green blotting paper by the teacher could be decorated by the children with gummed stars. A memo pad or a calendar or a bookmark could be decorated with Christmas seals or with pictures you have cut from old Christmas cards. With similar decorations, paper plates are transformed into pin trays or flowerpot stands. Keep materials you have prepared for such gifts out of sight, until you suggest that the children make a surprise for Daddy or Mother. (Some children may be living with an aunt or grandmother, so you will keep this in mind whenever family relationships are mentioned.)

With the Children in Church

As the children arrive, they are sure to observe preparations you have been making for Christmas, and will be eager to talk about these or to tell about preparations at home. Probably they will tell you what Santa Claus is going to bring them. Some of the children may want to proceed immediately to decorate the Christmas tree, while others will choose familiar materials with which to work or play. As they build with blocks or string beads or play with dolls or draw with crayons, their activities will reflect home experiences associated with Christmas. A box filled with blocks may be Santa Claus's sleigh. Their beads may be Christmas tree ornaments. Doll dishes may be used for making Christmas cakes. Pictures drawn with crayons may be anything they suggest. Share all such interests, recalling home songs or finger plays used in previous sessions as the children think about happy things that families do together. Sing also "Christmas Day" (page 233). Help the children feel that we are all playing Santa Claus at Christmas when we plan surprises for someone.

The story "A Baby Is Born" may very well be told as you sit quietly with one or two children and look at the pictures. You may also sing softly in such a group, "Shepherds Leave the Hillside" (page 233). This may mean that you repeat the story and the song several times, and some children may come each time to listen. If all the children hear the story in this way, the period after they have had a rest time could be used in making a Christmas gift for their fathers or mothers. While the children are resting, sing softly "Lullaby" (page 231) and "Shepherds Leave the Hillside." Before helping them to plan their surprise, you may say: "Christmas is Jesus' birthday, and that is why it is such a happy day. We help make it happy when we plan surprises for someone." A few children in the group will not be interested in working on a gift so we won't insist or make them feel ashamed.

With the Children at Home

Today you will give each child a copy of the nursery book *His Name Is Jesus* to take home. You might wrap it in tissue paper and fasten it with a Christmas seal, so that it will be a surprise when it is opened at home. If you have had a parent-teacher meeting as suggested a few weeks ago, parents will be prepared to make this book the center of their children's Christmas experiences at home as you are doing in church. Inform mothers and fathers that in nursery class you speak about "playing Santa Claus" when the children make and give gifts. Parents may wish to use the same idea as they discuss the jolly old saint at home.

SESSION 12. JESUS' BIRTHDAY

Thinking About the Children

If last session's activities in the nursery class were as simple and happy as they were in the planning, the children may want to repeat them this session. In the meantime, their Christmas experiences at home will have been enriched through hearing the stories and looking at the pictures in the nursery book *His Name Is Jesus*. Also any plans and preparations in which they have been sharing will be related to the thought of helping to make Christmas a happy day because it is the birthday of Jesus. This idea will underlie our planning again this session, and our special aim will be to help the children begin to discover the joy that comes through thinking of others.

Getting Ready for the Session

Have the same pictures you used last session low on the walls of the nursery room, and put evergreen sprays and the nursery book *His Name Is Jesus* on the special table. Have additional materials in readiness for decorating the small Christmas tree; also be prepared to provide large envelopes or sheets of folded paper in which the children may enclose their gifts for Daddy or Mother. Make sure that there are clean, soft blankets in the doll corner, since play centering around the care of a baby often follows naturally when the children have heard the Christmas story.

With the Children in Church

As the children arrive, some of them will be interested in continuing with Christmas preparations they were making last session, while others will want to play or work with familiar toys and materials. Whatever activities they may choose, share their interest and conversation. As they talk of Christmas, remind them that it is Jesus' birthday, and that we can all have a part in making it a happy time. By your comments, encourage friendly attitudes in play.

With children playing in the doll corner, suggest that they can hold their baby gently as Mary held her baby. Sing with them "Lullaby" (page 231) and "Shepherds Leave the Hillside" (page 233). With children decorating the Christmas tree, or perhaps making a Christmas tree with blocks or crayons, sing "Christmas Day" (page 233).

The story "A Baby Is Born" may be told again this session, as you sit quietly with one or two children and look at the pictures in the book *His Name Is Jesus*. The children will be interested to turn from the picture of Jesus and the children to the Nativity picture, and you will say, "This is when Jesus was a baby."

Allow plenty of time for the children to enjoy playing together, and for all to hear the Christmas story. When toys and play materials have been put away, and the children have relaxed, call their attention to the Christmas tree, and say, "You have helped make our church beautiful for Christmas by decorating this tree." The children could join hands with you, and dance around the tree as you sing "Christmas

Day." This might suggest that singing is a happy thing to do at Christmas time. Remind the children that Christmas is Jesus' birthday, and that they can sing about when Jesus was born. Sing with them "Shepherds Leave the Hillside."

Remark that planning surprises is another happy thing to do at Christmas, and look with the children at the gifts they have made for Daddy or Mother or Auntie. Allow time to put these in an envelope or in a sheet of folded paper before getting ready to go home. The edges of the paper can be fastened together with a Christmas seal.

With the Children at Home

The books that the children took home last session, and the gifts they are taking today, will help bring home and church close together during the Christmas season.

SESSION 13. CHRISTMAS TOYS

Thinking About the Children

Nursery children have little sense of time, and Christmas is not merely one day to them but includes all the experiences associated with the word. Thus the teaching opportunities offered by the Christmas season may be prolonged as we lead the children into recalling the happiness they found in making others happy. Our special aim for this session is to help them continue to find joy through further experiences in sharing.

Getting Ready for the Session

Pictures and decorations associated with Christmas should still be in place in the nursery room. Arrange favorite toys under the Christmas tree, as if it were Christmas morning. You might take a toy of your own from home to share with the children. If you have any toy sheep or lambs or a little donkey, place these near the blocks, where they will probably suggest the building of a stable such as that in which Jesus was born.

With the Children in Church

Some of the children may bring a new toy, and will be eager to show this to their friends. Encourage friendly sharing, at the same time reminding the children of the care with which we use things that do not belong to us. Give necessary supervision with toys that might be easily damaged or soiled, then put these safely aside, with assurance to the owners that they will be returned before it is time to go home. Remark on the love shown by the fathers and mothers and friends in giving toys to the children, and help the children recall their own happiness in planning Christmas surprises. Children who have not brought a toy might like to choose one to play with from under the Christmas tree, and you can encourage them in sharing and taking turns. Show them the toy you have brought from home, and let them play with it. Nursery Picture 10, which is of children playing together, may be used at this time.

If you have put toy animals near the blocks, the children who discover these may need no further suggestion that they build a stable. Talk with them about the animals in the stable when Jesus was born. Sing "Shepherds Leave the Hillside" (page 233). Children playing with baby dolls will like to talk about Mary caring for her baby. Ask them if their baby has any Christmas toys, and make these with your fingers as you recite "Here's a Ball for Baby" (page 235). Then sing "Lullaby" (page 231).

With whatever materials the children are playing, you will find opportunities for recalling with them their Christmas experiences, and encouraging them in friendly sharing. When it is time to sing "Putting Our Toys Away" (page 232), suggest that the children put their own toys under the Christmas tree. While the children have a brief rest, sing "Lullaby," then tell the story "Christmas Night" (page 224).

With the Children at Home

As children pick out their own toys to take home, remark on the happiness they gave to other children by sharing these, and say that they can share them with little friends who come to their house to play.

SECOND QUARTER

Book: *His Name Is Jesus*

CHRISTMAS is past, but its happiness is still with us, and during the next three months nursery children at home and at church should have repeated experiences in finding this happiness through doing things that are friendly and helpful. Such experiences will come as they are led to recognize the ways in which their mothers and fathers care for them, and their own part in contributing to the happiness of other members of the family. They may come also as the children are led to appreciate the many services that help them have food to eat, clothes to wear, and comfortable homes in which to live, and to grow well and strong so that they can help care for themselves. This appreciation will find expression in attitudes of friendliness and co-operation toward the milkman and the grocer and the postman and the doctor and other friends who help them.

Outdoors, there may be experiences in helping to care for birds that stay with us in winter, or that come back from the South in early spring. There may also be experiences in playing in the snow with little friends, or in working with Daddy as he rakes the leaves from the garden when frost and snow are gone. As days grow warmer, there will be increasing opportunities for outdoor play, and thus for finding happiness in God's beautiful world through experiences in friendliness and helpfulness.

All such experiences enter into our teaching plans for this quarter, which are based on the nursery book *His Name Is Jesus*. The story of when Jesus was a baby will be recalled as the children think of their homes and of ways in which their mothers and fathers care for them. The story of Jesus and the children follows naturally, and while this story emphasizes the love of Jesus for little children, it is used also to suggest the care of mothers and fathers for their children, happy times in which all the family share, how Jesus told little children about the birds and flowers, how he helped them to know that God loved them, and the happiness of Jesus in doing things that were friendly and helpful.

In planning for this quarter in your nursery class, read carefully the

teaching plans for Sessions 1-3, First Quarter, where detailed suggestions for procedure are given. Also, read again the introductory chapters of this handbook, in order to remind yourself of the needs of nursery children and the responsibility of the church to provide for such
needs in the nursery class. Make sure that children who were not in
the nursery class before Christmas receive a copy of *His Name Is
Jesus*. The stories from the book may be found on pages 217–219.

Suggestions for home co-operation are given in connection with
each session, but parents who read the teaching plans for themselves
will be better able to carry over the teaching of the nursery class into
the home.

SESSION 1. HAPPY TIMES AT HOME

Thinking About the Children

At this time of year when winds are cold and nights are long in many
parts of our country, children and grownups alike are conscious of
the warmth and fellowship of their home, and of happy times to be
had with members of their family. Fruits and vegetables that were
stored away for the winter give assurance of good things to eat, while,
with Christmas just past, there are new toys with which the children
can play and household gifts for fathers and mothers to enjoy. All
such experiences may be related to God's plan for people to live in
homes, where they love and help one another. Our special aim for
this session is to guide the children in a growing recognition of kind
and helpful things they can do for other members of the family.

Getting Ready for the Session

Read suggestions for relating happy home experiences to the
thought of God's plan for our care, Sessions 8 and 10, First Quarter.
Read also, in the Christmas sessions, suggestions for guiding the children into discovering the joy that comes through making others
happy. Plan to use Nursery Pictures 9, 10, and 11 in talking with the
children about their own home experiences, and Nursery Picture 4 in
telling of going to see Jesus as a happy time for all the family. The
Nativity picture will help recall the Christmas story and suggest their
experiences with a baby brother or sister. Fasten the picture of Jesus
and the children on the wall above the worship table, and plan to

leave it there during this quarter while our teaching plans are based on the reading book *His Name Is Jesus*.

With the Children in Church

The guidance suggested for Session 10, First Quarter, offers a good pattern for this session. As the children work or play in the homelike setting of the nursery class, many of their activities will be similar to ones they engage in at home, and the attitudes that make for happy relations with other children are those that produce happy relations with members of their family. Comment on friendly ways in which they share, take turns, or help, and remark that they have happy times at home when they show friendliness in these same ways.

Children playing with dolls may be encouraged in reproducing actual home experiences, and as they get dinner ready, or sweep the floor, or put the baby to bed, or make a dress, or knit a sweater, or go shopping, you may say, "Mother is always doing something for us, and when we help her, we have good times together." You might use the finger play "Here's a Ball for Baby" (page 235), as you suggest that children can help by playing with a baby brother, sister, or friend.

When it is time to sing "Putting Our Toys Away" (page 232), the children could pretend that they are doing this at home to surprise Mother. After their rest, look with them at the pictures of home experiences, and encourage them to tell about good times they have at home, including those they had at Christmas. The children may then sing "The Family" (page 234), and may make a house with their hands as you recite "This Is a Home" (page 235). They might like to say thank you to God as the pictures suggest. Help them feel that this is one of the things a family does. Sing "Thank You" (page 231).

You might remark that families enjoy stories together. Look at the picture and tell the story of fathers and mothers taking their children to see Jesus. Note that the mothers carried the babies in their arms, and the fathers took the little children by the hand. You might say, "Aren't you glad that God planned for us to live in families!" and the children may sing again "The Family."

With the Children at Home

The experiences of this session should carry over into the home. As you talk with parents, enlist their co-operation in helping their children to discover things they can do to contribute to the fellowship of their family.

SESSION 2. OUR MOTHERS AND FATHERS CARE FOR US

Thinking About the Children

The teaching of this session is closely related to that of the preceding one, in which we sought to guide the children in a growing recognition of their part in contributing to the happiness of their family. In this session our special aim will be to deepen their appreciation of the many ways in which their mothers and fathers care for them.

Getting Ready for the Session

Look through magazine advertisements for pictures of mothers and fathers caring for children in various ways, including fathers at work to earn money, and use these pictures in addition to the Nursery Pictures suggested for last session. Magazine pictures may be cut out and pasted on separate sheets of cardboard or mounting paper, or on one large sheet. Squares of corrugated cardboard, such as those used to protect phonograph records, make excellent mounts for pictures. Two or three of these fastened together with hinges of cellophane tape will stand up like a screen.

If additional housekeeping toys are desirable in the doll corner, this would be a good time for the children to find them there. Toys that encourage the reproduction of household activities will insure play through which the children may be led to recognize the many ways in which their mothers and fathers (or guardians) care for them.

With the Children in Church

Whatever kind of weather the winter season may bring in your part of the country, the clothes the children wear to nursery class will reflect the love and care of their parents in providing for their comfort. As the children begin to take off their outdoor clothing, comment on the care with which Mother has made a little coat, or knitted cozy mittens, or on the fact that Daddy has worked to earn money to buy rubbers or galoshes. Children enjoy variations of the couplet:

> "My snow suit is blue, your snow suit is red,
> My snow suit goes zip, zip, right down from my head."

When they are getting dressed to go home, the order of the zipping may be reversed so that it goes "right up to my head."

As children play in the doll corner, you will find many opportunities for remarking that the children are caring for their dolls as their mothers and fathers care for them. As children play with blocks, you might suggest that they build a garage or a store or a factory or a barn or an office building or some other structure associated with the way in which their fathers work to earn money.

As children look at the pictures used during this session, encourage them to tell about similar ways in which their mothers and fathers care for them.

After rest time, sit with the children on a rug, and look with them at the picture of the Nativity. Talk about Mary's care for Jesus when he was a baby, and the way in which their mothers care for them, or for a baby brother or sister. They may hold their arms as if rocking a baby, and sing very softly "Lullaby" (page 231). Then look with them at Nursery Picture 11, which shows a family group at bedtime. Sing "The Family" (page 234). Then encourage the children to say thank you to God for their mothers and fathers.

With the Children at Home

As the children put on their outdoor clothing, remind them that they can thank Mother and Daddy for the comfortable clothes they are wearing.

SESSION 3. WE CAN HELP CARE FOR OURSELVES

Thinking About the Children

During the past weeks, while we have been helping the children to discover ways in which they can assist at home, and to appreciate the many things their mothers and fathers do for them, they have been growing in ability to do things for themselves, and are finding increasing satisfaction with each new achievement in personal care. In this session our aim will be to provide experiences through which this satisfaction may be deepened, as the children are led to feel that in learning to help care for themselves they are also assisting their mothers and fathers.

Getting Ready for the Session

Arrange the nursery room as for previous sessions, leaving more materials on shelves or in cupboards for the children to bring out. Pictures of children dressing or eating or brushing their teeth or going to bed may be readily found in magazine advertisements, and may be cut out and pasted on sheets of mounting paper or corrugated cardboard. Fasten a long strip of paper low on the wall, and cut out the pictures so they will be ready for the children to paste on it. Plan to tell the story "Ready for Bed" (page 224), and to use Nursery Picture 11 to suggest saying thank you to God at bedtime. If you wish to buy a new book, either *Time for Bed* or *Bobbie and Donnie Were Twins* would be a good choice. (See page 94.)

With the Children in Church

If leggings and snow suits and galoshes are seasonable clothing in your part of the country, be sure to allow plenty of time at both ends of the session for the children to have some sense of achievement in helping to take these off and to put them on, and to manipulate buttons or zippers or other fasteners. You might recite with the children the little couplet suggested for last session as they slide zippers down or up, and, while encouraging them in helping themselves, be sure to give assistance where needed. As you do so, you might say, "Won't Mother be glad when you can put on your leggings to go out to play in the snow!"; or, "Mother will have more time to sew [or to knit, or to tell you stories] when you can dress and undress yourself"; or, "Perhaps you can surprise Daddy by taking your snow suit off by yourself when you go home"; or, "Your baby sister can't unfasten her buttons, can she, Donald?"

As children engage in various activities, encourage them in getting out and putting away the materials used. Ask them to help you carry or move something that is awkward to handle alone. To children playing in the doll corner, you might say, "Can your little girl dress herself yet?"; or, "Can your little boy put on his own shoes?"

If you have cut out pictures for the children to paste on a long strip of paper, call attention to these, and talk about the ways in which the children in the pictures are helping to care for themselves. Before pasting, the children might like to play doing some of these things.

When it is time for a rest, encourage the children in putting toys away more carefully. After their rest, tell the story "Ready for Bed." Then they might like to play that they are taking off each article of clothing, having a bath, and putting on their pajamas as Bobby did. Help them feel how pleased his mother must have been. Then look with them at the picture of a family at bedtime, and suggest that they can say thank you to God for all the things they are learning to do to help care for themselves.

With the Children at Home

Talk with fathers and mothers about providing plenty of opportunities for their children to grow in independence. Suggest that they express their pleasure in being helped in this way by the children.

SESSION 4. WE CAN HELP CARE FOR BIRDS

Thinking About the Children

Whether children live in the city or in the country, they are sure to have experiences in watching or listening to birds, and will always find joy in helping to care for them. This may be done very simply through providing pieces of bright-colored wool for nest-building in spring, a large shallow pan of cool water in summer, and seeds or crumbs for food when fields and trees are bare. Our aim for this session will be to guide the children into having a happy experience in caring for birds. Through this activity they begin to feel that in God's plan for birds in his world we play a part too.

Plans for this session can be used in any section of the country. However, it may be necessary to omit the dramatic play about snow and the reference to snow in the story "Wonders of God," printed on page 225. Or, in parts of the country where there is no snow, you might plan for other experiences in helping to care for birds and use the story "Feeding the Pigeons" (page 226) instead of "Wonders of God."

Getting Ready for the Session

If it is practicable for the children to make a little feeding station for birds outside the window of the nursery room, have a shallow wooden box or tray ready to fasten on the window sill; or a waxed carton, such as those in which ice cream is sold, to hang on the branch of a tree. Otherwise, provide envelopes so that the children may each make a packet of food for the birds near their own home. A bird seal, or a silhouette of a bird previously cut from colored paper by the teacher, could be used to decorate each envelope. Have a small jar of seeds and grain and crumbs and coarse cereals, and bits of suet and other foods attractive to birds, for the children to put in the feeding tray or carton, or in their envelopes.

If you are continually on the alert to find good pictures to use with nursery children, you will gradually be building up a file to supplement your Nursery Picture set, from which you can draw on any occasion. For this session look for a picture of birds feeding in winter, preferably a picture that shows children helping. Prepare to tell the story "Wonders of God." Birds cut from heavy colored paper, and placed with the small toys in the block corner, may suggest play in which the children think of ways to care for birds. On the book table you may wish to have a copy of *The Little Golden Book of Birds*.

With the Children in Church

Don't forget to encourage children's efforts in taking off their outdoor clothing, and comment on any new achievement in accomplishing this routine. If it is a snowy day, remark on the fun of playing in the snow. Whatever the weather, ask the children if they saw any birds on their way to church. In their play they will probably reproduce outdoor experiences of this season, and by your comments you may help them feel the beauty and wonder of God's world, and associate their happy times with God's plan for their care.

As you share the children's interests, sing (page 232):

> " 'Down, down, without a sound,
> Snowflakes are covering all the ground.' "

The children may imitate you in making the falling snowflakes with their fingers. They might like to play that they are getting ready to go outdoors, and may reproduce every procedure in putting on snow suits, galoshes, caps, and mittens. A good rhythmic play may be developed as they take high steps as if walking in deep snow. You might hum in slow march time as they do this. Remark that birds can't find food to eat when the ground is covered with snow. Then the children may play that they are scattering crumbs or seeds.

When toys and playthings have been put away and the children have had a rest, tell the story "Wonders of God." Sit quietly for a moment and look with the children at pictures of birds. Then say, "We can help feed the birds," and show materials you have in readiness for making a feeding station, or for planning to feed birds near home. As the children put food in the tray or carton or envelopes, you might say: "God has planned for birds to live in his world. Aren't you glad we can help care for them!"

With the Children at Home

Fathers and mothers who call for their children will be interested in the feeding station or in the little packets of food. Enlist their co-operation in helping their children to have happy experiences in feeding birds, and in bringing food for the feeding station next Sunday.

SESSION 5. JESUS TOLD ABOUT THE BIRDS

Thinking About the Children

During the past week, the children have probably been observing birds hunting for food, and may have helped feed them. Our aim in this session is to help the children find increasing happiness in such experiences. Through recalling the story of Jesus and the children in *His Name Is Jesus,* we will suggest the thought that when Jesus helped the children know how much God loved them, he told them about the birds and how God cares for them.

Getting Ready for the Session

If the children have made a birds' feeding station outside the nursery room window, be sure to have food with which to replenish it, and remember that this must be done each week. An abandoned birds' nest, and perhaps a tiny feather you have found on the ground, would be of special interest on the nature table. Look through your picture file or picture books for a picture of a mother and father bird building their nest, or caring for their babies.

With the Children in Church

Our guidance of the children's activities in this session will be much the same as in the last one. There will be opportunities for encouraging children in helping to care for themselves, and for fostering an appreciation of ways in which their mothers and fathers care for them. Experiences in feeding birds should be repeated, and perhaps reproduced in play. As children look at a birds' nest or a tiny feather or at pictures of birds, you may say: "See how carefully the father and mother bird made this nest for their babies. See how soft it is inside. God planned for birds to care for their babies like this"; or, "Aren't you glad God planned for birds to have soft feathers to keep them warm?" If the children's observations or questions should lead to further discussion of God's care for birds, guide them in thinking of ways in which they can help.

Some of the children might like to repeat the play of putting on snow suits and galoshes and caps and mittens, walking in deep snow, and scattering crumbs or seeds for birds. They might sing about the snowflakes falling down (page 232). If there is a feeding station outside the window, all the children will probably want to help in putting fresh food in it. Possibly they might see a bird come to feed there.

The story of Jesus and the children may be recalled after the rest period as you look with them at the pictures in *His Name Is Jesus*. Notice how the mothers carried the babies, and how the fathers took the little children by the hand. Call attention also to Jesus who held out his arms and said, "Let the children come." Then say: "Jesus is talking to the children, and telling them how much God loves them. Perhaps he is telling them about the birds too, and how God planned for them to have food to eat and feathers to keep them warm. Maybe those little children helped care for the birds, just as you do." Call attention to the picture of Jesus and the birds on page 23.

With the Children at Home

Remind the children that they can feed the birds near their homes every day.

SESSION 6. WE LEARN THAT GOD LOVES US

Thinking About the Children

Children naturally take for granted the many services that contribute to their welfare and happiness, but, with careful guidance, attitudes of appreciation and friendliness may be fostered toward all "helpers" with whom they come in contact. Such helpers may include the milkman, the storekeeper, the farmer, the minister, the doctor, and the man who brings the mail, whether he be a city postman or a rural mailman. Our aim for this session will be to help the children think of these people as friends, and begin to recognize that God shows love for us in planning for friends to help us.

Getting Ready for the Session

The activities for this session are planned in relation to several different helpers, but could be confined to one special helper if you think this would serve better to carry out your aim. Look for pictures of helpers with whom the children come into contact, or pictures that suggest friendly services. If you are planning to tell the story "Milk for Breakfast" (page 226), you could use a picture showing a milkman's truck or a farmer filling cans with milk for the dairy, or children drinking milk, or Nursery Picture 9, which shows a family saying grace—or you might use all these pictures. Nursery Picture 12 suggests ways in which doctors help to keep us well. Almost any picture in the children's picture books could be associated with some friend who helps them. Look through the nursery books on which these teaching plans are based, and note how many helpers are suggested by the pictures. *A Year on the Farm* or *The Little Farm,* and *Stop-Look-Listen* would be appropriate additions to the book table.

One or two small empty milk bottles near the blocks will direct the children's play to delivering milk. A few old envelopes, and a paper bag with a string to go over the shoulder, could be used for delivering valentines (made by pasting large red hearts on paper doilies). A basket in which blocks and cereal cartons may be carried provides materials for a shopping expedition. A board, to set up as a counter, might serve the grocer for a store.

See Session 10, Fourth Quarter, for activities related to the doctor.

With the Children in Church

Watch for opportunities to relate the children's play to someone who helps them. This is simply done in the block center. If a child has built a house, remark that the postman is coming down the street and may have a letter for that address, or that the baker or the milkman is at the door. You might ask if there is a grocery store nearby, and another child may proceed to build one. You might suggest that a doctor or a minister or a farmer lives in the house, and lead the children to think of ways in which these friends help them. A favorite building activity is to lay flat blocks on the floor to make a road or sidewalk. Toy trucks or cars running on the road could represent any kind of service.

Similar guidance may be given where children are playing with dolls. Also, the pictures you have chosen for this session will suggest things they can make. A picture of a postman might lead to pretending to write letters, putting them in envelopes, and mailing them in a box; or it might suggest that the children make and send valentines.

Be careful not to offer too many ideas, but to let the activities develop from the children's own experiences. Your guidance may consist in taking a role in their play, sometimes that of the mother in the home, and, by your remarks and attitudes, leading the children toward an appreciation of the friends who help them every day. You will find many opportunities for saying quite naturally, "Aren't you glad God plans for people to help us?"; or, "We know God loves us when he plans for so many friends who help us." Then sing "The Family" (page 234).

If you have a long session, the lunch period will offer an actual experience in enjoying tomato juice or fruit juice that the farmer and grocer have provided, and expressing thanks to God for these friends. Otherwise, as soon as the children have had a brief rest, you might look with them at pictures, and tell the story "Milk for Breakfast"; or you could tell the story of the doctor in the nursery book *I'm Growing* (and found also on pages 222, 223 of this handbook). Either of these stories might be followed by an expression of thanks.

With the Children at Home

The teaching of this session should be reflected in attitudes of appreciation and friendliness toward everyone who renders service. Help parents feel the importance of providing opportunities for the children to express such attitudes every day and to associate people who contribute to their welfare and happiness with God's plan for their care.

SESSION 7. JESUS TOLD LITTLE CHILDREN THAT GOD LOVES THEM

Thinking About the Children

During the past week the children have probably had a new interest in any "helpers" with whom they have come in contact, and will respond readily to further guidance in appreciating and being friendly toward them. During this session, we shall lead the children to feel more deeply that God loves them, and that these friends who help them keep well and happy are part of his plan for their care. Our aim will include a growing consciousness of Jesus as a friend who loved little children, and who told of God's love for them.

Getting Ready for the Session

Recall the activities that the children most enjoyed last session, and have materials on hand for repeating them. Be prepared to share the children's interest in any experiences they may have had with helpers during the week, and to relate these to the thought of God's care.

With the Children in Church

Your guidance in this session will be similar to that in the past one. Almost any activity in which the children engage may be related to someone who helps them, and you may enter into their play by taking a role. "These big blocks would make a fine grocery store," you might say. "I'd like to buy some oranges and some butter today!"; or: "I think I hear the milkman's truck coming along this street. Let us put out the empty bottles before it stops at our house"; or: "You are taking good care of your baby, Margaret. What does the doctor tell you to give her to eat? Would you like to get her ready to go to see him today?"; or: "Perhaps Bobby would like to be a postman, and bring us some letters in this bag. What will we say to him? Then we can write some letters, and mail them in this box."

Through play suggested by such questions or comments, the children will feel the friendliness of people on whose services we depend, and it will seem quite natural for you to say, "God has planned for friends to help us like this"; or, "Aren't you glad God planned for friends to help us?" As you look with the children at pictures on the wall or in picture books, your conversation may lead to a similar expression of gratitude to God.

As the children relax, you might recite with them the finger play "This Is a Home" (page 235). Ask them to tell about kind and helpful things their mothers and fathers do for them. Sing "The Family" (page 234).

Call the children's attention to the picture of Jesus and the children, and say: "Jesus was a friend. He told the children that God loved them." Tell the story, or talk about it with the children. Sing "Jesus and the Children" (page 232). Then say: "We know that God loves us too. He plans that our mothers and daddies and many friends shall do kind things for us."

With the Children at Home

Seek the co-operation of parents as suggested for last session.

SESSION 8. WE PRAY TO GOD

Thinking About the Children

As we guide little children in associating God with everything that contributes to their welfare and happiness, they will imitate the joyous way in which we say, "I'm glad God planned for this"; or, "Thank you, God." Gradually, as they begin to feel the nearness of God and his interest in all that concerns them, their expressions of thanks will become more and more spontaneous, and they will talk to God as naturally as they talk to Mother or Daddy. This is the way in which we are seeking to help little children pray and in which we should pray with them. Experiences in praying to God are closely related to our teaching of the past few weeks. Our aim for this session will be to help the children find increasing joy in such experiences, and feel that praying to God is one of the happiest things they do in church and at home.

Getting Ready for the Session

Choose carefully the books to be placed in the book center. These might include *My Bible Book, My Prayer Book, In Our Church, His Name Is Jesus,* and *From Crocus to Snowman.* Nursery Pictures 1, 9, and 11 present familiar situations in which children pray to God.

Picture 3 will help them recall that Miss Anderson prayed to God when Billy and the other children went with her into the big church, in the nursery book *In Our Church;* it will also remind them that fathers and mothers pray to God in church. The picture of Jesus and the children may suggest that when Jesus told little children that God loved them, they wanted to pray to God. This picture should be on the wall above the worship table. A few cones or evergreen branches or a little plant would be of interest on this table. Plan to tell again the story "Wonders of God" (page 225).

With the Children in Church

As the children arrive, and take off their outdoor clothing, and choose work or play materials according to their own interests, watch for opportunities to relate their activities to the thought of God's plan for their care as shown through mothers and fathers and all the friends who help them. This guidance will be similar to that for preceding sessions, and may lead naturally to simple expressions of thanks. These may be in the children's own words, or the children may sing "Thank You" (page 231), adapting the second line of this song to any special experience. This might be, "For clothes that keep us warm"; or, "For the milkman who brings the milk"; or, "For snow so soft and white."

With one child at a time, or with several, you may look at the picture books or pictures you have chosen for this session. Help the children recognize things in the pictures that tell of God's plan for our care, for which we say thank you to him. You might sing with them "Thank You" or "The Family" (page 234) or "At Church" (page 231).

When the toys have been put away, look with the children at Nursery Picture 11, and suggest that *they* can pray to God before they go to rest. Sing softly and reverently "Thank You." After a brief rest, tell the story "Wonders of God"; then let the children repeat the last line of this story with you.

With the Children at Home

In talking with parents, perhaps at a parent-teacher meeting, explain how their children are learning to pray to God in the nursery class, and how similar guidance may be given at home.

SESSION 9. JESUS PRAYED TO GOD

Thinking About the Children

In seeking to guide little children in joyous experiences in praying to God, we want them to feel more and more his love for them. As we tell the story of Jesus and the children over and over again, we may help our children to realize that love more fully. While our aim for this session is the same as for the preceding one, the thought is introduced that Jesus prayed to God because of his love for him; also, that when we pray to God, we can show love for him too.

Getting Ready for the Session

Pictures and picture books used last session will have equal teaching value in this one. Be on the alert for any signs of spring in your part of the country, so that you may be prepared to help your children feel the wonder of God's world at this season. If spring is early, you may want to use the stories in the third nursery book, *The Little Seeds That Grew* (see pages 219–221), before the end of this quarter.

With the Children in Church

The happier the children's play experiences in the nursery class, the more readily you can assist them in feeling that they are glad for their church, for the friends they meet there, for their mothers and fathers who bring them, for the birds and the sky and the sunshine they see on their way, for the milkman and the baker who contribute to their breakfast, for the doctor who keeps them well, and for any other of the many friends and wonderful things in God's world they are learning to associate with his love. Thus it will be quite natural for the children to express thanks or gladness to God while at play, and you may encourage them in such expression, either in their own words or in songs they have been learning to sing.

The story of Jesus and the children may be recalled at any time during the session as children look at the picture on the wall or the pictures in *His Name Is Jesus*. It might be retold, or recalled again, after the rest time. As you talk with the children about Jesus, you might say: "Jesus loved God, and often prayed to him. We pray when we say thank you to God, or when we tell God we are glad for something that makes us happy." Such conversation may be followed by singing "Thank You" (page 231) or "At Church" (page 231).

With the Children at Home

Remind the children that they can sing the prayer song "Thank You" at home every day.

SESSION 10. WE HAVE HAPPY TIMES WITH OUR FRIENDS

Thinking About the Children

Children who have been coming to nursery class for some time have been learning to share and to take turns and to consider the rights of others, and thus they are discovering that they can have friends to play with when they themselves are friendly. These children have an important role to play in helping newcomers feel at home in church. Friendliness is contagious and the happiness of children who are learning to work and play together will make the newcomers glad to be in the nursery class. With spring days just ahead, our aim for this session will be to help the children feel that friends with whom they play are part of God's plan for their happiness, and that both in church and out-of-doors they can have happy times with friends.

Getting Ready for the Session

Read suggestions for guiding the children in attitudes of friendliness and sharing, Sessions 3 and 4, First Quarter. Use Nursery Pictures 1, 2, 4, and 10 to fasten low on the wall. *My Prayer Book* is an appropriate picture book for the special table this session. The nursery books *In Our Church* and *His Name Is Jesus* ought to have a prominent place. *The Tale of Jeremy Gray* would add interest.

Fashion books that are out of date may often be procured from stores where dress patterns are sold. Cut pictures of little children from one of these, or from a mail-order catalogue, and have pieces of heavy paper in readiness to be used as mounting cards. Be sure there are a sufficient number of pictures for each child to have two.

A "party" might provide a specially happy time this session (see pages 90, 91). Have strips of colored crepe paper on hand so that the children may decorate the table.

With the Children in Church

The activities of the nursery class in any session should offer an actual experience in having happy times with friends. In this session be sure to comment on kind and friendly ways in which children are sharing or taking turns or helping one another. You might say, "We have happy times together when we share the blocks like this"; or, "It's fun for everyone when we take turns in rolling the ball"; or, "If we all help pick up our toys, we'll have more time for our party [or for looking at picture books or for singing together]."

In talking with the children, lead them to think of little friends with whom they play outdoors, or who come to their house to play. Help them recognize that they can have good times with these friends when they share and take turns as they do in nursery class.

Draw the attention of a few children at a time to the pictures you have cut out. Suggest that each choose two little picture children whom he thinks could play happily together, and paste these on a card to take home. If there are extra pictures, they might be pasted on cards for children who are absent.

With children in the book center, look at the pictures in the book *In Our Church* and talk about what Billy did with his new friends in the nursery class. Look also at the pictures of mothers and fathers taking their children to see Jesus in *His Name Is Jesus*. Talk about how glad they were to be going. Sing "Jesus and the Children" (page 232).

In connection with any activities in which children are engaged, you might say: "God plans for us to have friends. We can have happy times with them. Would you like to say thank you to God?" Sing "Thank You" (page 231), adapting the words as follows:

> " 'Dear God, thank you today,
> For friends with whom we play.' "

Sing "Putting Our Toys Away," when it is time for the children to do so, and remark that it is fun to work together. If you have planned for a "party," this may follow the rest period. Offer a grace: "Dear God, thank you for food to eat, and for the good times we are having with our friends."

With the Children at Home

The pictures of friends that the children have pasted on mounting cards will help remind them through the week of this Sunday's experiences.

SESSION 11. JESUS HAD HAPPY TIMES WITH HIS FRIENDS

Thinking About the Children

Through their experiences in the nursery class, children are beginning to discover that when they are friendly and ready to help, other children or grown-up people like to work or play with them. The thought of Jesus with his friends is introduced to suggest that people liked to be with him. Our special aim is to help the children think of Jesus as talking happily with his friends, and helping them to know that God loved them.

Getting Ready for the Session

Perhaps you can find branches of forsythia or pussy willows, or of other trees or shrubs, to bring indoors and put in water. If so, place a few of these on the worship or special table, and leave others for the children to assist in arranging. Nursery Pictures 1, 4, and 10 may be used to suggest happy times the children have together. March days provide the fun of playing outdoors with anything that will blow in the wind. Paper bags that come from the grocery store make excellent kites. Give one of these to each child, and let him color it or draw pictures on it. Help him fold down about an inch at the open top of the bag, and fasten a string through the folded edge. As he runs with this kite, the bag will fill with air so that it will float for a moment or two by itself.

With the Children in Church

The children will be interested in looking at budding branches, and helping to arrange them in water. Encourage the children to tell of the flowers or trees they have seen waking up outdoors, and remark that God planned for his world to wake up in springtime. Call attention to the buds you have placed on the worship table, and to the picture of Jesus and the children on the wall above it. Sing softly "Jesus and the Children" (page 232); then say: "Do you remember how Jesus told the children about God's care for the birds? He told them about God's care for the flowers too, and for everything that grows." Tell the story "Jesus and the Flowers" (page 227).

This simple story may be told at any time during the session to one child or to several. Meanwhile, other children may be engaged in activities of their own choosing, and you will want to encourage them in friendly ways of playing together.

After a rest time, the children might make kites, referred to above, from paper bags. It may be possible to fly them outdoors before going home.

With the Children at Home

Suggest that the children will enjoy flying their kites at home. Perhaps their mothers or fathers will help them make another kite to give to a little friend.

SESSION 12. WE LIKE TO SING

Thinking About the Children

Children like to sing, and the songs they are learning in nursery class are good songs for them to sing together. Sometimes the words will be changed to bring them closer to the children's experience, and sometimes the children will suggest words of their own to sing to familiar tunes. Our aim in this session will be to help the children have joyous experiences in singing together, so that they may think of this as one of the happy things they do in church. (See pages 88, 89.)

Getting Ready for the Session

Perhaps it is not too soon for the children's interest in winter birds to be transferred to birds that are coming back from the south to build their nests. An open-mesh bag made from string is a good container for nesting materials. Have this in readiness, also pieces of string, bright-colored wool, nonabsorbent cotton, and other suitable materials that the children can prepare to put in it.

Budding branches, or early spring flowers, or perhaps a bowl in which bulbs are growing will help bring the joy of springtime into the nursery room. Look through your picture file for pictures related to the children's outdoor experiences at this season. If spring is early, you might use Nursery Pictures 7 and 8, also the nursery book *The Little Seeds That Grew*. One or two copies of this book may be placed on the table in the book center, and you might plan to give the children their copies to take home.

With the Children in Church

As the children are taking off their outdoor clothing, you might sing "Good Morning to You" to the familiar "Happy Birthday" tune, naming the child whom you are helping, or one whom you turn to greet. Some of the children will join in this friendly greeting, and will want to sing to each little friend as he arrives. This joy in singing may be carried over into other activities, and as children build with blocks, or play with housekeeping toys, or color with crayons, or look at pictures or picture books, you may find occasion to sing with them any of the songs they have been learning in nursery class.

If nesting materials are laid out on a low table, children will need little suggestion to unravel pieces of wool and string and to pull non-absorbent cotton into small pieces. They may put these in the open-mesh bag you have provided, drawing pieces of string and wool out through the holes so that the birds will see them. Perhaps they can take the bag outdoors to hang on a low tree, or on a shrub or fence.

Singing "Putting Our Toys Away" (page 232) might be followed by "This Is the Way We Pick Up Our Toys," to the tune of "Here We Go Round the Mulberry Bush." During rest time, sing very softly "Lullaby" (page 231). When the children "wake up," remark that singing is one of the happy things we do in church. Open the book *In Our Church*, and help them recall that the children in Billy's church sang "Church Bells" (page 231). Sing this song, then other songs the children choose, concluding this "singing time" with "At Church" (page 231).

With the Children at Home

Give each of the children a few strands of colored wool to hang on a shrub or a fence near home.

SESSION 13. WHEN CHILDREN SANG FOR JESUS

(Matthew 21:15)

Thinking About the Children

During the past three months, while our teaching plans have been based on the nursery book *His Name Is Jesus,* the children have been learning to know Jesus as he loved little children, and helped them know that God loved them. In this session, the thought of the children going to church with Jesus, and singing happy songs for him, may be related to the nursery children's own joy in singing in church. Probably they are hearing much at home about preparations for going to church on Easter, and may want to talk about these. As we share their interest, we may help them feel that Easter is a specially happy day when people like to go to church to sing together and to remember how Jesus helped little children, and grown-up people too, to know that God loved them. Our aim in this session will be the same as in the last one, with emphasis on our gladness in singing thank you to God.

Getting Ready for the Session

At this season of the year, each session should bring some new discovery of awaking life. Be on the alert for treasures of springtime to put on a nature table, and for pictures related to the children's experiences outdoors. Use Nursery Pictures 7 and 8. The nursery books *In Our Church, His Name Is Jesus,* and *The Little Seeds That Grew* should be on the table in the book center.

With the Children in Church

In this session as in the last one, allow plenty of time for the children to enjoy singing together, and watch for opportunities to sing with them as they play. As they look at the picture of Jesus and the children, or at pictures in the book *His Name Is Jesus,* introduce the thought of children singing for Jesus. You might say: "In the Bible we read of another day when children were with Jesus. They sang their happiest songs for him. They went with him to a beautiful church, and sang their songs there. They liked to be with Jesus, for he told them stories about the birds and the flowers, and he helped them know how much God loved them."

This story may be told several times as children come to the special table or to the book center. Draw their attention to the nature table, and talk about God's care for birds and flowers in springtime. Help them feel that this is part of God's plan for their care, and suggest that they sing "At Church" (page 231). Before they go home, they might repeat this song, substituting the words, "In our home."

With the Children at Home

Give each child a copy of *The Little Seeds That Grew*, if you have not already done so. You may wish to send home a note to mothers and fathers explaining the meaning of Easter for the little child (see page 86).

THIRD QUARTER

Book: *The Little Seeds That Grew*

SPRING is in the air, and with the whole world waking to new life and beauty, even a little child may be led to feel the wonder of God's love. As the story of God's continuing care is told in every opening bud, each new discovery in field or garden may be interpreted as part of his plan for our welfare. For children who live in the country or in a favored section of the city, experiences with growing things will be rich and varied, and there may be many opportunities for helping to care for birds or for baby animals. But even where city pavements leave little room for grass or flowers, there may be trees with budding branches, the warmth of spring sunshine, the twitter of sparrows, the patter of raindrops, and the wonder of watching the moon or the stars in the sky at night.

For this quarter, April to June, our teaching plans are based on the nursery book *The Little Seeds That Grew*, and the activities of the nursery class are closely related to the children's experiences in the outdoor world. (See pages 85, 86.) The teaching of previous sessions in the nursery class is recalled as opportunities for further guidance are offered. In the light of your growing experience and understanding, read again the teaching plans for Sessions 1-3, First Quarter, also the first two sections, "When Nursery Children Are Three" and "In the Nursery Class." Probably the children already have their copies of *The Little Seeds That Grew;* otherwise these may be given to them in the first session. The stories from the book may be found on pages 219–221 of this handbook.

Be sure to seek the co-operation of the home as suggested in connection with each session, and encourage parents to read the child's book and these teaching plans so that they may understand how their children's experiences are being guided in the nursery class.

SESSION 1. GOD'S PLAN FOR SEEDS TO GROW

Thinking About the Children

Children's experiences with things that grow will vary greatly according to the community and the part of the country in which they live. But, however rich or meager these experiences may be, through our own consciousness of the greatness and the love of God, we may help our children feel the wonder of his world and of his care for us. In this session, our special aim will be to help the children feel the wonder of God's plan for seeds to grow.

Getting Ready for the Session

Look for budding branches or spring flowers to take to nursery class. Perhaps you can plan for the children to experience the joy of planting seeds as Jerry did in *The Little Seeds That Grew.* Flower seeds planted in paper drinking cups could be taken home. Bulbs of the paper-white narcissus will sprout quickly if planted in a bowl of small pebbles, and require no preliminary rooting in the dark. Fasten Nursery Pictures 7, 8, and 9 low on the wall, and leave them there throughout this quarter. Use the picture of Jesus and the children on the wall above the special table, with something from outdoors, and a book such as *My Bible Book* on the table. This would be a good time to add toy gardening tools to the nursery class equipment, if these are not already included. The books *From Crocus to Snowman, A Year on the Farm,* and *The Little Farm* might be placed on the book table. (See page 94.)

With the Children in Church

Watch for opportunities to relate the children's play to outdoor experiences. Toy garden tools suggest that the children play raking leaves from the garden or lawn, preparing the soil, and planting seeds.

Blocks might be used to build a fence around a field where a farmer is plowing. Nested blocks and large wooden beads and toy cars or trucks may all be used in garden or farm play. Children in the doll corner may be busily engaged in spring cleaning, and you might suggest that they take time to go out for a walk with their babies in the sunshine. Children looking at pictures or picture books will be glad to have you share their interest in these.

With any of the above activities, you could find occasion to say: "God planned for seeds to grow in springtime. He planned for flowers to grow to make the world beautiful. He planned for beans and peas and corn to grow so that we may have food to eat. He planned for the sunshine and raindrops to help." Sing about the raindrops falling down (page 232), as the children make them patter with their fingers.

Share with any child his pleasure in a new coat or shoes, and say: "We like to wear clothes that are fresh and clean when God's world is fresh and new in springtime. Your mother and father must have thought of that." As there are children who will not have *new* clothes, speak too about the pretty color of a hair ribbon or the soft material of a suit that is *not* new.

Sit quietly with the children after they have relaxed and look at the pictures in *The Little Seeds That Grew*. Tell the first story page by page. Then say: "Jerry's seeds that grew were a wonder of God, weren't they? We can plant some little seeds to grow too."

Flower seeds planted in paper drinking cups could be taken home as an Easter gift for Mother. Tell the children to care for them as Jerry did. Perhaps Mother would like to watch with them for the surprise. Narcissus bulbs could be left to grow in the nursery room.

With the Children at Home

A new picture book for his very own is a delight to each little child, and offers his parents a share in his nursery class experiences. Their share will be greater if he takes home seeds he has planted. Explain to them that the paper cup could be set in a flowerpot or window box, or in a garden when the seeds have started to grow. Suggest to parents that at appropriate moments they say with their child, "Dear God, thank you for seeds and flowers that grow."

SESSION 2. HELPING SEEDS GROW

Thinking About the Children

Last session the children were guided in feeling the wonder of God's plan for seeds to grow, and during the week they have probably observed tiny green shoots pushing up above the ground. Perhaps they have been watering little seeds they planted in a paper cup, and are watching eagerly for them to sprout. Our aim in this session will be to lead the children from a feeling of wonder to a joyous recognition that they can share in God's plan for seeds to grow.

Getting Ready for the Session

Growing things have an important place in the nursery class at this season, and from week to week the nature table should reflect the children's experiences outdoors. Use Nursery Pictures 7 and 8 to suggest ways of helping seeds to grow indoors and out. A small watering can such as Jerry used would be of special interest in either actual or play experiences in caring for seeds. Perhaps you could plan to go for a short walk to see where someone has been helping seeds to grow.

With the Children in Church

Guidance in this session will be similar to that in the last one, relating the children's play to experiences with things that grow. As children look at the nature table, lead them to observe how tiny leaves are unfolding from buds, and how bright are the colors of spring flowers. Perhaps there are narcissus bulbs that are sprouting, and need more water and sunshine. "God has planned for us to help seeds grow," you might say. "That is why we must remember to water them, and to put them near a sunny window." Help the children recall that this is what Jerry did in *The Little Seeds That Grew*. Look at the pictures in this book, and tell the first story. This may be repeated several times as other children come to listen. After rest time, you might go for a short walk, or develop a little finger play of making a garden. The children will imitate you as you dig, rake, and plant seeds; then move your fingers to suggest flickering sunbeams or pattering raindrops. Hold your hands palms together, then separate the fingers slowly to make an opening flower.

With the Children at Home

Speak with parents about the importance of planning further experiences for their children in helping seeds to grow.

SESSION 3. BIRDS AND THEIR NESTS

Thinking About the Children

At every season of the year there is joy for little children in watching or listening to birds, and in caring for them. Our aim in this session will be to lead the children into feeling the wonder of God's plan for birds to come back from the south to build their nests, and the happiness of watching and helping.

Getting Ready for the Session

Read Sessions 4, 5, and 12, Second Quarter, to recall your guidance of the children's previous experiences with birds. Plan to repeat the activity of preparing nesting materials. If you have a birds' nest, put it on the nature table with a copy of *The Little Golden Book of Birds*.

With the Children in Church

The children may play that they are birds flying back from the south and looking for a place to build their nests. This may suggest preparing nesting materials as in Session 12, Second Quarter. Draw attention to the nest on the nature table, and wonder with the children at the care with which it is made; then say: "The little birds that made this nest didn't need it any more. They flew away to the south for the winter. Now they are back and are making a new nest. God planned for them to make a cozy home like this."

The children's interest in birds may be related to other happy experiences of springtime. If they didn't go for a walk last session, they might do so today, and look for birds or a birds' nest; or they might develop the finger play of making a garden, perhaps planting string beans as Jerry did in *The Little Seeds That Grew*. Sing about the raindrops pattering down (page 232).

The children might express their wonder and happiness in the evidences of springtime all around them, as you sing with them "At Church" (page 231).

With the Children at Home

The children may take home pieces of colored wool for birds to use in building their nests. Suggest that Mother might give them other materials for this purpose.

SESSION 4. THE RAIN IS FALLING

Thinking About the Children

For children who have raincoats and hats and rubber boots, rainy days bring the fun of playing in the rain, walking on shiny sidewalks, and splashing through puddles. But for children who have to stay indoors, any tendency to resent the rain may be turned to appreciation as they are led to recognize how the rain helps seeds grow, gives the birds a drink, and makes all outdoors fresh and clean. Our special aim in this session will be to help the children think happily of the rain as part of God's plan for our care.

Getting Ready for the Session

Fasten a large sheet of poster or wrapping paper on the wall. Make strokes on it with a crayon to suggest the falling rain, or paste narrow strips of tin foil such as used on Christmas trees to secure this effect. Look through magazines or seed catalogues for pictures of fruits and vegetables and flowers, or use a simple outline pattern to cut these from colored paper. Little umbrellas might also be cut out in various colors. Plan to tell the story "The Rain Is Falling" (page 227).

With the Children in Church

Help the children feel responsibility to assist in watering growing things that have been brought indoors. As they proceed with play activities, these will offer many opportunities for recalling and reproducing outdoor experiences so that your teaching of the past few weeks will carry over into this session. You will find occasions to refer to the rain as helping flowers and vegetables and trees to grow, and to associate this with God's plan for our care. As children observe the falling rain on the wall poster, draw attention to the pictures you have in readiness to paste on it, and say: "Here are some things that need the rain to help them grow, and here are umbrellas for people who go out in the rain. You can make a big picture with these." Sing "Rain" (page 232).

Children may take turns in pasting pictures on this poster. When they have had a turn, suggest that they come to the book corner and look at the picture of Jerry with his umbrella and rubbers, and of the rain falling on the seeds in his garden. (*The Little Seeds That Grew.*) You might tell this story.

After rest time, tell the story "The Rain Is Falling." Then the children might play that they are putting on raincoats and hats and rubber boots and going out for a walk in the rain. Let them suggest outdoor things they are observing. Their play might end as they come indoors and sit down to sing together. Sing with them "Rain" and "At Church" (page 231), which might suggest that they pray softly, "Dear God, thank you for the rain."

With the Children at Home

Talk with parents about the happiness of watching and listening to falling rain with their children, and the opportunities this offers for feeling the greatness and the love of God.

SESSION 5. THE SUN IS SHINING

Thinking About the Children

Last week our guidance was directed toward helping the children to feel God's care in his plan for rain to fall. In this session our aim will be to help them feel God's care in his plan for the sun to shine.

Getting Ready for the Session

Prepare a poster similar to the one suggested for last session, but with lines to suggest the rays of the sun instead of falling rain. Have the same kinds of fruits and vegetables and flowers for the children to paste on this poster, but substitute for the little umbrellas pictures of children cut from fashion books or mail-order catalogues. Plan to recall the story of Jesus and the children in *His Name Is Jesus.*

With the Children in Church

This session will proceed much the same as the last one, with guidance seeking to relate the children's play activities to outdoor experiences. As children look at the poster they made last session, and question about the new one, you might say: "All these flowers and fruits and vegetables need the sunshine too. So do little children. God planned it that way. You can make a big picture to tell about it."

Share the children's interest in the poster as they take turns in working on it. When all have had a turn, draw attention to the picture of Jesus and the children, noticing that the sun was shining when the children went to see Jesus. Look at the pictures of this story in *His Name Is Jesus,* and help them recall it. Note that the children gathered flowers to take to Jesus. Sing "Jesus and the Children" (page 232).

When the toys have been put away and the children have relaxed, they might develop the finger play of making a garden, as described in Session 2 of this quarter. When the flowers have bloomed, you might say softly, "Dear God, thank you for the rain and the sunshine that helped the flowers grow."

With the Children at Home

Suggest to the children that they say thank you to God when they are playing outdoors on sunny days.

SESSION 6. FLOWERS ARE BLOOMING

Thinking About the Children

Rain, sunshine, and flowers all enter into our thinking at this season, as we seek to guide little children toward God. During the past two weeks our emphasis has been on God's plan for rain and sunshine in helping seeds of all kinds to grow. In this session our aim will be to lead the children into feeling God's love in his provision for flowers to bloom, thus making this world a beautiful place in which to live.

Getting Ready for the Session

Leave the rain and sunshine posters on the wall, also the picture of Jesus and the children. Plan to recall this story as you did last session, and tell how Jesus talked about the flowers, as suggested in Session 11, Second Quarter. For the special table, have a few spring flowers from the woods or garden, or a bowl in which bulbs are blooming.

Either this Sunday or next is Mother's Day. If it should be this Sunday, adapt suggestions in Session 7 to your plans for this session.

With the Children in Church

Play activities may include building a fence around a garden with blocks, and using large wooden beads for flowers blooming there; making "pictures" of flowers; making flowers in a garden with modeling clay; digging and hoeing and raking and planting with toy gardening tools. As you share the children's interest in such play, or look with them at pictures or picture books, or a garden that can be seen from the nursery room window, you may say, "Aren't you glad God planned for flowers to grow!" You might sing "Flowers, Bright and Gay" (page 232):

> " 'Flowers, bright and gay,
> This is a lovely springtime day.' "

This song may be repeated with different groups of children. It might be sung softly as children look at the picture of Jesus and the children, and at the flowers on the special table. Tell the story "Jesus and the Flowers" (page 227). This story may be told also in the book center, as children look at pictures in *His Name Is Jesus* or in *The Little Seeds That Grew*. You might add, "We know that God loves us because he planned such a beautiful world for us to live in." Sing "At Church" (page 231).

If there are flowers blooming in the church garden or in a garden nearby, you might go to see them after rest time.

With the Children at Home

Remind the children to care for seeds or bulbs that are growing in sunny windows or in gardens at home.

SESSION 7. A SURPRISE FOR MOTHER

Thinking About the Children

Spring is a time for surprises, and the children's interest in the surprise that Jerry planned for his mother in *The Little Seeds That Grew* may suggest that they plan something special for their mothers too. Although Mother's Day can have little significance for a nursery child, he may hear his father or older brothers or sisters talking about it, and it may be to him, "My mother's day," as one little girl announced in nursery class. With this interpretation in mind, our aim for this session will be to help each child have a happy time in planning a surprise for Mother or *someone else who cares for him*. The book *Ask Mr. Bear* tells about a special kind of present for a mother. It might be added to your book collection.

Mother's Day is being increasingly emphasized as a family festival, so you may wish to refer to the sessions on the family in the fourth quarter.

Getting Ready for the Session

In addition to pictures referred to in preceding sessions of this quarter, use Nursery Pictures 10 and 11 to suggest happy times at home. Read carefully the teaching plans for Session 10, First Quarter, and plan similar guidance for this session. Cut circular table mats from colored mounting paper or blotting paper, using pinking shears if available, and provide seals or pictures with which the children may decorate these.

With the Children in Church

Follow in general the suggestions for guiding the children's play activities, Session 10, First Quarter. Use the same songs and finger plays, and lead the children to think of ways in which they can help Mother every day, and contribute to the happy times they have at home.

After rest time, talk with the children about the surprise Jerry planned for his mother. Ask them to tell how seeds they planted for their mothers are growing. It is important to place the little round table mat you have decorated under a bowl or vase of flowers to show how it can be used, and suggest that each of the children can paste pictures on one of the little round mats as a surprise for his mother or someone else who loves and cares for him. Help him anticipate her pleasure in receiving it. After the mats are decorated, sing "The Family" (page 234), then say, "Let us tell God that we are glad for Mother, and say thank you to him."

With the Children at Home

In talking with mothers, speak of the "surprise" the children have been making. Suggest that to please the children the mats be used under vases or bowls at home.

SESSION 8. GOD'S SHINING STARS

Thinking About the Children

Even a little child may begin to feel that "the heavens declare the glory of God," and these words should be in our hearts as we share our children's wonder at the moon and the stars, and help them feel God's love and care through the night. This may be our special aim for today's session, but it should be our aim in any session when the children tell of experiences in watching the moon or the stars.

Getting Ready for the Session

Take time to look and wonder at the sky at night. In addition to pictures related to the stories in *The Little Seeds That Grew,* use Nursery Picture 11. If you have a copy of *My Prayer Book,* place this book on the worship table, leaving it open at the picture of a starry night. Fasten a large sheet of black paper on the wall, and cut stars from yellow paper for the children to paste on it.

With the Children in Church

As the children engage in activities of their own choosing, watch for opportunities for guidance in friendly ways of helping and sharing. Happy experiences in church and at home and outdoors should be associated with God's love and care. Watch also for opportunities to relate their play to nighttime experiences. Children playing with dolls might sing "Lullaby" (page 231) as they put doll babies to bed. Remind workmen building with blocks that they can have a quiet rest at night when their work is done. Some children will want to paste stars on the black wall poster. Talk with them about watching the stars at night. You might sing the first stanza of the familiar nursery song "Twinkle, Twinkle, Little Star." With children in the book center, suggest that Jerry and his daddy were glad of the nighttime to rest. With children at the worship table, say softly: "God planned for the moon and stars to shine at night through the darkness. They help us remember that he loves us."

When the toys have been put away, and the children are ready for a rest, suggest that they hold their hands high above their heads, and make their fingers twinkle like the stars. Say softly: "God planned for the stars to shine while we sleep. That is part of his care for us." Sing "Lullaby" while the children are resting.

After a rest, there might be time to tell the story "Ready for Bed" (page 224). Then look with the children at the picture of a family at bedtime and sing "At Church" (page 231), changing the words to say, "In our home." The prayer "Thank You" (page 231) might follow naturally.

With the Children at Home

Watching and wondering at God's shining stars is a home experience in which parents and children can share.

SESSION 9. THE WIND THAT BLOWS

Thinking About the Children

It is fun for little children to play in the wind, and they are always ready to test its strength with things that will float or turn. In this session we will plan for such experiences, and at the same time we will seek to help the children feel the wonder of the wind as part of God's plan for seeds to grow.

Getting Ready for the Session

Have materials in readiness for play in the wind—long strips of colored paper, squares of white paper, a balloon, a pin wheel, and plenty of string. Collect seeds that are scattered by the wind for the nature center or for the worship table.

With the Children in Church

Share the children's interest in their play and, while keeping in mind your aims in preceding sessions, watch for opportunities to relate activities to experiences with the wind. You might provide a small flag to float on top of a tall building in the block center, and a clothesline on which clothes may dry in the wind in the doll corner. In the book center talk with children about the pictures in *The Little Seeds That Grew,* and remark that the wind must have helped blow the rain clouds so that the rain would fall on Jerry's garden.

Pick up a square of white paper in the art center, and fold it diagonally. Place it on the floor or on a table where a breeze from the window will make it sail like a boat. Children will quickly imitate you. Meanwhile, other children may be experimenting in holding long strips of paper near the window to see them wave. Suggest that they tie several strips of paper together and leave a long string so that these will sail like a kite. Other children will be attracted by this play. They might help you fasten up a balloon and a pin wheel near the window; then you could help them make a sailboat or a kite. If practicable, the children could take these playthings outdoors for a few moments, and then come in for a rest. If so, fasten a string to the sailboats so that they won't float away.

After rest time, talk with the children about the fun they had with the wind. Draw their attention to the seeds and let them observe how these can float in the wind. Remark that this is one way in which God planned for seeds to be planted. Talk about the seeds that Jerry planted, and about the wind blowing the rain clouds to water them. Say that this is another part of God's plan. You may pray softly, "Dear God, thank you for the wind." Or the children might sing "At Church" (page 231) and then the prayer song "Thank You" (page 231).

With the Children at Home

The children may take home the sailboats and kites they made. Remind them that they can make kites with paper bags as they did one other Sunday.

SESSION 10. WE HELP CARE FOR THINGS THAT GROW

Thinking About the Children

Throughout this quarter our guidance has been concerned with helping the children to feel God's plan for their welfare and happiness, as revealed in his world in spring. While we are still giving such guidance, our aim in this session will be to help the children feel that they have a part in caring for things that grow so that these may be used as God has planned.

Getting Ready for the Session

Read again the teaching plans for Sessions 1 and 2 of this quarter, and recall how they were carried out. Plan to repeat activities related to experiences in helping seeds to grow. Put flowers from your garden or from the field or woods in a large container of water, in readiness for the children to arrange in vases or bowls. Any vegetables or fruits that ripen at this season should be in evidence on the nature table or elsewhere. Use pictures suggested for preceding sessions of this quarter.

With the Children in Church

Children who come early may help in arranging flowers in vases and bowls, and in placing these around the room. Lead them to observe that you put the flowers in water as soon as you brought them indoors, and that you handle them very gently. Perhaps there are growing plants in the room. As the children water these, you may say: "We must always remember to water plants that grow indoors, for there is no rain to water them. And we must put them near the window so the sun will shine on them."

As the children engage in play activities, you will find occasion to suggest ways in which they can help care for things that grow. These may include watering the grass, weeding the garden, picking flowers from plants to keep them blooming, putting cut flowers immediately in water, sharing them with someone who hasn't a garden, picking small fruits or vegetables when these are ripe, eating them without waste, sharing them with others, being careful not to walk where new grass is growing, and being careful not to break flowers or shrubs in their play.

When toys have been put away, and the children have had a rest, look with them at the pictures in *The Little Seeds That Grew* and help them recall that, after Jerry had cared for the seeds while they were growing, the flowers were given as a surprise to his mother, and the string beans were used for food. The children might reproduce in a finger play (see page 174) either of these stories. Help them feel the wonder of God's plan for seeds to grow, and their part in helping. They might pray with you, "Dear God, we are glad that you planned for things to grow, and that we can help care for them."

With the Children at Home

Remind parents to provide opportunities for their children to assist in caring for things that grow, even though it is only a matter of planting a few seeds in a small box of earth.

SESSION 11. GOOD THINGS TO EAT

Thinking About the Children

Through the story of the string beans that grew in Jerry's garden, in *The Little Seeds That Grew,* the children are being led to feel God's love in his plan for good things to grow for us to eat. Our aim in this session is to deepen their appreciation of the friends who help.

Getting Ready for the Session

Read the teaching plans for Sessions 6 and 7, Second Quarter, in order to recall your guidance of the children's experiences with friends who help us. Plan to use materials and activities suggested in relation to experiences with friends who contribute their part in supplying good things to eat. Read also the teaching plans for Session 8, Fourth Quarter. Look through your picture file for a picture of a farmer or a grocer or a milkman, or of food they help provide. Use Nursery Pictures 1 and 9 to suggest thanking God for food. Plan to tell the story "Going to the Store" (page 228). Have samples of fruits and vegetables that ripen at this season, and arrange a few of these attractively on the worship or special table. A "party" would be a specially happy experience with good things to eat (see pages 90, 91). Fruits and vegetables you have cut from colored paper could be used by the children to decorate paper place mats. If you have the books *The Little Family* and *Time for Bed,* make them available for this session.

With the Children in Church

Relate any gardening or housekeeping play experiences with good things to eat, and talk with the children about the farmer's care for fruits and vegetables, the grocer's care in keeping these fresh, and their mother's part in cooking them for the family to eat. The children might build a field for the farmer, or a store for the grocer, or play that they are keeping house and getting supper ready. As you take a role in their play, you may say, "The farmer [or the grocer, or your mother] helps in God's plan for us to have food to eat." As children look at the pictures in *The Little Seeds That Grew,* they may observe that Jerry and his daddy are helping too. Suggest that fathers also help by working to earn money to buy good things to eat.

After quiet time you might tell the story "Going to the Store" (page 228). Look with the children at the picture of a family saying grace. Sing "Thank You" (page 231). If you have planned for a "party," some of the children may help decorate the napkins while others help get the food ready. Use "Thank You" as a grace.

With the Children at Home

Remind children and parents that "Thank You" is printed on the end paper of *The Little Seeds That Grew*, and may be used as a grace at home.

SESSION 12. "HAPPY PLAY IN GRASSY PLACES"

Thinking About the Children

In all the activities of the nursery class, the children are learning to play in friendly ways, and to find their happiness in that of others. In this session our special aim will be to help them feel the joy of playing in God's beautiful world as part of God's plan for their care.

Getting Ready for the Session

If possible, plan for this to be an outdoor session, perhaps in the church grounds, or in a nearby park, or in a neighbor's garden. Choose suitable toys and other materials for outdoor activities, and have small baskets or cartons in readiness so that the children can help in carrying these. Several parent assistants will be glad to accompany the group. Blankets or motor rugs may be advisable for sitting on the grass or on church steps. Read the teaching plans for Sessions 3 and 4, First Quarter, also Session 10, Second Quarter, for suggestions for guiding the children in playing together.

With the Children in Church

Where the whole session can be held outdoors, the children may help in carrying out materials and arranging these ready for use. Some of the children will proceed with usual play activities, while others will probably wander around investigating a new environment. If an outdoor session is not practicable, the children might take turns in going out with a teacher for a few minutes, just to look around, and feel the wind and the sunshine, and observe the grass, or flowers, or trees, or birds, or sky, or other lovely things in God's world. Indoors or out, the same guidance may be given in fostering friendly attitudes, and in helping the children to feel God's love.

Introduce rhythmic play, suggested by outdoor play on swings or seesaws, or in bouncing a ball. The children will quickly imitate you as you hum gaily and sway back and forth with one foot forward, and hands outstretched as if holding the ropes of a swing. They will imitate you also as you stretch both arms sideways, and bend from the waist, first to one side, then to the other, as you sing "Seesaw" (page 232). This tune may be hummed as you pretend to bounce a ball or throw it up in the air and catch it.

The children may sit or lie on a rug for a rest, then may have a time for singing, choosing songs they have learned in nursery class. Conclude with singing "Thank You" (page 231), changing the second line to "For friends with whom we play."

With the Children at Home

Speak with parents about the importance of happy outdoor play, and the opportunities it offers for helping their children to feel God's love and care.

SESSION 13. THANKING GOD FOR HIS WONDERFUL WORLD

Thinking About the Children

In this session, we will help the children recall experiences of spring-time through which they have been led to feel God's love and care. Our aim will be to guide them in spontaneous expressions of thanks to God as they think of the wonders of his world as part of his plan for our welfare and happiness.

Getting Ready for the Session

Read Sessions 8 and 9, First Quarter, to recall previous experiences through which the children were guided in expressions of thanks to God. Read also Session 13, Fourth Quarter, for suggestions that might be adapted in this session. Use pictures and picture books and nature materials that help children feel the wonder of God's world at this season, and suggest how they can assist in God's plan for our care. Plan to tell the story "Jesus and the Flowers" (page 227).

With the Children in Church

If an outdoor session proved a satisfying experience last week, this might be repeated. Use the same toys and other materials, with similar guidance, allowing plenty of time for the children to feel the wonder and beauty all around them. They might sing "Flowers, Bright and Gay" (page 232):

> "'Flowers, bright and gay,
> This is a lovely summer day.'"

Repeat rhythmic plays that were introduced. Looking at pictures and picture books, talking about these, telling stories, and singing songs are pleasant things to do outdoors. The children may ask you to tell again any of the stories in *The Little Seeds That Grew* or *His Name Is Jesus* or *In Our Church*, and to sing some of the songs they have been learning in nursery class. Thus they may be led to feel the wonder of God's world and his plan for our care, and to express thanks to him. Reserve the story of "Jesus and the Flowers" until after rest time and tell it in such a way that saying, "Thank you," or "I'm glad," to God may be a natural response.

If the session is held indoors, the same plan may be followed.

With the Children at Home

If children are going away for summer vacation, or if your church school program is changed for the summer months, copies of the nursery book *I'm Growing* might be given at this session.

FOURTH QUARTER
Book: *I'm Growing* 7

THE NURSERY CHILD takes a natural delight in growing as registered in terms of height and weight on the doctor's chart, and he has a sense of achievement with each discovery that he is tall enough or strong enough to do some new thing by himself. But he must be led to feel that growing is something more than merely increasing in stature, and involves acceptance of responsibility for helping to care for himself and doing things for others. As we guide him into thinking of God as planning for his welfare and happiness, we must help him recognize that God's plan includes his growing ability to care for himself, and to live in friendly ways.

If the program for your church school includes promotion in autumn, plan in plenty of time to help children who are going into the kindergarten anticipate this. Suggestions for promotion will be found on page 74. If possible, plan for promotion at any time through the year as individual children are ready for it.

For the next three months, July, August, September, our teaching plans are based on the nursery book *I'm Growing*. The activities of the nursery class are related to experiences at home and outdoors through which the children may be led to feel God's plan for growing, and to find increasing satisfaction in doing their part. The teaching of the nursery class should be closely linked with that of the home, where it may find expression in willing co-operation in daily routines of eating and sleeping and outdoor play that are conducive to health and growth. Review the first two sections in this handbook, noting especially references to facts of development and individual differences, in the chapter "They Grow as *Persons*."

The teaching plans for Sessions 1-3, First Quarter, give detailed suggestions for procedure in the nursery class. Read these again, carefully. The stories from *I'm Growing* may be found on pages 221-223. The children should be given their copies of the nursery book in the first session of this quarter.

SESSION 1. OUR FAMILY

Thinking About the Children

Little children need the feeling of security that comes through recognizing their family as a social group to which they belong. This is specially important at this season when family routines are often interrupted by having visitors, or going visiting, or living away from home. Our aim in this session will be to deepen this feeling of confidence through guiding the children into thinking of God's plan for people to live in families and to love and help one another.

Getting Ready for the Session

Read the teaching plans for Sessions 8 and 10, First Quarter, and Sessions 1 and 2, Second Quarter, in order to recall previous guidance in helping children to appreciate the love and care that surround them in their home, and to associate this with God's plan for their welfare and happiness. Use Nursery Pictures 4, 6, 9, and 11.

Take several large sheets of paper and cut the tops to suggest the pointed roof of a house. Fasten these "houses" low on the wall to form a "street." Cut pictures of men and women and children from magazines or fashion books or mail-order catalogues, and have these "families" in readiness for the children to paste. Pictures of dogs or cats or other family pets would add to the children's interest.

Prepare to tell the first story in the nursery book *I'm Growing. In Our Church, His Name Is Jesus,* and *The Little Seeds That Grew* should be in the book center; *The Little Family* would add interest.

Wherever practicable, plan for the summer sessions, or part of them, to be held outdoors.

With the Children in Church

Children's play activities are sure to suggest home experiences, and will provide opportunities for talking about the members of their family, and things they do for one another. As you share their interest, you will find many occasions for saying quite naturally, "Aren't you glad

God planned for you to live in a family where you have such happy times together?"; or, "Betty's family have happy times too"; or: "John's family are going away on the train. John will have lots of things to tell us when he comes back"; or: "There is a new baby brother in Donna's family. I saw Donna helping her mother put him to sleep."

Some of the children are sure to be interested in the row of paper houses you have fastened on the wall. Suggest that a family lives in each of these houses, and draw attention to the pictures you have cut out. The children may choose a father and mother and children, and perhaps a grandmother, to paste in each house. They might also include a family pet. Encourage taking turns in this activity as other children join you. As you share their interest in each family, say the words of "This Is a Home" (page 235), or sing "The Family" (page 234). You might say: "God plans for people to live in families, and to love and help one another. I wonder how the children in this family help!"

Meanwhile other children may be looking at the pictures or picture books suggested for this session. Lead them to observe the family group in the Nativity picture, also the mothers and fathers taking their children to see Jesus. Note the family saying grace, and talking to God at bedtime. Sing "Shepherds Leave the Hillside" (page 233), or "Lull-aby" (page 231), or "Jesus and the Children" (page 232), or "Thank You" (page 231).

After rest time look with the children at the pictures illustrating the story of Timothy's grandmother coming to visit, in *I'm Growing*, and tell this story. You might suggest that the children say, "Thank you, God," as Timothy did.

With the Children at Home

If the children were not given their copies of *I'm Growing* last session, these should be taken home today. Draw the attention of parents to the message that is printed in it for them.

SESSION 2. WHEN FRIENDS COME TO VISIT

Thinking About the Children

Even nursery children can begin to share in family plans for friends who come to visit. In this session our aim will be to help the children feel that entertaining guests is one of the happy things a family can do together and that each member can find satisfaction in taking a part.

Getting Ready for the Session

Nursery Pictures 4 and 6 may help recall friends who came to visit Jesus when he was a baby, and children who came to see Jesus when he had grown to be a man. Use Nursery Pictures 9 and 10 to suggest family experiences in which guests can share. Make sure that housekeeping and gardening toys are ready for use. Flowers will help make the nursery room attractive, and may be used by the children in pretending to get ready for guests in the doll corner.

With the Children in Church

Play with blocks will probably lead to building a house and planning for friends to come to visit. The house might have a garden, with outdoor furniture, where supper could be served. Play with dolls also might lead to planning for guests, as the children sweep, or dust, or make the beds, or cook, or set the table, or dress the dolls in their best clothes. Arranging flowers in the guest room or on the table is an appropriate part of such play. As you share in it, lead the children to think of ways in which they can help make guests happy, and remind them that helping in these ways is part of growing.

In play with other toys or equipment encourage the children in friendly attitudes, and mention that such attitudes in their homes make friends like to come to visit. You might open the Bible and say that you can read there, "Be kind," or, "Love one another." As children look at pictures or picture books, these might suggest the finger play "This Is a Home" (page 235), or that you sing "Shepherds Leave the Hillside" (page 233), or "Jesus and the Children" (page 232), or "Lullaby" (page 231), or "The Family" (page 234), or "Thank You" (page 231). "Seesaw" (page 232) might be sung and played as a happy game to play with little friends who come to visit.

After quiet time tell the story of Timothy's grandmother coming to visit, in *I'm Growing*. Part of this story could be reproduced in play as the children pretend they are making a bed, and sweeping up the grass, and getting dressed, and driving to the station to meet Grandmother.

With the Children at Home

Suggest to parents that they encourage their children in helping to prepare for guests and to make their visit happy.

SESSION 3. GOING VISITING

Thinking About the Children

Going visiting may involve a long journey, with experiences in living away from home, or may be merely going to the house next door. Wherever they go, children may discover that they are welcome visitors when they show friendliness in sharing and taking turns, are careful with things that do not belong to them, co-operate in routines of the family they are visiting, and are ready to assist where they are able. Our aim in this session will be to help the children begin to recognize that they can grow in these ways, and to associate such growing with happy experiences in going visiting.

Getting Ready for the Session

Nursery Pictures 4, 8, 9, and 10 may be related to experiences in going visiting. Fasten the picture of Jesus and the children on the wall above the worship table. Make sure that there are small travel toys, such as cars or trains or boats or airplanes, in the block center. If you do not have these toys, cut pictures of these from magazines and mount them on heavy cardboard for travel play. Add a small suitcase, or a box fitted with a handle, to the equipment in the doll corner.

With the Children in Church

With travel toys near the blocks, play about going somewhere is sure to develop; you may suggest going visiting. Perhaps you can be the person visited, and by your comments you may help the children think of friendly and considerate and helpful things they can do for you. To children who have discovered the suitcase in the doll corner, you might say: "Perhaps you could take your family to visit their grandmother. What clothes will you pack in your suitcase? What will you take for a present?" As this play develops, you might be the grandmother, and express pleasure in the friendly, helpful ways in which your grandchildren are growing.

As children look at pictures or picture books, they may observe that children took flowers to Jesus when they went to see him, and that Grandmother took presents to Timothy and Susan. Help them think of someone for whom they could gather flowers or plan a present. You might suggest that they sing one of the songs they are learning in nursery class when they go to visit Grandmother. Let them choose and sing songs they think she would like to hear. You might say, "Grandmother will be glad you are growing big enough to remember this song to sing for her." Remind the children that people do not always bring a present when they come to see us. We are glad that *they* have come to talk and play with us.

Sing "Putting Our Toys Away" (page 232). Remark on the care with which the children have been learning to put their toys away in nursery class, and that they can show similar care in putting things away when they go visiting. Suggest that remembering to do this is one way of growing. As the children rest, say that learning to be quiet while other people are resting is also a way of growing.

Look at the pictures and recall with the children the story of Grandmother's visit in *I'm Growing*. They might like to reproduce part of this story in play, as suggested for last session.

With the Children at Home

Talk over with parents the idea that the simplest experiences in going visiting offer opportunities for religious growth as children are led to show friendliness and helpfulness and consideration for others.

SESSION 4. HELPING ONE ANOTHER

Thinking About the Children

During the past few weeks the children have been learning to help in their own homes and when they go visiting as one way in which they are growing. In this session we will lead them to feel satisfaction in their increasing ability to do things that are helpful, and to associate this with God's plan for their care.

Getting Ready for the Session

Use pictures and picture books and play materials as suggested for preceding sessions of this quarter, and plan to repeat activities that seemed to have special interest and value. Read the teaching plans for Session 5, First Quarter, for suggestions in guiding the children in learning to be helpful.

With the Children in Church

This session should provide many opportunities for the children to help one another in church, and reproduce in their play experiences assisting at home. Be sure to show appreciation of their helpfulness, and remark on things they have learned to do since first coming to nursery class. Their achievements may include filling a vase with water without spilling too much, fastening pictures on a wall or screen, and remembering where things belong. Readiness to share and take turns and play in friendly ways is also evidence that children are learning to help. Remark that God has planned for us to grow and to help one another.

Activities related to entertaining guests and going visiting may be repeated. As you comment on the children's growing ability to do things that help, remark that remembering to do these is also part of growing. You might recall, with the children, the Bible verses "Be kind" and "Love one another." Suggest that remembering to help is one way of being kind and showing people that we love them, and that it is part of God's plan for us to grow.

Sing "Putting Our Toys Away" (page 232), and allow time for this activity to be a happy experience in helping one another. After the children have relaxed, tell the story of Jerry and his father planting string bean seeds in *The Little Seeds That Grew*, or the story of Grandmother's visit in *I'm Growing*. You might suggest that the children say thank you to God because they are growing more and more able to help.

With the Children at Home

In talking with parents, enlist their co-operation in the teaching of the session by asking them to provide satisfying opportunities for their children to assist at home. If they have a copy of this book, WHEN THEY ARE THREE, suggest that they read especially about the needs of nursery children (pages 43-46). Sharing in small tasks at home with Mother or Daddy will help children feel needed and important as *persons*.

SESSION 5. CARING FOR PETS

Thinking About the Children

Little children have much to learn before they can be entrusted with the care of pets, and careful guidance is necessary in teaching them to be gentle and thoughtful and considerate of their needs. Our aim in this session will be to give such guidance, and to help the children feel that learning to care for pets is one way in which they are growing.

Getting Ready for the Session

In the teaching plans for Sessions 4 and 5, Second Quarter, and Session 3, Third Quarter, suggestions were given to help the children feel that God's plan for birds in his world includes our part in helping to care for them. Read these teaching plans, and be prepared to give similar guidance in experiences with pets and other animals. Use Nursery Picture 8 to suggest care for a little kitten; also note pictures of a dog in *I'm Growing* and of a lamb in *His Name Is Jesus.*

A bowl of goldfish would be of special interest this session, or perhaps you know a dog, kitten, or rabbit that would be a welcome visitor for a short period. A large, shallow pan or bowl could be set out in a safe place for a birdbath. Look through your picture file for pictures of pets. Large wooden button molds, or empty spools colored with vegetable dyes, and a ball of string might suggest simple playthings to make for a pet kitten. If toy animals are not included in your nursery class equipment, plan to borrow a few for this session. *Animals for Me, Toby's House,* or *Anybody at Home?* would be useful in the book center.

With the Children in Church

If there is a bowl of goldfish or a real pet in the nursery room, the children's first interest will center in this. They might feed the goldfish (be sure the fish aren't given too much food), or give a saucer of milk to a kitten, a drink of water to a puppy, or some lettuce to a rabbit. As you talk with them, help them feel the responsibility of having a pet to care for, and remembering to give it food and water and a comfortable place to sleep. Similar conversation will take place as children play with toy animals, or look at pictures of pets, or recall what Fluffy did in *The Little Seeds That Grew*, or Jock in *I'm Grow-ing*, or the little lamb that the shepherd boy carried in *His Name Is Jesus*. The children might recall how they fed birds in winter and pro-vided nesting materials for them in spring, and you might suggest that they can set out a birdbath for them now, when days are hot. Tell the children that you know they are growing when they remember to care for birds and animals, and that God planned for them to help in this way.

You may find occasion with one child or with several to tell the story of "David and His Sheep" (page 228), or "Three Little Kittens" (page 229). Then repeat the story with different groups. Perhaps some of the children would like to make a plaything to take home to a pet kitten or puppy, by tying a button mold or an empty spool on the end of a piece of string.

After rest time you might open the Bible and show the children where you can read, "Be kind." Let them tell of different ways in which they can be kind to pets, and play that they are caring for them in these ways. They might recite the familiar nursery rhyme "I Like Little Pussy."

With the Children at Home

The teaching of this session will carry over into the home as children care for pets of their own. If they have no pets, suggest that they re-member to keep a shallow pan filled with water for birds.

SESSION 6. WE HAVE EYES TO SEE HOW WE CAN HELP

Thinking About the Children

From week to week children in the nursery class have been growing in ability to do things that are helpful, and have been encouraged in discovering such things to do. Through our guidance in this session we may lead them to feel the wonder of having eyes to see, and to find a growing satisfaction in using their eyes to see how they can help.

Getting Ready for the Session

Flowers, pine cones, shells, colored stones, and other lovely things to see should have a place on the nature table. Use Nursery Pictures 7, 8, and 10 to suggest ways in which children can help. Plan to let them assist in setting cupboards in order. Have new boxes or other containers in readiness for holding play materials. Aprons cut from newspaper, with strings attached for tying, will add to the children's interest in helping.

With the Children in Church

As the children arrive, encourage them to help by saying, "Can you find a vase for these flowers?"; or, "I need a thumbtack for this picture"; or, "What else should go on the nature table?"; or: "Margaret hasn't been here long enough to know where everything belongs. Perhaps you can help her find what she wants." Such questions or comments will lead the children to use their eyes, and you may say, "Aren't you glad God planned for you to have eyes to see how you can help?"

Similar guidance may be given as children play. "Have you left room for Jimmy's blocks?" you might ask; or, "Has Jane enough beads?"; or, "Would Allan like to use one of your crayons?"; or, "Where is the basket for these scraps of paper?"; or, "Has Evelyn had a turn yet?" Comment upon the ways the children find to help. Lead them to feel the wonder of having eyes to see.

Draw attention to new boxes or containers for beads or crayons or small blocks or other materials, and begin to set cupboards in order. As children come to assist you, suggest that they find aprons to wear. Help them feel satisfaction in sorting materials and putting them in their proper place. When it is time to sing "Putting Our Toys Away" (page 232), children who have been playing may also experience this satisfaction.

After rest time tell the story "A Letter for Daddy" (page 229). Remark that Betty used her eyes to know how to send a letter to make Daddy happy. Develop the finger play "This Is a Home" (page 235), and let the children imitate in play the kind and helpful things they can do at home.

With the Children at Home

Suggest to the children that they use their eyes to see something they can do to help Mother or Daddy. They might carry one of Mother's packages from the grocery store, or remember especially to pick up their toys. They might help sweep the sidewalk or hold the big screws for Daddy when he fixes a wagon or a table.

SESSION 7. WE HAVE EARS TO HEAR HOW WE CAN HELP

Thinking About the Children

In this session we may lead the children to feel the wonder of having ears to hear, and to find a growing satisfaction in using their ears to hear how they can help.

Getting Ready for the Session

Use Nursery Pictures 2 and 9 to suggest that children can hear church bells ringing and father saying grace at table. Use Nursery Picture 5 to help them recall that little children heard Jesus saying, "Let the children come." If you have rhythm sticks, plan to use them. Short lengths of window shade sticks or Venetian blind slats could be used for this purpose (see pages 88, 89, 100).

With the Children in Church

If your church has bells, ask the children if they heard them today, and remark that bells help us know when to come to church. Some of the children might like to play that they are ringing church bells as they sing "Church Bells" (page 231). Say: "Aren't you glad God planned for us to have ears? We can hear church bells ringing, and birds singing, and we can hear when we talk to one another."

As the children choose materials with which to play, watch for opportunities for suggesting that they can use their ears. You might say: "Do you hear Barbara singing to put her baby to sleep, John? If you play quietly with your blocks, you won't waken her"; or, "I'm glad you heard Lois asking you to help her, Jean"; or: "I hear Billy blowing the horn on his car. Let us get out of the way quickly."

Sing "Putting Our Toys Away" (page 232). Remark that when the children hear this song, they know what to do. Then say that you are going to sing another song that will tell them something to do. Sing "Lullaby" (page 231).

After rest time sit with the children and look at the pictures of the church in the book *In Our Church*. Suggest that they hear the bells ringing, and sing "Church Bells." Then look at the picture of a family saying grace. Suggest that they can hear what the family are saying, and sing "Thank You" (page 231). Look at the picture of Jesus and the children, and ask what these children heard Jesus saying. Sing "Jesus and the Children" (page 232). Say that we have ears to hear when someone asks us to do something to help. Suggest that you would like to hear how well the children are learning to use their ears. Hum or play a familiar tune to which they can make some attempt to keep time with rhythm sticks.

With the Children at Home

Remind the children that they have ears to hear when Mother or Daddy asks them to help.

SESSION 8. GOOD FOOD HELPS US GROW

Thinking About the Children

At each season of the year children may be guided in associating the food they eat with God's plan for their care, and in appreciating the many friends who help in this plan. Our aim in this session will be to emphasize the children's own part in helping so that they will find increasing satisfaction in co-operating in routines of eating that will keep them well and strong.

Getting Ready for the Session

Use Nursery Pictures 1, 7, 8, 9, and 12. Cut pictures from advertisements of fruits and vegetables and wholesome food products with which the children are familiar. Cut a large sheet of poster or wrapping paper in the shape of a picnic basket, and fasten this low on the wall. Perhaps you could plan a "picnic" for this session, and serve fruit or tomato juice and crackers outdoors. Read the teaching plans for Session 11, Third Quarter, for suggestions in guiding experiences related to good things to eat. Arrange a small basket of fruits and vegetables on the worship or special table, and fasten the picture of a family saying grace on the wall above it.

With the Children in Church

Play activities provide many opportunities for children to help one another and to do things for themselves. By your comments lead them to associate their ability to do these things with the thought that the good food they eat is helping them to grow. As they play with blocks, suggest that they build a barn for the farmer, or a store for the grocer, or a garage for the milkman's truck. Lead them to recall how these friends help in God's plan for us to have good food to eat. Children in the doll corner may play that they are getting breakfast ready for their family. Suggest that they give them orange juice and milk and cereal and other foods that will help them grow.

One group of children might like to paste pictures of good things to eat in the picnic basket you have fastened on the wall. Help them recognize the foods they must eat to grow strong and tall. When the basket is filled, they might play that they are growing tall. Other children will probably join in this play. They will imitate you as you stoop down, then rise gradually, taller and taller, until you are right up on tiptoes. Recite these lines as you play, or sing the first line going down the notes of the scale, and the second line going up:

> "Now I am quite small, I know,
> But green spinach will help me grow."

Repeat this play, naming fresh milk, or fresh eggs, or carrots, or potatoes, or orange juice, as the children may suggest. Remark that they are helping in God's plan for growing, by eating these foods. Avoid overstressing this point, as allergy or other causes may prevent some children from eating any one of the foods.

When toys have been put away, and the children have had a rest, have a "picnic" outdoors or tell the story "Going to the Store" (page 228). In either case there may be a moment of worship as the children sing "Thank You" (page 231).

With the Children at Home

Tell parents how you are seeking to guide their children in eating food that is good for them, so that the teaching of the nursery class may be carried over into the home.

SESSION 9. FRESH AIR AND SUNSHINE HELP US GROW

Thinking About the Children

Little children delight to play outdoors in the fresh air and sunshine, with little concern beyond the enjoyment of the activities in which they are engaged. Our aim in this session will be to help them recognize that the fresh air and sunshine are part of God's plan for them to grow.

Getting Ready for the Session

If possible, plan for this to be an outdoor session. The teaching plans for Session 12, Third Quarter, suggest a pattern that may be followed, and describe rhythmic plays. Be prepared to tell the story "The Baby Samuel" (page 230), with emphasis on the baby's enjoyment in being outdoors. Suggest that the fresh air and sunshine helped him grow. You might plan for the children to make little packages of paper napkins, fastening them together with a band of colored paper and a seal, for a picnic supper at home. Choose several poems about air and sunshine from a poetry collection (see page 95), and have them ready to read at any time during the session.

With the Children in Church

Follow in general the procedure suggested for Session 12, Third Quarter. As you share in the children's play, comment on the fresh air and sunshine and blue sky and flowers and trees, and everything that makes it a lovely day. Sing "Flowers, Bright and Gay" (page 232). Comment also on rosy cheeks and sun-tanned skin, and say, "I think you have had lots of sunshine to help you grow strong this summer." To children playing with dolls, suggest that they take their babies walking in the sunshine, and that they leave their window open at night so they will have fresh air while they are sleeping. Suggest to children building with blocks that they put plenty of windows in their house to let in the fresh air and sunshine. Look with others at the pictures in *I'm Growing*. Note that Timothy played outdoors, and that Dr. Brown was pleased with the way he was growing. Some of the children might like to make little packages of paper napkins to take home for a picnic supper. With any group of children, you may find occasion to say: "The fresh air and sunshine are part of God's plan for us to grow. We can say thank you to him."

There might be time to develop the rhythmic play of growing, described last session. Include "fresh air" and "sunshine" among the things that help us grow.

When it is time for a rest, suggest that the children play that they are putting on their sun suits and having a sun bath. Remind them that they must do their part by not staying too long in the sun. If you are outdoors, find a shady spot or a sunny spot, according to the temperature, and tell the story "The Baby Samuel." Indoors, the children might pretend they are sitting on the grass. After the story they may play that they are Hannah taking Samuel for a walk to enjoy all the lovely things the story tells about. Then they might sing "Lullaby" (page 231) as they hush him to sleep.

With the Children at Home

Help parents recognize the many opportunities they have every day for guiding their children in associating experiences in eating and sleeping and playing with God's plan for them to grow and to do things for themselves and for others.

SESSION 10. FRIENDS WHO HELP US

Thinking About the Children

In order that the services of the doctor may be effective, children must be led to regard him as a friend who cares for them when they are sick or hurt, and who helps their mothers and fathers know how to care for them from day to day so that they may grow according to God's plan. Our aim in this session will be to foster such appreciation, also a feeling of satisfaction in growing old enough to co-operate with the doctor in his care.

Getting Ready for the Session

Suggestions for guiding experiences in relation to friends who help us may be found in Session 6, Second Quarter. Use Nursery Pictures 1, 7, 8, and 10 to stimulate thinking about happy ways in which children can play and help when they are well and strong. Use Nursery Picture 12 as you talk about the doctor's care in helping them to keep well, and to grow more and more able to do things. A toy stethoscope and pieces of bandage in the doll corner would encourage doctor play.

With the Children in Church

You might suggest to children playing with blocks that they build a hospital, or a house or office building for their doctor, or a garage in which he can keep his car. Toy cars might suggest pretending that the doctor is driving to the hospital, or to the home of someone who is sick. Children playing with dolls might phone for the doctor to come to see a sick baby, or they might take their family to the doctor's for a checkup. As you share in such play, help the children feel that the doctor is their friend. Perhaps you could take the role of the doctor, and by your comments suggest ways in which the children can co-operate when you are trying to help them.

With children in the book center, look at the pictures of Timothy at the doctor's in *I'm Growing,* and tell the story. You might repeat it several times as other children come to listen. Emphasize the thought that Timothy's finger hurt, but he let Dr. Brown take the splinter out. Also when Dr. Brown was "checking up," Timothy did just what he was asked to do.

When it is time for a rest, sing "Putting Our Toys Away" (page 232) and remark on special thoughtfulness shown in doing this. Help the children feel satisfaction in growing in these ways. Remark also that our doctor tells us we need lots of rest to make us grow. Sing "Lullaby" (page 231) while the children are resting. After their rest look with them at the pictures suggesting happy ways in which they can play and help. You might say that God has planned for us to grow so that we can do these things, and that our doctor is one of the friends who helps us.

Develop the little rhythmic play of growing described in Session 8 of this quarter. Remark that our doctor helps us know that all these things will make us grow, and that they are part of God's plan for our care. "Thank You" (page 231) might be a natural expression of thanks.

With the Children at Home

Tell parents how you are seeking to guide their children in appreciation of their doctor, so that similar guidance may be given at home. Ask them to read especially the story "Our Doctor" in the children's book *I'm Growing.*

SESSION 11. DOING THINGS BY MYSELF

Thinking About the Children

During the past few weeks the children have been guided in recognizing different ways in which they are growing, and to find satisfaction in things they can do for themselves and others. In this session emphasis will be placed on things they can do by themselves, so that they may begin to accept responsibility for co-operating in routines that are planned to help them grow.

Getting Ready for the Session

Use Nursery Pictures 7, 11, and 12. Read the teaching plans for Session 3, Second Quarter, for suggestions in guiding children in learning to care for themselves. Pictures of babies may suggest the many things we do for babies that nursery children have learned to do by themselves. Plan to tell the story "Ready for Bed" (page 224). If you have *Bobbie and Donnie Were Twins,* place it on the book table.

With the Children in Church

As the children work or play, comment on things they are doing by themselves that they couldn't do when they first came to nursery class, and help them have a feeling of achievement. Encourage them to tell of things they do by themselves at home, and suggest playing these. To the tune of "Here We Go Round the Mulberry Bush," the children may sing, "This is the way we wash our hands" (or "comb our hair," or "put on our socks," or "pick up our toys").

With children in the book center, draw attention to the picture in *The Little Seeds That Grew* of Jerry caring for the flower seeds he had planted. Remark that he remembered all by himself to water the seeds and put them near a sunshiny window. In *I'm Growing* note that Timothy and Susan put on their own clothes. In *In Our Church,* Billy took off his own coat and hat, and put them on again. In *His Name Is Jesus,* it was the little children themselves who thought of gathering the flowers to take to Jesus.

In putting toys away, encourage the children to do as much as possible by themselves. After rest time look with them at pictures of babies, and encourage them to tell of things they can do by themselves that babies can't do. They may play about things that help them grow as described in Session 8 of this quarter. Lead them to feel their responsibility to eat and sleep and play in ways that will help them grow.

Tell the story "Ready for Bed." Look with the children at the picture of a family group at bedtime, and remark that they can say thank you to God for things that help them grow. Sing "Thank You" (page 231).

With the Children at Home

Suggest that the children can surprise Mother or Daddy by doing things by themselves.

SESSION 12. DOING THINGS WITH OTHERS

Thinking About the Children

As children are learning to do things by themselves, they must also learn to do things with others. This is one of the most important teachings of the nursery class, for it means growing in friendliness and helpfulness and in other attributes of Christian character. While such growth is our aim in every session, our special aim in this one will be to help the children begin to feel some responsibility for the happiness of others.

Getting Ready for the Session

In teaching plans for Sessions 3 and 4, First Quarter, and Session 10, Second Quarter, detailed suggestions are given for guiding the children in friendly ways of playing together. Plan to give similar guidance today. Use Nursery Pictures 4, 9, and 10, and fasten the picture of Jesus and the children on the wall above the special table. Arrange a few garden flowers, and place them on the table. Look through magazines or your picture file for pictures of familiar situations in which children are doing things with others. If you have them, place *Bobbie and Donnie Were Twins* and *The Tale of Jeremy Gray* on the book table.

With the Children in Church

The children's usual play activities should provide many experiences in doing things with others. Be on the alert to encourage cooperative play in building with blocks or playing with dolls or using creative materials or manipulative playthings. Children looking at pictures or picture books may show these to one another and talk about them. Lead them to observe how Susan and Timothy, in *I'm Growing*, both helped get ready for Grandmother's visit, and played together with their new toys. In *His Name Is Jesus*, the children went together to see Jesus. In *The Little Seeds That Grew*, Jerry worked with his father in planting the string bean seeds. In *In Our Church,* Billy had a happy time because the other children were ready to do things with him.

Whatever the children are doing, you may remark, "I know you are growing when you play together like this"; or, "I'm glad you can remember to let everyone have a turn." To one child, you might say softly: "That was kind to let Dickie have the red truck. He'll soon learn to play with other children"; or: "Doris hasn't been here before. Can you help her find something she would like to play with?"

Putting toys away may be a happy experience in doing things with others. Help the children feel responsible for being quiet while other children are relaxing. After rest time you might tell the story of Timothy's grandmother coming to visit, in *I'm Growing,* or you might suggest that playing on a swing or a seesaw, singing, playing in a band, and so forth, are happy things to do with others. Let the children choose what they would like to do. Help them feel satisfaction in using rhythm sticks or other musical instruments together. They might sing "At Church" (page 231). Help them feel the happiness of saying thanks to God together.

With the Children at Home

Speak with parents about the many opportunities their children have at home for doing things with others, and for growing in friendliness and helpfulness.

SESSION 13. REMEMBERING TO SAY THANK YOU TO GOD

Thinking About the Children

Throughout the year in the nursery class, children have been learning to associate everything that contributes to their welfare and happiness with God's plan for their care, and to express thanks to him. In this session our special aim will be to help them feel that remembering to say thank you to God should be part of every happy experience at home and at church.

Getting Ready for the Session

In Sessions 8 and 9, First Quarter, and in Session 13, Third Quarter, suggestions were given for leading the children to recognize God's love and care, and to express thanks to him. In this session help them to recall experiences of the summer months through which they have been growing. Choose from pictures suggested for preceding sessions of this quarter. Use the picture of a family saying grace, or praying at bedtime, for the wall above the worship table. Fruits, vegetables, shells, colored stones, or other lovely things from outdoors should have a place in the nature center.

With the Children in Church

As the children work or play with materials of their own choosing, you will find many opportunities for leading them to think of God as planning for them to have food to eat, or clothes to wear, or homes in which to live, or little friends to play with, or big friends to help them. Your own consciousness of God will lead you to say quite naturally, "God planned for us to have friends so that we could have happy times together like this"; or, "God planned for the sunshine and fresh air to help us grow"; or, "Aren't you glad God planned for you to grow so that you can do things for yourself and for your friends too?"; or, "Aren't you glad God planned for you to have eyes to see how you can help?" (or, "ears to hear how you can help?").

Such comments may suggest that the children sing "Thank You" (page 231). You might remark that saying thank you to God is one of the things we do both at home and at church. Some of the children might like to sing "The Family" (page 234), then play that they hear the church bells ringing, and sing "Church Bells" (page 231); or they may sing "At Church" (page 231). Remark that we are happy when we remember to say thank you to God. The children may sing "Thank You" again, perhaps changing the last line to name other things for which they want to give thanks. Children playing with dolls or looking at picture books will probably also express thanks in this way.

After their quiet time you might tell the story of Jesus and the children in *His Name Is Jesus*. Sing "Jesus and the Children" (page 232). Suggest that the children in the story would want to say thank you to God for the happy time they had with Jesus. Ask the children to tell of something for which they want to say thank you. Do not expect an answer from every child.

With the Children at Home

Talk over with parents the importance of remembering to say thank you to God with their children at mealtime and bedtime, and when something makes them especially happy. Children are in the church school for such short periods of time that these and other experiences need repetition in the home if they are to become part of their lives.

EXTRA SESSION. THE FRIENDLY DARK

(To be used in special situations, or when there are fourteen sessions in a quarter.)

Thinking About the Children

At any season of the year children may have experiences of being alone in the dark. Sometimes they may become frightened or lonely. Our aim in this session will be to help them feel the friendliness of the dark as they associate it with happy experiences, and are led to feel that it is part of God's plan for their care.

Getting Ready for the Session

Guidance and activities suggested in the teaching plans for Session 8, Third Quarter, may be followed in this session. In making the nighttime poster, you might plan to add one or two houses cut from dark paper, with yellow paper windows to suggest the light shining from these at night. Fasten Nursery Picture 11 on the wall above the worship table. Use Nursery Picture 6, and plan to tell the first story from *His Name Is Jesus*. (The story is found also on pages 217, 218.)

With the Children in Church

As the children play, watch for opportunities for suggesting friendly aspects of nighttime. With children using blocks, remark on the peace and quietness at night when no building operations are going on. If they are playing with toy cars, say that some people like to drive at night when it is cooler than in the daytime. Suggest to children in the doll corner that a story at bedtime, looking at the moon or stars from the window, and talking to God are happy things to do at night. Sing "Lullaby" (page 231) as they rock doll babies to sleep.

Children pasting stars on the nighttime poster will be interested in the little houses with lighted windows. Help them think of the good times they have at night when Daddy comes home from work.

When it is time to put toys away, remark that everyone is glad when we remember to pick up things before going to bed, so that no one will step on them in the darkness.

Some of the children might like to play that it is nighttime and they are getting ready to go to bed. Let them suggest and imitate the various steps in getting undressed, washing, brushing their teeth, putting up their window, and making other preparations. You might say: "God planned the quiet nighttime for us to sleep. Let us say thank you to him." They might sing "Thank You" (page 231). Sing "Lullaby" as they relax on the rug or rest their heads in their hands as if sleeping.

After rest look with the children at the picture of Jesus as a baby. Tell the story about the wonderful night when Jesus was born. Look at the pictures of the starry skies in *His Name Is Jesus*. Then sing very softly "Shepherds Leave the Hillside" (page 233).

With the Children at Home

Suggest to the children that they sing "Thank You" at night before they go to sleep.

EXPERIENCES THROUGH WHICH LITTLE CHILDREN MAY GROW TOWARD GOD

The following classification of experiences, indicating quarters and sessions in which activities related to them are suggested, offers a guide to teachers who may prefer to make their own teaching plans. It may also serve as a guide in changing suggested plans for any session, according to the immediate experiences of the children.

1. *Experiences Associated with the Church*

These experiences may be guided so that the children will feel at home in the church and find happiness in helping and worshiping there.

Quarter I: Sessions 1, 2, 3, 5, 7, 9; Quarter II: Sessions 8, 10, 12; Quarter III: Session 13; Quarter IV: Session 13.

2. *Experiences Related to Jesus*

Through carefully chosen stories, and through our own Christian faith, children may gradually learn to know Jesus and to love him.

I: 6, 11, 12, 13; II: 5, 7, 9, 11, 13; III: 5, 6; IV: 1, 2.

3. *Experiences Related to the Bible*

Bible truths underlie all our teaching in the nursery class. Bible stories or verses, or specific references to the Bible, may be found in the plans for the following sessions:

I: 2, 6, 10, 11, 12; II: 1, 2, 5, 7, 9, 11, 13; III: 5, 6; IV: 2, 4, 5, 9, 13.

4. *Experiences in Belonging to a Family*

The everyday experiences of little children in the home offer our greatest opportunity for religious guidance.

I: 8, 10; II: 1, 2, 8; III: 7; IV: 1, 2, 3, 4.

5. *Experiences in Relation to Other Children*

Through these experiences, children may grow in friendliness and helpfulness and in other attributes of Christian character.

I: 3, 4, 13; II: 10, 12; III: 12; IV: 2, 3, 4, 12.

6. *Experiences in Relation to Grown-up Friends*

These experiences may be guided so as to foster attitudes of appreciation and co-operation.

I: 1, 3; II: 6, 7; III: 2, 11; IV: 2, 3, 10.

7. *Experiences in Caring for Pets*

There is only one session in which activities are definitely related to caring for pets, but caring for birds is emphasized in several sessions.

II: 4, 5, 12; III: 3; IV: 5.

8. *Experiences with Toys and Other Playthings*

Such experiences enter into every session, but occasionally are given special emphasis.

I: 2, 3, 4, 13; II: 10; III: 12.

9. *Experiences Related to Food*

These experiences may be guided so that the children will grow in appreciation of God's provision for our care at all seasons.

I: 8; II: 2, 10; III: 1, 10, 11; IV: 8.

10. *Experiences Related to Clothes*

Children's interest in clothes may be guided toward appreciation of their mother's and father's care, and satisfaction in their growing ability to care for themselves.

I: 5; II: 2; III: 1; IV: 11.

11. *Experiences in Learning to Do Things for Themselves*

Nursery children may find satisfaction in learning to do things for themselves, and associating this with God's plan for growing.

I: 5; II: 3; IV: 6, 7, 11.

12. *Experiences of the Wonder of God's World*

Such experiences should be guided so that the children may feel the greatness and the love of God, and may give thanks to him.

I: 8; II: 4, 5; III: 1-13; IV: 9; Extra Session.

*
STORIES TO TELL
AND
SONGS TO SING
*
*

Stories to Tell
and Songs to Sing

The stories in the children's four quarterly reading books are reprinted below:

BOOK: IN OUR CHURCH

THE NURSERY CLASS

It was Sunday morning. Billy and Mother and Daddy were finishing their good breakfast of orange juice and cereal and toast and milk.

"Soon time for church school," said Daddy as he took a last bite of toast.

"Soon time for church school," sang Billy, sliding down off his chair.

In a little while they all were ready and they started on their way. Billy walked between Mother and Daddy and took their hands. Sometimes he went hop, hop, hop and jump, jump, jump. That made Mother and Daddy and Billy laugh.

Soon they saw the church. It stood straight and tall against the blue sky.

They went in the side door to the nursery room. Miss Anderson was there. She smiled and said, "Good morning, Billy; it's good to see you today."

Billy took off his coat and hat. He hung them up on his very own hook; a picture of a red ball was just above it.

Billy waved good-by to Mother and Daddy.

"We'll see you later," they said.

Other children were already at work in the nursery room. Stephen was there, and Carolyn, and John, and Dorothy.

First Billy built a tower with blocks. Carolyn said it looked like a church and she put a high steeple on the top. Miss Anderson brought some bells and the children sang:

> "Ding dong, ding dong, the church bells ring;
> Ding dong, ding dong, come to church."

Then Billy sat down at the table. He made a yellow-and-blue picture for Mother.

Miss Anderson and several children were in the doll corner. Billy went over to see what they were doing.

Miss Anderson asked: "Will you join us, Billy? We're cooking breakfast for our doll family."

Billy helped Stephen set the table with the little green and yellow dishes.

Miss Anderson said: "We are all very glad that we had real food for *our* breakfast this morning. Would you like to say thank you to God the way you do at home?"

"Yes," answered the children. So they said, "Dear God, thank you for our good food."

It was time to put the toys away. The children helped carry blocks and cars and books to the shelves, and tucked the dolls in bed.

They lay down on the rug for a few minutes to rest. Miss Anderson closed her eyes and sang very softly:

" 'Lullaby, lullaby; sleep, dear baby, sleep.
Lullaby, lullaby; sleep, dear baby, sleep.' "

After rest Billy sat on a chair near Miss Anderson. She had a picture of a church and she said: "We are glad for the nursery class in our church. We hear about God and we are happy with our friends."

Billy saw Mother and Daddy at the door. He ran over to them and gave Mother her picture. He put on his hat and coat.

"Good-by, Billy," said Miss Anderson. "I'll see you next Sunday."

"Good-by, Miss Anderson," said Billy. "I'll be back!"

THE BIG CHURCH

One Sunday, after a good rest time, Miss Anderson and the children went outdoors. Miss Anderson said: "Today we are going into our *big* church. There your mothers and daddies sing and pray and hear about God."

Billy and John and Dorothy and the other children walked with Miss Anderson to the steps of the church.

They bent their heads way back so they could look up, up at the *very* tiptop of the tower.

Miss Anderson started to sing:

"Ding dong, ding dong, the church bells ring;
Ding dong, ding dong, come to church."

They went through the high brown doors. It was cool and dark inside, and someone was playing the organ. It was a nice place to be.

Billy sat down with Miss Anderson and the other children in the back of the church.
He saw the songbooks standing in a row.
He saw the purple and red colors shining through a window.

He listened to the clear bell sounds of the organ music. He looked at his shiny shoes; they were swinging back and forth, back and forth, very, very lightly.

Soon the music stopped. Everyone walked tiptoe to the front of the church.

There they saw white and yellow flowers in a vase.
They saw a big Bible. Miss Anderson held the Bible so all the children could have a turn to see. Billy touched the smooth gold edges.
Miss Anderson said, "We read about Jesus in the Bible."

Then Miss Anderson and Billy and the other children walked tiptoe to the back of the church. They turned around and looked.
Miss Anderson said quietly: "Dear God, thank you for this beautiful place where mothers and daddies and children may come. Thank you, God, for *our* church."

—*Sara G. Klein.*

BOOK: HIS NAME IS JESUS

A BABY IS BORN

One night on a hillside shepherds were taking care of their woolly sheep. A shepherd boy was with them; his little pet white lamb was snuggled close beside him as he rested on the ground.

The shepherds heard that a new baby was sent from God and that he was born in Bethlehem.
Two of the shepherds said, "We are going right away to Bethlehem to see the baby."

"May I go too?" asked the shepherd boy.
"Yes," answered one of the shepherds. "You may go. I should like you to see the little child who was born today."

The shepherd boy picked up his white lamb and tucked him carefully inside his coat.
"I think the baby would like to see *you*," he said, as he gently touched the woolly head of the lamb.

They started down the road. They walked very fast; sometimes the shepherd boy skipped along the way. They were hurrying to see the baby.

The stars were bright in the sky as they came to Bethlehem. The shepherds found the stable where the baby was staying.

They went to the door and pushed it open very, very slowly.

There they saw Mary holding a tiny baby in her arms. She was singing. Joseph was standing near.

The shepherds went inside and quietly closed the door. The shepherd boy tiptoed over to Mary and sat on the floor.
Everyone listened as Mary sang her song:
> "Go to sleep, dear baby,
> God has sent you here;
> Go to sleep, dear baby,
> You bring love to all the earth."

Three gray doves were perched on the rafters. They listened to the song, cooing softly, "Coo-roo, coo-roo." Then they put their heads under their feathered wings and went to sleep.
A shaggy little donkey rested nearby in some straw. He listened to the song. His eyes were bright. But soon he closed his eyes and went to sleep.

The white lamb lay on the shepherd boy's lap. He listened to the song as he looked up at Mary. Then he snuggled down inside the shepherd boy's coat and went to sleep.

Soon the baby was sleeping too. The shepherd boy watched Joseph take the baby carefully from Mary's arms and lay him in a manger bed.
"What is the name of the baby?" asked the shepherd boy.
"His name is Jesus," Joseph said.
Matthew, ch. 1; Luke 2: 1-20.

LET THE CHILDREN COME

When Jesus grew to be a man, he was a friend to everyone. He told people about God's love for them.

One day some mothers and fathers said, "Let us take our children to see Jesus."
So the mothers picked up the little babies and carried them in their arms.
The fathers took the children by the hand. They were on their way to see Jesus.

Along the road they met a man riding on a camel.

"Where are you going?" he asked them.

"We are going to see Jesus," said the children happily. "We are going to see Jesus."

They walked until they came to a field; yellow flowers were growing there. The children stopped and gathered the flowers to take to Jesus.

The babies reached out their hands toward the bright yellow petals. They wanted to carry the flowers too!

Soon the mothers and fathers and children came near the place where Jesus was talking to his friends. The children ran toward Jesus.

One of the men turned and saw the children. He said: "Sh-h-h! Don't disturb Jesus now. He is very busy talking."

But Jesus heard the children's voices. He saw the children and the babies and the mothers and fathers. He smiled at them.

Jesus held out his arms and said: "Let the children come to me; never send them away. Always let the children come, for they too must learn about how much God loves them."

Mark 10: 13-16; Luke 18: 15-17; Matthew 19: 13-15.
—Sara G. Klein.

BOOK: THE LITTLE SEEDS THAT GREW

THE SURPRISE

Once there was a little boy named Jerry. He decided to give a surprise to his mother.

So he went outdoors and dug up brown, crumbly earth with his shovel.

He put the earth in a box. He patted it carefully.

With his finger he made three holes in the earth: one—two—three! He had three little hard brown seeds. He dropped the seeds into the holes: one—two—three!

He covered the seeds with the earth.

He put some water in a watering can and sprinkled the earth lightly.

Every day he sat watching beside the box. Every day he filled the watering can and sprinkled a little water on the earth. But it looked just the same.

Then one morning Jerry saw three little green stems poking up in the box. The seeds were growing!

Jerry remembered to sprinkle water on the earth to keep it wet. He put the box near a sunshiny window.

The stems were growing taller; green leaf buds opened on the stems.

Then one day, when Jerry looked again, he saw *three flowers* on the stems— a red flower and a blue flower and a yellow flower.

The little hard brown seeds had grown into beautiful flowers!

Jerry ran to Mother with the surprise.

"Oh, thank you, Jerry," said Mother. "Thank you for the beautiful flowers. You planted the little seeds and took care of them. You sprinkled the seeds with water; you put the box in the sunshiny window. God planned for the seeds to grow."

Then Mother and Jerry carried the flowers out to the garden for Daddy to see.

PLANTING TIME

Daddy said, "I think Jerry and I could plant string bean seeds in our garden today."

Daddy used his big hoe to loosen the earth. Jerry used his little shovel to help. Then Daddy smoothed the earth with the rake. Jerry picked up the biggest stones and threw them out of the way.

Daddy and Jerry dropped the slippery bean seeds along the rows. They covered them with earth and watered them.

"Now,' said Daddy, "we must wait for the seeds to grow."

One day it rained. "Fine," said Daddy. "The wet rain will help to make the string beans grow. That's the way God planned it."

One day the sun was shining. "Fine," said Daddy. "The warm sunshine will help to make the string beans grow. That's the way God planned it."

Soon the green stems pushed above the earth. They grew and grew. There were leafy bushes along the ground.

One afternoon, when Jerry was playing outdoors with Fluffy, he looked carefully at the green bushes in the garden. And he saw—a string bean! He saw another string bean, and another, and another.

Jerry called to Mother and Daddy. They brought a basket. Jerry and Mother and Daddy picked a whole basketful of string beans.

Mother washed the string beans and cooked them for supper.

Jerry and Mother and Daddy sat down at the table. Daddy said: "Dear God, thank you for sending rain and sunshine to make the seeds grow. Thank you, God, for our good food. Amen."

—*Sara G. Klein.*

BOOK: I'M GROWING

OUR FAMILY

"Grandmother is coming today," said Mother. So Timothy helped make the bed in Grandmother's room. He smoothed the covers very carefully.

"Grandmother is coming today," said Daddy. So Susan helped sweep away the fresh green grass from the sidewalk and pile it into a basket.

The house looked clean and shining.

Then Mother said, "It's time to get dressed." Timothy put on his blue suit and his shiny brown shoes.

Susan put on her yellow dress and her shiny *black* shoes. Mother helped them with the littlest buttons.

Mother and Daddy and Timothy and Susan climbed into the car. They were going to the station to meet Grandmother.

Jock ran out to the car. He wanted to go along. "Woof, woof," he barked, and he wagged his tail. He jumped in the car and sat beside the window.

"All aboard, family!" called Daddy. "All aboard for the station to meet Grandmother!"

They waited at the station for the train to arrive. In a little while they heard the whistle: toot, toot, too-oo-oot! Then they saw the engine come chug-chug-chugging into the station.

They saw people getting off the train. Soon they saw Grandmother; she was carrying a suitcase and a big package. She waved at them, and they ran to meet her.

Grandmother kissed Mother. She kissed Daddy. She hugged and kissed Timothy and Susan at the same time. She patted Jock on the head.

"What a nice *family!*" said Grandmother.

They drove Grandmother back to their clean and shining house. They went inside and showed Grandmother her room.

Grandmother opened the big package. There was—a baby doll for Susan and—a red truck for Timothy!

"Thank you, Grandmother," said Susan and Timothy.

"I shall call my baby Betsy Anne," said Susan, and she held her very close.

"I like my big red truck," said Timothy.

After supper Mother and Daddy and Grandmother sat in the living room and talked. Timothy pushed his truck round and round on the rug. Susan made a warm bed for Betsy Anne in a cardboard box. Jock was curled up with his head on his paws.

Timothy said, "I need something to put in my truck."

Mother had an idea. She said, "Timothy, why don't you and Susan take turns giving Betsy Anne a ride in your truck?"

So they did just that. First Timothy gave Betsy Anne a ride up one side of the room. Then Susan gave Betsy Anne a ride down the other side of the room.

It was fun to share the new toys!

When it was bedtime for Timothy and Susan, Mother and Daddy tucked them in.

"What is a family, Daddy?" asked Susan.

"A family is you and Timothy and Mother and I," answered Daddy.

"And Grandmother," said Timothy.

"Yes, indeed, and Grandmother," said Daddy. "God plans for people to live in families and to love and help one another."

"I'm glad," said Susan.

"Thank you, God," said Timothy.

OUR DOCTOR

The next morning Daddy went to work and Susan went to kindergarten. Timothy played in the yard. He started to build a house with stones and pieces of wood. Suddenly a little wooden splinter went right into his finger. He began to cry because it hurt.

Timothy ran in to Mother. Mother patted Timothy and looked at the splinter. She said, "We'll go to see our Dr. Brown and let him take care of it."

So Timothy and Mother walked down the street to Dr. Brown's office. They went inside. People were sitting there. Timothy and Mother waited their turn.

After a while Timothy and Mother were called in to see Dr. Brown.

"Hello, young man," said Dr. Brown.

"Timothy has a splinter," said Mother.

"We'll soon have that splinter out," said Dr. Brown.

He lifted Timothy up on a high table. He took hold carefully of Timothy's finger. "It will hurt a little," said Dr. Brown.

Then—*zip*—out came the splinter! Dr. Brown put some medicine on Timothy's finger and wrapped a white bandage loosely around it.

Timothy's finger began to feel better!

"Now for a checkup!" said Dr. Brown. "First, let's have a look at your teeth."

Timothy opened his mouth wide.

"Say 'A-ah,' " said Dr. Brown and he put a little stick in Timothy's mouth and used a light so he could see.

"Good," said Dr. Brown.

Next Dr. Brown put his stethoscope to his ears and listened to Timothy's chest. Everything was very still and quiet for a few minutes.

Dr. Brown winked at Timothy. "Good," he said.

Timothy stood up straight so Dr. Brown could measure him and see how tall he was. "Timothy, young man, you're *growing*," said Dr. Brown.

"Timothy is growing in many ways," said Mother. "He's learning to be a helper at home; he's learning to share his toys."

"Good," said Dr. Brown.

Timothy and Mother said good-by and started home.

"See my finger," said Timothy.

Mother looked at the white bandage. "It feels better, doesn't it, Timothy?" said Mother.

"I like Dr. Brown," said Timothy.

—*Sara G. Klein.*

WHEN BETTY WENT
TO NURSERY CLASS

It was Sunday. Ronnie had news for his teacher in nursery class. "There is a new little girl next door to our house," he said. "Her name is Betty, and she is three years old. She is coming to nursery class next Sunday."

"Then we must help her have a happy time," his teacher said. "I wonder what she would like to do!"

"I think she would like to build a house with blocks," said Gordon.

"I think she would like to play with our new doll," said Joan.

"I think she would like to draw with crayons," said Teddy.

"I think she would like to look at a picture book," said Ann.

Ronnie pointed to a picture on the wall. It was a picture of Jesus with the little children who came to see him. "I think she would like to hear that story," he said.

The teacher took the picture down from the wall so that all the children could see. They sang very softly:

"One day Jesus said so kindly,
 'Let the children come.'
 Little children heard him saying,
 'Let the children come.'"

When Betty went to nursery class the next Sunday, she built a house with blocks. She played with the new doll. She drew a picture with crayons. She looked at a picture book. And the teacher told her the story of Jesus and the children. Then Betty and Gordon and Joan and Teddy and Ann and Ronnie all sang the song that tells about Jesus' saying, "Let the children come."

—Elizabeth Cringan Gardner.

CHRISTMAS NIGHT

It was Christmas night. Barbara and Mother and Daddy were in the living room.

Mother put out all the lights except the tiny ones on the Christmas tree. They made it sparkle with red and blue and green and silver and gold. Barbara looked up at the bright star shining at the top.

"Stars shone in the sky when Jesus was born," Daddy said. "Perhaps there are stars shining in the sky tonight. Let us look and see."

Daddy lifted Barbara up to the window. They saw many stars shining brightly in the sky.

"Listen!" said Mother. "I can hear Christmas music. The children across the road are singing carols."

Barbara looked across the road. She saw the children singing. She listened to their song.

"Shepherds leave the hillside,
 And their woolly sheep.
 In a crib they find Him,
 Jesus, fast asleep!"

"I like Christmas," Barbara said softly.

—Elizabeth Cringan Gardner.

READY FOR BED

It was time for Bobby to go to bed.
"I can undress myself," he said to Daddy.
Pull, pull, and one little shoe was untied.
Tug, tug, and one little shoe came off.
Slip, slip, and off came one little sock.
Pull, pull, and the other little shoe was untied.
Tug, tug, and the other little shoe came off.
Slip, slip, and off came the other little sock.

Down, down, and Bobby's woolly trousers went over his feet.
Up, up, and Bobby's woolly sweater went over his head.
Daddy was running the water for Bobby's bath.
Splash, splash, and Bobby was in the tub.
Scrub, scrub, and Bobby was out again.
Rub, rub, and Daddy helped dry him with a big soft towel.
"I can put on my pajamas, myself," Bobby said.
Slippity, slip, and one little foot was in.
Slippity, slip, and the other little foot was in.
Slippity, slip, and in went one little arm.
Slippity, slip, and in went the other little arm.
Daddy helped fasten the buttons.
Then he tossed Bobby up on his shoulder. "Come on," he said.
"Let's go tell Mother you're ready for bed."

—Elizabeth Cringan Gardner.

WONDERS OF GOD

(A Story Suggested by Job 37: 14)

It was bedtime, and Anne had just climbed into bed. It was wintertime outside Anne's window, and she wanted to be warm all night. She had on warm pajamas. She pulled the covers up tight, and her mother tucked them in.

"What shall we pray tonight?" Anne asked her mother.

"We could pray 'Thank you.'"

"But we always pray 'Thank you,'" Anne said.

"Then tonight let's just be still and think about the wonders of God."

For a little while Anne and her mother were very still.

And then Anne said, "This morning when I saw the sun on the snow, that was a wonder of God, wasn't it, Mother?"

"The sun shining brightly
On the new white snow?
Yes, that's a wonder of God."

And then Anne said, "This noon, when the little birds came to eat our bread, was that a wonder of God?"

"The little cold birds
Finding bread crumbs to eat?
Yes, that's a wonder of God."

And then Anne said, "This evening, when we watched the fire in the fireplace, was that a wonder of God?"

"The great black logs
Burning in the fireplace?
Yes, that's a wonder of God."

Then Anne and her mother said their prayer together.

"Be still and think about the wonders of God."

—Mary Louise Ellis.

FEEDING THE PIGEONS

One day Teddy was watching the pigeons. They were flying high above the barn.

Teddy ran into the barn and got a handful of corn. He began to scatter it on the ground.

A little white pigeon came flying down. A little gray pigeon came flying down. A little brown pigeon came flying down. Soon all the pigeons came flying down from the barn, and crowded around Teddy.

Peck, peck, peck! They ate up the corn he scattered on the ground. Teddy ran into the barn to get some more.

"I will get some too," said Mother.

Mother sat on a bench while Teddy scattered his corn on the ground. She gave him some of her corn to scatter too. She held the rest in her hand.

A little white pigeon saw the corn in Mother's hand. He flew up on the bench beside her. Mother sat very still.

Peck, peck, peck! The pigeons ate up the corn Teddy scattered on the ground.

Peck, peck, peck! The little white pigeon ate up the corn Mother held in her hand.

Then all the pigeons flew up to rest on the top of the barn.

"Coo-oo-oo-oo!" they sang softly. And Teddy and Mother knew that they were saying thank you.

—*Elizabeth Cringan Gardner.*

MILK FOR BREAKFAST

It was early in the morning. The milkman's truck was coming down the street. Shirley lay in bed and listened.

The milkman stopped at Teddy's house.

Clink! Clink! Clink! He was taking away the empty bottles. He was leaving bottles of fresh, sweet milk.

The milkman stopped at Mary's house.

Clink! Clink! Clink! He was taking away the empty bottles. He was leaving bottles of fresh, sweet milk.

The milkman stopped at Shirley's house.

Clink! Clink! Clink! He was taking away the empty bottles. He was leaving bottles of fresh, sweet milk.

Shirley heard Mother open the door. She heard her bring in the bottles of milk. "Is breakfast ready?" Shirley called.

"It will be ready as soon as you are dressed," Mother answered.

Shirley jumped out of bed and dressed herself. Mother helped fasten the buttons. "Come and see what the milkman has brought for your breakfast," she said.

Shirley looked at the table where breakfast was ready.

There was fresh, sweet milk in her own little pitcher.

There was fresh, sweet milk in her own little cup.

"I'm glad for the milkman who brings the milk," Shirley said.

—Elizabeth Cringan Gardner.

JESUS AND THE FLOWERS

One day Jesus was out in the country. A great many people were with him. They were sitting on a hillside.

Jesus looked at the bright flowers that were blooming all around. They were red and yellow and white and blue. He could smell their sweet perfume. He could reach out and touch their soft petals.

"See how beautiful the flowers are," Jesus said. "No one was ever dressed in lovelier colors. God planned for them to have their sweet perfume. He planned for the rain and the sunshine to help them grow. God is caring for the flowers, and I know he is caring for you."

The mothers and fathers who were with Jesus looked at the flowers. The little children looked at them too. They smelled their sweet perfume. They touched their soft petals.

"God is caring for the flowers," the mothers and fathers said happily to one another.

"God is caring for the flowers," said the little children.

Jesus spoke very softly. "When you look at the flowers, always remember that God is loving and caring for you."

—Elizabeth Cringan Gardner.

THE RAIN IS FALLING

Teddy and Joan were standing at the window. They were watching the rain. It was tapping on the windowpane and splashing in shiny puddles at the edge of the garden.

Teddy's dog, Toby, jumped up to watch too. Joan held her doll so that she could see.

The raindrops kept coming faster and faster. They chased one another down the windowpane. They made tiny streams that ran among the flowers.

"The flowers are having a drink," said Joan.

"So is the grass," said Teddy. "See how green and shiny it is!"

The raindrops began to come slower and slower. The sun peeped out from behind a cloud.

"Cheer-ee! Cheer-ee! Cheer-ee!" sang a little robin. And it flew down from the branch of a maple tree. It began to drink the raindrops from a tiny stream.

"Look!" said Teddy. "The rain has stopped. Let's go out and play."

The sun was shining when Teddy and Joan ran out to the garden. The raindrops were sparkling on the flowers and on the grass and on the leaves of the trees.

"Bow-wow! Bow-wow! Bow-wow!" barked Toby.

"Cheer-ee! Cheer-ee! Cheer-ee!" sang the little robin.

"I like the rain," said Joan.

"And I like the sunshine," said Teddy.

They were happy in God's beautiful world.

—Elizabeth Cringan Gardner.

GOING TO THE STORE

Gwen and Tommy were going to the grocery store. They were going to the store for Mother. Gwen carried a piece of paper in her hand. Tommy pulled his little red wagon.

When they reached the store, Gwen gave the piece of paper to the grocer. He read the words that Mother had written on it: "One package of oatmeal, one dozen oranges, one dozen eggs, one pound of butter." Then the grocer looked at Gwen's and Tommy's rosy cheeks.

"Your mother knows the kind of food that helps you grow," he said. "I'm glad the farmer helps me have it here for you."

The grocer took a package of oatmeal from his shelf. He put it in a big bag. He counted one dozen oranges, and put them in the bag with it. He reached under his glass counter, and brought out a carton of eggs and a pound of butter. He put them in the bag too. Then he lifted up the big bag, and carried it out to the door of his store. He put it carefully in Tommy's wagon.

"Thank you," said Gwen.

"Thank you," said Tommy.

Then Gwen and Tommy pulled the little red wagon home together.

—Elizabeth Cringan Gardner.

DAVID AND HIS SHEEP

("And, behold, he keepeth the sheep."—Part of I Samuel 16: 11)

David had some white, woolly sheep and some baby lambs. Every morning he took them out to the fields. He walked in front of them to show them the way.

Trippity, trippity, trippity went their little feet over the ground.

Soon they came to a field where the grass was fresh and green.

The sheep began to nibble the fresh, green grass.

The baby lambs began to nibble the fresh, green grass.

David sat down nearby and watched them.

A little stream of water was flowing through the field.

The sheep stood on the edge of the stream and drank the cool water.

The baby lambs stood on the edge of the stream and drank the cool water.
David stood nearby and watched them.
A shady tree grew beside the little stream.
The sheep lay down under the shady tree to rest.
The baby lambs lay down under the shady tree to rest.
David lay down nearby and watched them.
By and by it was time for the white, woolly sheep and the baby lambs to go home. David walked in front of them to show them the way.
Trippity, trippity, trippity went their little feet over the ground.
And soon they were all safe at home again for the night.

—*Elizabeth Cringan Gardner.*

THREE LITTLE KITTENS

Tabby Gray was a mother cat. She lived at Ruth's house. Every day Ruth gave her a saucer of milk. Tabby Gray had three little kittens. There was one black kitten, and one gray kitten, and one kitten that was black and white.

Tabby Gray and the three little kittens slept in a basket. At first the kittens slept all day long. But one morning their eyes were open.

"Meow-meow-meow!" said the little black kitten, and it scrambled up the side of the basket.

Ruth took the little black kitten in her arms. She held it very gently. Then she put it back in the basket.

"Meow-meow-meow!" said the little gray kitten.

"Meow-meow-meow!" said the kitten that was black and white.

Ruth took the little gray kitten in her arms. She held it very gently. Then she put it back in the basket.

Ruth took the black-and-white kitten in her arms. She held it very gently. Then she put it back in the basket.

And the three little kittens cuddled down beside their mother, and were soon fast asleep.

—*Elizabeth Cringan Gardner.*

A LETTER FOR DADDY

Daddy was going away on the train. He waved good-by to Mother. He waved good-by to Betty. "Be sure to write me a letter," he called.

There was a piece of white paper on Betty's own little table. There was a box of crayons too. Betty took a red crayon and drew a picture for Daddy.

"What would you like me to write on the back of it?" Mother asked. And this is what Betty told Mother to write:

"*Dear Daddy,*
This is a picture for you. We want you to come home soon.
With love and kisses,
Betty."

Betty folded the letter and put it in an envelope. Mother wrote Daddy's name on it. She gave Betty a stamp to paste in the corner.

Betty carried the letter out to the mailbox. She stood up on tiptoes and dropped it inside.

Then one morning the postman knocked at the door of Betty's house. He had a letter from Daddy.

Mother opened the letter and read it to Betty:

"*Dear Betty,*

Thank you for your good letter. The postman brought it to me. I like the picture. I am coming home tomorrow.

> *With love and kisses,*
> *Daddy.*"
>
> —*Elizabeth Cringan Gardner.*

THE BABY SAMUEL

(*Based on I Samuel, Chapter I*)

Elkanah and Hannah had a new baby.
They named him Samuel.

Every day they took loving care of their baby.
They gave him food.
They bathed him and dressed him in soft linen.
They liked to play with him.
He smiled and cooed.
He waved his arms and kicked with his sturdy legs.

When Samuel grew, he learned to walk and to speak words and to sing.
He often laughed and sometimes he cried.
He liked to look at the yellow flowers and the blue sky.
He listened to the songs of birds.
He clapped his hands when the wind blew the little leaves on the
    olive trees.

Samuel's mother and father were very happy.
They said, "Thank you, God, for our baby."

> —*Sara G. Klein.*

LULLABY

Sara G. Klein

S. G. K.

Lull - a - by, lull - a - by; Sleep, dear ba - by, sleep.

Lull - a - by, lull - a - by; Sleep, dear ba - by, sleep.

THANK YOU

Sara G. Klein

Elizabeth Cringan Gardner

Dear God, thank you to - day For food and rest and play.

CHURCH BELLS

Sara G. Klein

S. G. K.

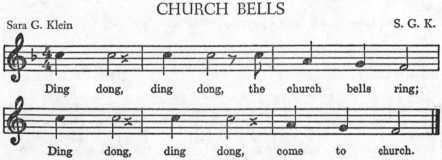

Ding dong, ding dong, the church bells ring;

Ding dong, ding dong, come to church.

AT CHURCH

Elizabeth Cringan Gardner

Arr. from 13th century French Melody

In our church we like to sing, And some - times we soft-ly pray,

Thank-ing God for ev-'ry - thing, God who loves us ev-'ry day.

SEESAW

Anonymous   Anon.

See - saw, up and down, Off to the coun - try, back to the town.

With a slight variation in the rhythm, these seasonal songs may be used with the melody above:

FALLING LEAVES

Down, down, with rustling sound,
Leaves are falling, all around.

RAIN

Down, down, with pattering sound,
Raindrops are falling on the ground.

SNOWFLAKES

Down, down, without a sound,
Snowflakes are covering all the ground.

FLOWERS, BRIGHT AND GAY

Flowers, bright and gay,
This is a lovely springtime [summer]
day.   *Elizabeth Cringan Gardner.*

PUTTING OUR TOYS AWAY

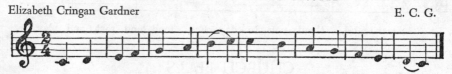

Elizabeth Cringan Gardner   E. C. G.

We have had a hap - py play, Now we'll put our toys a - way.

JESUS AND THE CHILDREN

Elizabeth Cringan Gardner   Melody from Reinecke

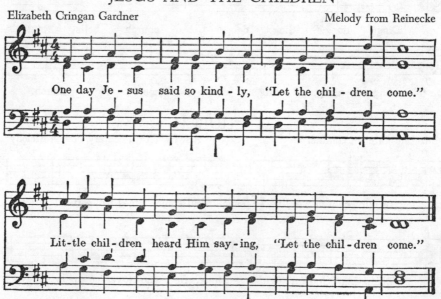

One day Je - sus said so kind - ly, "Let the chil - dren come."

Lit-tle chil - dren heard Him say - ing, "Let the chil - dren come."

CHRISTMAS DAY

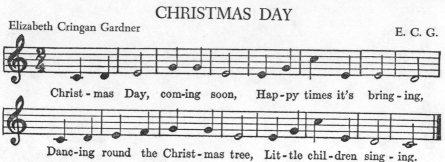

Christ-mas Day, com-ing soon, Hap-py times it's bring-ing,

Danc-ing round the Christ-mas tree, Lit-tle chil-dren sing-ing.

SHEPHERDS LEAVE THE HILLSIDE

Shep-herds leave the hill-side, And their wool-ly sheep.

In a crib they find Him, Je-sus, fast a-sleep!

THE FAMILY

Anonymous

Traditional Melody

We're glad we live in our fam - i - ly, We're glad we live in our fam - i - ly, We're glad we live in our fam - i - ly, Fa - ther and moth - er and chil - dren too.

The following words may be used with the melody above:

THE NURSERY CLASS

We're glad we're here in the nursery class,
We're glad we're here in the nursery class,
We're glad we're here in the nursery class,
Helping each other in work and play.

FINGER PLAYS

HERE'S A BALL FOR BABY *

Here's (1) a ball for baby, big and soft and round,
Here's (2) the baby's hammer, oh, how he can pound;
Here's (3) the baby's music, clap, clap, so,
Here (4) are baby's tenpins, standing in a row;
Here's (5) the baby's trumpet, toot, toot, toot, toot, too!
This (6) is how the baby plays at peekaboo.
Here's (7) a big umbrella to keep the baby dry,
Here's (8) the baby's cradle, rock-a-baby-by.

Action:

(1) Cup hands, fingertips together.
(2) Clench fists, left stationary, pound with right.
(3) Clap hands.
(4) Fingers outspread, palms outward, upright position.
(5) Fists clenched, left placed over mouth, right moving back and forth, to the rhythm of the words.
(6) Hands crossed; placed in front of face; play "peek."
(7) Left hand cupped for umbrella top; forefinger of right hand placed in palm of left for handle of umbrella.
(8) Fingers interlaced; hands in cradle formation.

THIS IS A HOME **

This (1) is a home where people (2) live,
    Each one helps the other;
They do such kind and helpful things,
    They love one another.

Note: "Church" may be substituted for "home."

Action:

(1) Fingers interlaced to represent roof of house; thumbs erect to represent door.
(2) Open door and show "people" inside.

---

* From *Finger Plays*, by Emilie Poulsson. Copyright by Lothrop, Lee & Shepard Co., Inc. Used by permission.
** Copyright by the United Church Publishing House, Toronto, Canada. Used by permission.

STUDY GROUP
OUTLINE

FOR PARENTS AND TEACHERS

*
*

Study Group Outline

For Parents and Teachers

THE TOPICS suggested in the following outline, to be used in a series of informal parents' or parent-teacher study groups, are merely "springboards" for further thinking, reading, and discussion. Reference may be made to material in this handbook, to more detailed presentations in books or pamphlets listed in the bibliography, and to the experience of the parents and teachers themselves. Occasionally a speaker or consultant might be brought in when the group feel they need special help. (See pages 107-109.)

I. What ought we to consider about the nursery class in the church?
   A. Parents and teachers must have a continuous mutual understanding of the program and the teaching plans.
   B. Preparation of the child for this new experience begins in the home, and parents contribute, day by day, to the Sunday teaching.
   C. Teachers make the child feel at home in the church.
   D. Parents and teachers work together.

II. What can we do to set up an attractive physical environment for the three-year-olds in the nursery class?
   A. We can paint walls and furniture.
   B. We can construct equipment.

III. How can we better understand the activities through which our children learn in the home and church?
   A. We can observe children at play.
   B. We can provide them with at least a minimum number of satisfactory materials.
   C. We can ourselves enjoy music and art and literature on the child's level as well as on the adult's.

239

IV. How do children grow?
  A. They grow as complete persons—physically, emotionally, socially, mentally, and spiritually.
  B. They all do not develop at the same rate of speed.
  C. They grow well only when certain basic needs are met.
  D. They learn best when their stage of growth and principles of learning are recognized.
  E. They must sometimes be helped to meet "problems," such as fears, shyness, and overaggressiveness.

V. How, more specifically, can we best guide nursery children in their religious development?
  A. We, who live and work with them, provide a Christian atmosphere for their nurture.
  B. We help them grow toward God and understand his plans.
  C. We acquaint them with Jesus.
  D. We see that they have opportunities to pray.
  E. We encourage loving and helpful attitudes toward others.

VI. Are our own faith and attitudes worthy of influencing the personalities of our children?
  A. As we study the Scriptures, God reveals himself to us through great leaders and prophets, and through Jesus Christ.
  B. We re-examine and enrich our satisfactions and interests as they are measured against the Christian standard of living.
  C. We take care of our bodies, temples of the Holy Spirit.

VII. Is our home a Christian fellowship?
  A. Each one of us respects and honors the others as individuals.
  B. The parents do not bestow favoritism on one child.
  C. We take time for group worship.
  D. We discuss plans and problems in a family council.
  E. We are concerned with a Christian use of money.

VIII. Is our church a Christian fellowship?
  A. *Everyone* is welcome.
  B. We seek to bring others into its fellowship.
  C. We remember vows taken at the baptism of the children.
  D. The teachers in the church school are honored, and every effort is made to supply them with materials and to send them to training or laboratory schools.

E. There is a good working relationship among the various boards and councils of the church.

F. The best possible use is made of the facilities available.

IX. Is our community a Christian fellowship?

A. A spirit of neighborliness and consideration exists among all the people.

B. There are healthful living conditions for everyone.

C. Unwholesome influences contributing to delinquency are eliminated.

D. Schools, libraries, and playgrounds are given interested attention.

E. Social services, clinics, health units, and hospitals receive adequate support.

F. There is friendly co-operation among the churches.

Bibliography
for Parents and Teachers

BOOKS * FOR BIBLE STUDY AND SPIRITUAL ENRICHMENT

Bowie, Walter Russell, *The Story of the Bible*. The Abingdon Press, $2.95. The content of the Bible.

Goodspeed, Edgar J., *The Story of the Bible*. The University of Chicago Press, $2.50. The content of the Bible.

Hunter, Archibald M., *Introducing the New Testament*. The Westminster Press, $1.50. An aid to finding one's way around the New Testament quickly.

Richardson, Alan, *A Preface to Bible Study*. The Westminster Press, $1.50. Shows our need to wait before God in the Scriptures.

Rowley, H. H., *The Re-discovery of the Old Testament*. The Westminster Press, $3.50.

Smyth, J. Paterson, *How We Got Our Bible*. Harper & Brothers, $1.50. The making of the Bible.

The following reading books for young people published by The Westminster Press provide quick review reading for the adult:

    Men Called Him Master, by Elwyn A. Smith.

      The life of Jesus. (Junior high age.) $2.00.

    The One Story, by Hulda Niebuhr.

      The story and message of the Bible. (Junior high age.) $2.00.

---

* May be ordered through your nearest denominational bookstore. Prices subject to change.

God Has Spoken, by David Noel Freedman and James D. Smart. Introductions to all the books of the Old Testament. (Senior high age and young people.) $2.00.

Baillie, John, *A Diary of Private Prayer.* Charles Scribner's Sons, $2.00. Morning and evening prayers for personal and, with some adaptation, group worship.

Bainton, Roland H., *The Church of Our Fathers.* Charles Scribner's Sons, $3.75. A very readable presentation for young people of the history of the Christian Church.

Trueblood, Elton, *The Common Ventures of Life.* Harper & Brothers, $1.00. A discussion of marriage, birth, work, and death as Christian sacraments.

CHILD DEVELOPMENT AND GUIDANCE

Bradbury, Dorothy E., and Amidon, Edna P., *Learning to Care for Children.* D. Appleton-Century Company, Inc., $1.32. This book was prepared to help high-school boys and girls who take care of children. It is a guide for parents and teachers also.

Duff, Annis, *"Bequest of Wings."* The Viking Press, $2.50. Delightfully written presentation of how a family share together experiences in art, music, and literature.

Gesell, Arnold, *et al, Infant and Child in the Culture of Today:* The Guidance of Development in Home and Nursery School. Harper & Brothers, $4.50. Dr. Gesell has been doing research for many years at the Yale Clinic of Child Development. He offers in concrete detail the growth characteristics of the preschool years. This book is "a must" for the church school library.

Hymes, James L., Jr., *Enjoy Your Child* (ages 1, 2, and 3). Public Affairs Pamphlet No. 141, 20 cents. Write to Public Affairs Committee, Inc., 22 E. Thirty-eighth Street, New York 16, New York, for additional titles.

Rice, Thurman B., *Those First Sex Questions.* American Medical Association, 535 N. Dearborn Street, Chicago, Illinois, 25 cents.

Ridenour, Nina, in collaboration with Isabel Johnson, *Some Special Problems of Children.* New York Committee on Mental Hygiene of the State Charities Aid Association, 105 E. 22d Street, New York 10, New York: single copies, 10 cents each; packet of eight different subjects, 50 cents. Discussion of fears, unpleasant habits, hurting other children (ages 2 to 5). Write for list of publications.

Smith, Richard M., *Between Two Years and Six.* John Hancock Mutual Life Insurance Company, Boston, Massachusetts, free. Questions concerning food, rest, and mental habits are answered by a physician.

Spock, Benjamin, *Baby and Child Care.* Pocket Books, Inc., New York, 35 cents. Another "must" for the library or the home. Physical care especially discussed in great detail.

What Makes Good Habits—The Beginnings of Discipline. Child Study Association of America, Inc., 132 E. Seventy-fourth Street, New York 21, New York, 15 cents. Write to Association for book and pamphlet list.

When Children Ask About Sex. Child Study Association of America, Inc. (above), 25 cents.

Your Child from One to Six. Publication 30, Children's Bureau, U. S. Department of Labor, 15 cents. (For sale by Superintendent of Documents, Government Printing Office, Washington, D.C.) Write for list of titles.

THE NURSERY PROGRAM *

Alschuler, Rose H., editor, *Children's Centers.* William Morrow & Company, Inc., $2.50. Useful guide for organizing a nursery school, day nursery, or child care center.

Children and Music. Association for Childhood Education International, 1200 Fifteenth Street, N. W., Washington 5, D. C., 75 cents. The place of music during the first years and in regard to the growing child. Write to Association for booklet list.

Essentials of Nursery Education. National Association for Nursery Education, Roosevelt College, 430 S. Michigan Avenue, Chicago 5, Illinois, 50 cents. Presents the needs of the child and how they can be met in the curriculum.

First Aid. Metropolitan Life Insurance Co., New York, New York, free.

Foster, Josephine C., and Mattson, Marion L., *Nursery-School Education.* D. Appleton-Century Company, Inc., $3.00. Discusses the young child and the philosophy and program of the nursery school. A basic book.

Good Education for Young Children. New York State Council for Early Childhood Education, Box 98, Queens College, Flushing, New York. 60 cents. A description of children during each year of the preschool age as a basis for organizing a curriculum.

Landreth, Catherine, and Read, K. H., *Education of the Young Child.* A nursery school manual. John Wiley & Sons, Inc., $2.75. Prepared especially for the training of nursery school teachers.

Norton, Edith N., *Parent Education in the Nursery School,* Association for Childhood Education International (see address above), 50 cents.

Portfolio for Nursery School Teachers. Association for Childhood Education International (see address above), 75 cents. Each packet contains twelve leaflets that deal with the program, guidance, and material for the age group.

Shedlock, Marie L., *Art of the Story-teller.* D. Appleton-Century Company, Inc., $2.25.

Some Ways of Distinguishing a Good Nursery School. National Association for Nursery Education, 2 cents each. Distribution center, 430 S. Michigan Avenue, Chicago, Illinois.

The Group Living of Children, Citizens' Committee on Children of New York City, Inc., 136 E. Fifty-seventh Street, New York 22, New York,

---

* The books in this section have been prepared primarily for the secular nursery school but offer valuable suggestions for any preschool program. Church school teachers should be acquainted with them.

25 cents. Handy booklet on program, administration, and equipment for groups of children under six years of age.

What Nursery School Is Like, How a Child Feels About Entering a Nursery Center (two pamphlets for parents), and *The Child's First Days in Nursery School* (a pamphlet for nursery staff), by Doris Campbell. New York Committee on Mental Hygiene (see address in preceding section), 15 cents each.

Working with the Child from Two to Six (Curriculum Bulletin No. 5). State Department of Education, Columbus, Ohio, free. Suggestions for work with the child of nursery school and kindergarten age.

Write also to 69 Bank Street, New York 14, New York, for list of packets and articles for teachers and parents.

RELIGIOUS EDUCATION

(In the Church and Home)

Brown, George W., and Ruth McAfee, *Teaching Religion in the Home*. The Westminster Press, 75 cents. A practical study course for use at home or in a parents' class.

Carl, Dorothy, *The Family Celebrates Christmas*. The Pilgrim Press, 50 cents. Includes suggestions about worship, gifts, songs, stories, sharing.

Carlson, Jessie B., *Guiding Children in the Nursery Class*. The Judson Press, 60 cents.

International Council of Religious Education, 206 S. Michigan Avenue, Chicago 4, Illinois. The following pamphlets are 3 cents each:
  Parents—First Teachers of Religion.
  Helping Your Child to Know God.
  You Are Teaching Your Child Religion!
  Family Worship with Young Children.
  Visiting in the Home.
  The Church and Children of the Community.

Jones, Mary Alice, *The Faith of Our Children*. Abingdon-Cokesbury Press, $1.50. Answers the question, How may we lead our children into life-enriching faith in God?

Kramer, Emma Jane, *Equipment and Arrangement*. The Methodist Publishing House, 20 cents. Helpful suggestions for planning the physical setup of children's departments in the church school.

Lloyd, Mary Edna, *Nursery Children in the Church*. The Methodist Publishing House, 20 cents.

Nursery Children in the Church. The Pilgrim Press, 40 cents.

Odell, Mary Clemens, *Our Family Grows Toward God*. Abingdon-Cokesbury Press, 50 cents. Discussion of spiritual values in the family.
    Our Little Child Faces Life. Abingdon-Cokesbury Press, 50 cents. Parents educate their little boy on the topics of God, life, and death.

Rosser, Pearl, compiler, *Your Child Grows Toward God*. The Judson Press,
15 cents. A condensation of the goals of the religious education of children
of each age group.

Sweet, Herman J., *Opening the Door for God*. The Westminster Press, $1.50.
Stresses parents' own faith and life, but also includes concrete and practical suggestions for the religious guidance of the child.

Thomas, Mazelle W., *The Family Worships Together*. Companion to *The
Family Celebrates Christmas* (above).

Whitehouse, Elizabeth S., *Opening the Bible to Children*. The Bethany
Press, 60 cents. Suggestions for intelligent use of the Bible with different
age groups.

    The Nursery Department at Work. The Judson Press, 40 cents.

Wiegmann, F. W., *Christian Happiness in the Home*. The Bethany Press, 45
cents. A study course to show how young married couples can make better
homes by using the Church's resources.

Wood, Leland Foster, *Harmony in Marriage*. Round Table Press, New York,
$1.00. Discussion, by a doctor and a minister, of all aspects of marriage,
including the religious.

PERIODICALS

Child Study. Child Study Association of America, New York, New York,
132 E. Seventy-fourth Street, New York 21, New York, $2.25 a year. A
professional magazine.

Childhood Education. Association for Childhood Education International,
1200 Fifteenth Street, N. W., Washington, D. C., $3.50 a year. A pro-
fessional magazine.

Children's Religion. The Pilgrim Press, 14 Beacon Street, Boston 8, Massachusetts, $1.50 a year.

National Parent-Teacher. The official magazine of the National Congress of
Parents and Teachers, 600 S. Michigan Boulevard, Chicago 5, Illinois,
$1.25 a year.

Parents' Magazine. The Parents' Institute, Inc., 52 Vanderbilt Avenue, New
York 17, New York, $3.00 a year.

The Child. Division of Reports, Children's Bureau, $1.00 a year. (Send re-
mittance to the Superintendent of Documents, Government Printing
Office, Washington 25, D. C.)

The Christian Home. The Graded Press, 810 Broadway, Nashville 2, Tennes-
see, $2.00 a year.

45-01-08